Sauerkraut Yankees

*Pennsylvania-German
Foods and Foodways*

William Woys Weaver

Foreword by **Don Yoder**

*Dann lacht juscht fort ihr englisch Volk,
    Ihr meescht eier dumme Schpuchte dreiwwe,
Gebt uns juscht Schpeck un Graut genunk,
    Dann wolle m'r luschtig Deitsche bleiwwe.*

E. L. KEMP, 1883

UNIVERSITY OF PENNSYLVANIA PRESS
Philadelphia, 1983

Design by Lawrence Didona

Copyright © 1983 by William Woys Weaver

Library of Congress Cataloging in Publication Data

Weaver, William Woys.
 Sauerkraut Yankees.

 Bibliography: p.
 Includes index.
 1. Cookery, American—Pennsylvania. 2. Cookery,
German. I. Title. II. Title: Pennsylvania German foods
and folkways.
TX721.W38 1983   641.59748   82-40488
ISBN 0-8122-7868-2
ISBN 0-8122-1145-6 (pbk)

Printed in the United States of America

4

Fish and Shellfish

(36) Fish (Cleaning and Cooking), (37) To Poach Salmon, Bass, and Other Large Fish, (38) To Fry Trout and Other Small Fish, (39) Cod Fish, (40) Fried Clams, (41) Fried Oysters, (42) Fried Oysters.

5

A "Karrich" of Vittles and Herbs

(43) Vegetables (Cooking), (44) Cauliflower, (45) Celery, (46) Carrots, (47) Parsnips, (48) Red Beets, (49) Asparagus, (50) Green Peas, (51) Tomatoes, (52) Spinach, (53) Squash, (54) A Good Cabbage Salad, (55) To Preserve Parsley, (56) To Make Good Mustard.

6

Soups, Broths, and Stews

(57) Chicken Soup, (58) Mutton Soup, (59) Veal Soup, (60) Beef Soup, (61) Calf's-Head Soup, (62) Rice Soup, (63) Apple Soup, (64) Huckleberry Soup.

7

Puddings, Pies, and Other Sweets

(65) Plain Rice Pudding, (66) Bread Pudding, (67) Flour Pudding, (68) Plum Pudding, (69) Apple Pudding, (70) Transparent Pudding, (71) Potato Pudding, (72) Calf's-Foot Jelly, (73) Raised Crust for Pies, (74) Mince Pie, (75) Apple Pie, (76) Apple Puffs, (77) Sweet Patties, (78) Dried-Apple Pie, (79) Dried Cherry Pie, (80) Sour Cherry Pie, (81) Peach Pie, (82) Cranberry Pie, (83) Rhubarb Pie, (84) Huckleberry Pie, (85) Cream Pie, (86) Custard Pie, (87) Rice Pie, (88) Pumpkin Pie, (89) Johnny Cakes, (90) Cornmeal Muffins, (91) Waffles, (92) Jumbles, (93) Soft Gingerbread, (94) Composition Cake, (95) Almond Cake, (96) Yellow Lady Cake, (97) Pound Cake,

Contents

1

DIE GESCHICKTE HAUSFRAU
Its Author and Its Setting

2

Meats
and Hearthside Savories

(1) To Roast a Suckling Pig, (2) Sauce for Suckling Pig, (3) Roast Mutton, (4) Roast Beef, (5) To Roast Veal, (6) Stewed Beef, (7) Beef Steaks, (8) Beef Steak, French Style, (9) Roast Pork, (10) Venison, (11) Marinated Pot Roast, (12) Roast Veal, (13) Stuffing for Roast Veal, (14) Stewed Veal, (15) Boiled Calf's Head, (16) Veal Cutlets, (17) Veal Cutlets Another Style, (18) Baked Calf's Liver, (19) Boiled Ham, (20) To Bake Ham, (21) Tripe, (22) Pig's Feet Soused, (23) An Excellent Recipe for Prepared Tongue, (24) Sausages, (25) Scrapple, (26) To Cure Beef and Pork, (27) To Cure Ham, (28) Excellent Brine for Curing Meat.

3

What the Dutch Call
"Gefliggel"

(29) To Roast a Turkey Cock, (30) To Roast a Goose, (31) Roast Pigeons, (32) Fricasseed Chicken, (33) Chicken Pie, (34) Roast Duck, (35) To Tenderize Old Chickens Quickly.

For William Groke Mickey

Foreword

❧

They were called "Sauerkraut Yankees" during the Civil War. It was meant to be unflattering, but the name stuck and, for a time, became a byword for their entire culture. William Woys Weaver has revived it in the title of this thoroughly original book that is both a factual guide and a first-person tour through one of the most colorful of American ethnic cookeries: the cookery of the Pennsylvania Dutch.

When he invited me to write this foreword, I was pleased to accept, because I have watched the project grow over the past five years from orderly notes to final manuscript, never realizing that when I "discovered" *Die geschickte Hausfrau* nearly ten years ago, it would eventually serve as the basis for a book. But it is a happy event, because in terms of American food history, this ethnic kitchen classic, around which William Weaver has written his book, appeared at a time when Americans were experiencing major shifts in their eating habits and taste preferences. Thus, *Sauerkraut Yankees*, as a culinary study, as a peregrinating essay through early American foods and foodways, pinpoints both an end and a beginning. As a study of hearth cookery, it closes the final chapter on a way of cooking that flowered in America during colonial times. As an essay—actually a series of vignettes—the book leads us over a great deal of new ground on a recipe-by-recipe basis. Numerous line illustrations chosen from rare nineteenth-century sources garnish the visual impact of this book immeasurably. Thus we come to know the nineteenth century not only as the Pennsylvania Germans saw it in their daily lives, but also as a time of new and exciting changes that eventually affected all of us. We are given not just a taste of good food history, but also a portrait of the Sauerkraut Yankees as a people; and more importantly, their ethnic experience becomes a reflection of ourselves.

Long forgotten in farmhouse attics, *Die geschickte Hausfrau*—this rarest of American ethnic cookbooks—is now available to us in a new setting, after years of persevering research, endless country sales and dusty flea markets, and the selfless collaboration of a varied crew of scholars in this country and abroad. To say nothing of the author's culinary sensitivity as the tenth-generation in a long line of expert Pennsylvania-German cooks.

Don Yoder

University of Pennsylvania

Die Geschickte

Hausfrau

Eine Sammlung

Guter Recepte und Vorschriften

zum

Kochen, Braten,

Kuchen-Backen,

und

Einmachen von Früchten.

Harrisburg, Pa.
Gedruckt und zu haben bei Lutz und Scheffer,
1851.

The fourth edition of *Die geschickte Hausfrau*

Preface

"When the great architect had finished building the earth, he dumped the chips and debris into the centre of Pennsylvania, and men called the heap the Seven Mountains."[1] So wrote Fred Lewis Pattee in *The House of the Black Ring*. The Seven Mountains are still there. That is where I spent my childhood summers, only to realize these many years later that those great stone heaps and their folkloric origin symbolize the very culture of Pennsylvania in its broadest sense. For Pennsylvania was built with the chips and debris of Europe's humanity sent here centuries ago, stirred together, and allowed to flower into a people uniquely diversified and especially gifted.

The Pennsylvania Germans were only a part of this fascinating process, but their culture still represents one of the largest and most influential chapters of the story. Even where their language is no longer spoken, or where there are no longer Pennsylvania-German names in telephone directories, people still cook Pennsylvania-German foods and celebrate Pennsylvania-German festivals. It is about the culinary legacies of the Pennsylvania "Dutch" that this book is concerned.

Sauerkraut Yankees explores this heritage as it has been preserved for us in the pages of *Die geschickte Hausfrau* (The Handy Housewife), an apron-pocket cookbook of special importance not only to Pennsylvania-German cookery, but also to the history of American cookery in general. Originally published in Harrisburg, Pennsylvania, in 1848, *Die geschickte Hausfrau* was one of the first truly ethnic cookbooks to appear in this country.[2] For reasons quite unforeseen by its author, it became a best seller among the Pennsylvania Dutch and ran through many editions over a twenty-year period. It was plagiarized heavily—sections of it appeared in *Der neue Reading Calender* (The New Reading Almanac) for 1881—and as late as 1883, *Die geschickte Hausfrau* was still being sold by its original publisher, Theodore F. Scheffer. Scheffer was the key figure behind the popularity of the cookbook. He not only took advantage of its ethnic aspects, he was also the principal heir of its anonymous author, Gustav Sigismund Peters (1793–1847). In fact, since Peters died before the book was published, *Die geschickte Hausfrau* owed its existence to Scheffer and his temporary partner, Martin Lutz. These two men turned Peters's rough manuscript into a popular cookbook.

Having said that, I should hasten to add that the best seller was not perfect. It was extensively corrected from one edition to the next in order to remove the vagaries that plagued the earliest printings.

These language difficulties have been completely eliminated in *Sauerkraut Yankees* because I have translated *Die geschickte Hausfrau* into English for the first time since its appearance in 1848.

This translation was fraught with a number of unusual linguistic obstacles, not the least being the awkwardness of the original German. There was evident haste in the way the book was put together for publication. Several hands were involved in editing or reediting the recipes. All of this contributed its share of odd spellings and strange grammar that can be deadly in any cookbook, but especially in one that must be translated. In more than one instance, it was not clear from the German whether a thing was being fried or baked, and worse, there were a few recipes that simply would not work as Theodore Scheffer had published them. Correcting such problems required second guessing, no little amount of research into cooking techniques of that period, and more importantly, a thorough look at Peters's own recipe sources. His plagiarism had one benefit: In time, it could be traced.

In any case, I believe the recipes as they now stand are much clearer than in the original German. I have taken great pains to be specific. Furthermore, in order to insure that my translation of *Die geschickte Hausfrau* was as accurate as possible, I used P. J. Kunst's classic dictionary of Pennsylvania High German: *Ein amerikanisches Wörterbuch der englischen und deutschen Sprache*. This dictionary was actually compiled by Gustav S. Peters himself, who first published it in 1836. I checked the Lutz and Scheffer edition of 1850, because it was closest to the edition of *Die geschickte Hausfrau* used for this book.

Why was *Die geschickte Hausfrau* written in German? That is a question many people unfamiliar with the settlement of Pennsylvania may not understand. Because it has direct bearing on the way I translated the recipes and on the type of vocabulary I preserved in the text, an explanation is in order.

During the 1840s, when Gustav Peters was gathering material for his cookbook, as much as 40 percent of Pennsylvania's population spoke a dialect of German that the Pennsylvania Dutch themselves call *Deitsch*. The Pennsylvania Dutch were so thickly settled in some parts of the state that many of them had no contact with English. Even the road signs were in German. Since *Deitsch* was a spoken language rather than a written one, the Pennsylvania Germans used for literary purposes a hybrid language called Pennsylvania High German. This was a peculiar mixture of archaic High German (what some linguists call "Bible German"), Pennsylvania-German dialect, and English loan words. This was the language of *Die geschickte Hausfrau* and most of the other books written by the Pennsylvania Dutch during this period. Today, Pennsylvania High German is almost extinct.

In order to preserve some of the personality of the original cookbook, the name of each recipe is supplied both in English and Pennsylvania High German. Whether it is grammatically correct or not, the German appears exactly as it is in the original. In addition to the Pennsylvania High German, I have often included the *Deitsch* equivalents, particularly where the dialect name reveals a cultural attitude toward the dish or food discussed. These terms have been garnered from a variety of period sources and represent standard usage at the time *Die geschickte Hausfrau* was at the height of its popularity (1850–70). Since then, the Pennsylvania-German language has changed considerably. Today, it is rapidly disappearing, although there are efforts here and there to keep it alive. Where it is spoken, English loan words are now much more prevalent than a century ago. Thus, *Sauerkraut Yankees* is an attempt to preserve some of the linguistic heritage of the Pennsylvania-German people, at least in terms of their rich and varied culinary experience.

But *Sauerkraut Yankees* is also much more than that, certainly much more than a translation. It is a new book written around an old one. Taking the recipes from *Die geschickte Hausfrau*, I have arranged them into chapters with introductory comments, an attempt at order that is totally lacking in the original cookbook. Nearly every recipe I have chosen serves as a point of departure for a remark or extended sketch treating some aspect of that particular dish, its history, origin, or context in terms of Pennsylvania-German culture. Furthermore, I have added illustrations—mostly wood engravings—selected from nineteenth-century sources to create visual allusions to my remarks, to foods, or to period cooking implements.

Because I wanted to keep this study within the limits of cookery, seven recipes from the original *Geschickte Hausfrau* have been omitted. They dealt with such household activities as candlemaking, mixing whitewash, and making soap, and are similar to the sort of directions found in other American cookbooks of the period. To compensate for this, I have included in translation nineteen rare recipes from other period sources, particularly from George Girardey's *Höchst nützliches Handbuch über Kochkunst* (Practical Manual of Domestic Cookery), first published in Ohio in 1841; and from Friederike Löffler's *Oekonomisches Handbuch für Frauenzimmer* (Economical Manual of Domestic Arts: Stuttgart, 1791), a Swabian cookbook that gained wide popularity here. Girardey's recipes represent the sort of classical Pennsylvania-German cookery found mostly in city hotels (he was a confectioner by trade) and the households of upper-class "Dutchmen." They are a useful contrast to the middle-class cookery of *Die geschickte Hausfrau*. Löffler's cookery, however, preserves many of the dishes once common in Pennsylvania during the eighteenth century. In fact, she includes several well-known Pennsylvania dishes, such as *Buweschenkel* (stuffed noodles) and *Mauldasche* (a form of "pocket" dumpling). Therefore, her cookbook is useful in terms of Pennsylvania-German culinary roots. But most important, her cookbook was eventually published in Pennsylvania under the title *Voll-ständiges Kochbuch für die deutsch-amerikanische Küche* (Complete Cookbook for the German-American Kitchen: Philadelphia, ca. 1856).

Looking back over the five years that went into the making of *Sauerkraut Yankees*, I can only say that the undertaking was no easy task, for I was dealing not only with another language, but also with another way of thinking. Of necessity, most of my references involved material in German, some of it very technical. Extensive footnoting would have deprived me of space for the numerous illustrations in the text and would have put off the general reader for whom this book was written. So I have placed my notes and sources at the end of this book. Any direct or indirect reference to an author, book, or article will be found there. While perhaps interesting only to specialists, some of this material does make excellent reading for those who wish to explore the origins of Pennsylvania-German cookery more deeply.

Food historians will not be surprised to learn that many recipes in the original *Geschickte Hausfrau* came from sources outside the Pennsylvania-German community—I have already used the word "plagiarism" in connection with Peters's name. Actually, such borrowing occurred in all household books used by the Pennsylvania Dutch, and the process of assimilation is often extremely revealing. Where this has occurred in *Die geschickte Hausfrau*, I have tried to furnish some explanation as to how the dish worked its way into Pennsylvania-German cookery. When possible, I have also noted which recipes were reprinted in *Der amerikanische Bauer* (The American Farmer), a short-lived but widely read Pennsylvania-German agricultural magazine published by Lutz and Scheffer in the 1850s. I also mention which recipes were plagiarized by other Pennsylvania Germans. One recipe for curing meat, for example, appeared as late as 1932 in a state grange cookbook.

This brings me to another point: Unquestionably, *Die geschickte Hausfrau* had an impact on later Pennsylvania-German culinary literature. Yet its influence was sometimes indirect, because after 1883 the book itself was more or less forgotten. Its importance was not noted again until novelist Ann Hark and Professor Preston Barba of Muhlenberg College joined forces to publish their *Pennsylvania German Cookery* (Allentown, 1950). Although this was a cookbook, it also included one of the first critical attempts to analyze Pennsylvania-Dutch cuisine. It even provided a few recipes from *Die geschickte Hausfrau*. It was not until 1971, however, that the true significance of Peters's cookbook was finally recognized.

In his article, "Historical Sources for American Traditional Cookery," published in 1971 in *Pennsylvania Folklife*, Don Yoder of the University of Pennsylvania discussed *Die geschickte Hausfrau* and concluded that it was one of the earliest Pennsylvania-German works devoted exclusively to cookery. Dr. Yoder reproduced the front cover of what was then the only known copy of the book.

By chance, Eleanor Lowenstein, who was working at the time on a revised edition of the *Bibliography of American Cookery Books, 1742–1860,* located two editions of *Die geschickte Hausfrau* and included them in her bibliography in 1972. Thus, through the work of Dr. Yoder and Mrs. Lowenstein, *Die geschickte Hausfrau* became known to historians and collectors. Nevertheless, there are only about six recorded copies of the cookbook scattered in various library collections around the country, so *Die geschickte Hausfrau* has been virtually inaccessible to the general reader until now.

A Technical Note on the Recipes and Cooking Implements

The recipes in the original *Geschickte Hausfrau* were collected by Gustav Peters because they had one technical feature in common: They were all based on open-hearth cookery. This sets *Die geschickte Hausfrau* apart from the more progressive cookbooks of its period, which promoted the use of cast-iron stoves. This emphasis on hearth cookery is particularly significant in view of the fact that cooking ranges were being manufactured in Pennsylvania as early as 1812.

A cookstove of the 1840s

Long faithful to traditional cooking techniques, Pennsylvania-Dutch housewives were suspicious of newfangled indoor stoves. They considered them a fire hazard. They also thought that cookstoves gave food a "stovey" taste. Most women believed that their outdoor bake ovens gave better texture and flavor to bread, cakes, and pies—a culinary judgment that many professional chefs support today. Pennsylvania-German housewives were so loyal to open-hearth and bake-oven cookery that there are accounts of women still cooking the old way as late as the First World War. Today, alas, only the "Nebraska Amish," a small traditionalist sect in central Pennsylvania, still preserve the use of outdoor bake ovens, but even they have given up the hearthside kitchen.

Of course, hearthside cookery requires a certain degree of experience and expertise. This is alluded to in the title *Die geschickte Hausfrau*. *Geschickt* can mean many different things, but specifically, it implies dexterous hands: in a culinary sense, the ability to make something from nothing. With that in mind, most of the recipes in *Die geschickte Hausfrau* represent the type of cookery once characterized as "practical and substantial." In several cases, the recipes are mere outlines for dishes a cook could elaborate upon according to her talents and means—and cultural inclinations. Whether elaborate or plain, most of the recipes in this book are surprisingly tasty in a hearty, up-country way.

Naturally, to make this discovery, one must test the recipes, which is no easy matter, for nearly all of them need adjusting for any degree of success in the modern kitchen. Furthermore, they represent a system of taste that is strange to the modern palate. I have tried to convey as accurately as possible old nuances of taste, particularly those characteristically Pennsylvania German, or at least characteristic of southeastern Pennsylvania. Among these, for example, was the extensive use of saffron; the use of cassia instead of cloves; and, throughout the nineteenth century, the use of vanilla instead of sugar in certain types of boiled puddings.

At various places in the text, I have also noted those fireplace utensils that may not be familiar to modern cooks. In the chapter on soups, I have included brief instructions on how to manage soups over an open hearth because soups were one of the specialties of Pennsylvania-German cookery. Actually, there is more romance than mystery to hearth cookery. The problems are the same as those faced by campers. They are overcome not by reading about them, but by practical experience.

Acknowledgments

This book would never have taken shape over the past five years without the help and advice of innumerable people. Their enthusiasm for my project kept me going forward at times when I thought I would never see the end. To this category belongs Don Yoder of the University of Pennsylvania. He watched the book grow and was always ready to offer valuable advice. I owe him a special debt of gratitude for his willingness to write the foreword to this book.

Don's help is only surpassed by the patience of Groke Mickey of Charlottesville, Virginia, who must accept the *blame* for inadvertently getting this project started. Groke gave me the copy of *The Virginia House-Wife* that led to the discovery of recipe plagiarism in *Die geschickte Hausfrau*. That spark set in motion the research that culminated in these pages. Groke has waited five years to see my work in print; to him I dedicate this book.

There is another person, however, who deserves almost as much credit for *Sauerkraut Yankees* as I do. He is my agent, Martin Stanford. I must admit, when Martin came into this project, he took on a halfborn book and midwifed it into existence. In the process, he has become a genuine friend.

As far as the actual research for this book is concerned, I shall always remain grateful to the following colleagues for their sincere interest and especially for sending me material that was unavailable in this country: Maria Dembińska, of the Polish Academy of Science (Warsaw), for material on medieval diet; my friend Edith Hörandner, of the University of Vienna, for a valuable array of studies on Central European foods and foodways, including her own important articles on rural diet; Kevin O'Danachair, University College, Dublin, for research on Celtic foodways and flat cakes; Hans-Jürgen Teuteberg, University of Münster (Federal Republic of Germany), for material on German sugar and meat consumption—I am still reminded of our pleasant discussions over dinner at my home not many years ago; Anke Wijnsma, of the Rijksmuseum voor Volkskunde (Arnhem, Holland), for material on scrapple; and finally, Maria Van Winter of the University of Utrecht, a specialist on medieval cookery with whom I have had the pleasure of sharing scarce native herbs from my garden.

On this side of the Atlantic, I should like to thank Christine Richardson, of the German Society of Pennsylvania, for allowing me to dig for rarities in that remarkable but only partially catalogued collection. By the same token, the staff of the Library Company of Philadelphia deserves special credit for extending a friendly, courteous, and professional hand in assisting me with my work.

Karen Hess, editor of Martha Washington's *Booke of Cookery*, and, more recently, of a new edition of *The Virginia House-Wife*, must be given special thanks for her review of my manuscript. She caught inconsistencies and made observations that threw new light on several aspects of my research. She called me one night from New York to tell me that there was no butter in the pound cake recipe—as there ought to be! Well, I didn't leave it out, and neither did Gustav Peters, because he copied his recipe verbatim from another book. It was just one of those mysteries that often crops up in food research and makes the exchange of opinions between writers so thoroughly engaging.

Next, I should like to mention Ingalill Hjelm and Lee Ann Draud at the University of Pennsylvania Press. They kept me on schedule with my *Quaker Woman's Cookbook*, labored with me over page corrections, and made the whole business of book-birthing an art and a pleasure.

Speaking of art, I simply cannot fail to mention Lawrence R. Didona, a sensitive artist and designer who put so much of himself into the visual aspects of this book. To him I owe a special word of thanks.

Finally, I should like to express my gratitude to all the Pennsylvania-Dutch housewives who have been so helpful to me in the course of my research. Their willingness to supply observations, recipes, and heirloom cookbooks provided me with insights that were available nowhere else. Because of them, my work continues. So I should like also to hear from my readers if they have information about foods, implements, cooking techniques, or old cookbooks that might shed additional light on Pennsylvania-German foods and culture.

August 1982   **William Woys Weaver**

Devon, Pennsylvania
USA 19333

1

DIE GESCHICKTE HAUSFRAU
Its Author and Its Setting

In a very real sense, the original *Geschickte Hausfrau* reflected all the quirks and color of its unassuming but highly unusual maker, Gustav Sigismund Peters. Born in 1793 at Langenbrück, Saxony (now in the German Democratic Republic), Peters was a Dresden-trained printer who in 1828 set himself up in business at Harrisburg, Pennsylvania's state capital. There he embarked on a nineteen-year career as printer and publisher of books and reading matter for the Pennsylvania Dutch, particularly for Pennsylvania-Dutch children. His gemlike toy books with color plates, his charming woodcuts and delightful broadsides, are now among the most sought-after prizes on the American rare-book market.

But there was another, little-known side of Gustav Peters, for lurking beneath his amiable pottering with toy books and games was a resolute recipe pirate. When he put his printing tools aside and donned his beaver hat for a stroll around Harrisburg's Market Square, Gustav Peters assumed the role of a cookery buff, a gourmet of a very peculiar sort.

Described by his contemporary William H. Egle as short and fat (well fed), with blond hair and the features of a "jolly old elf," Peters lived in a community that accepted his bachelor lifestyle with good-natured reserve.[3] He lived alone in Nagel's Hotel and dined out often, for it was possible in those days to find a decent meal in Harrisburg— as even Charles Dickens once noted with a grumble of surprise.

Peters was not a creative cook and probably understood very little about some of the finer points of culinary technique. The closest he came to an oven was to sleep in an armchair in the office of his bookstore, with his feet propped up on an old ten-plate stove. To him belonged the avocation of light-fingered collector, the inveterate recipe snipper whose "master work" surfaced upon the world in the form of *Die geschickte Hausfrau* only after he was safely in the grave.

At the time of his death in March of 1847, Peters had already prepared for publication *The Family's Guide*, a little cookbook that was nothing short of blatant piracy on his part, since word for word, it belonged to a New York State printer. *Die geschickte Hausfrau* was not so baldly illegal; its garnered composition was more diverse and more adroitly hidden beneath the murky veneer of German. Perhaps there are some gourmets whose penchant leans more toward savoring intrigue than flavors. If so, Peters belonged to that class.

His love of stomach took a remarkable twist in the end—unique in Pennsylvania's history, I think—and for reasons quite lost upon Peters's friends and heirs, the press, the state capital, and posterity. No doubt he enjoyed a thousand laughs among the angels when it was discovered in his will that his stomach was to be removed from his corpse, stuffed with snuff, and placed between his legs for the public to admire at his viewing. This added a wonderfully morbid note of hocus-pocus to what otherwise would have been an unspectacular departure. The day after Peters was buried at Harrisburg's Mt. Kalma Cemetery, his executors discovered the will and out of duty, duly exhumed the corpse to carry out this bizarre last request, much to the scandal of everyone involved.*

These gruesome details would be of little value to our sketch of Gustav Peters and *Die geschickte Hausfrau*—and would have caused a much greater scandal at the time—if they had not been quickly clouded up in mystery or, rather, quietly suppressed by Peters's trusted friends and executors, Johann Martin Lutz and Theodore F. Scheffer, who were also his legal heirs and the actual publishers of the cookbook. Gustav Peters died on March 22, 1847, just as he had *predicted* two years earlier in his will. One could wonder whether he did not guarantee his speedy end as specified with an artful potion concocted from one of his innumerable books on chemistry. Or was it uncanny coincidence?

During most of 1846, Peters worked on *Die geschickte Hausfrau*, probably with the help of one or two of his employees. The manuscript was rough and incomplete when he died. Although the first edition was undated, it did not appear until over a year after his death. The only names on the title page were those of its publishers, Lutz and Scheffer.

A native Pennsylvania German, J. Martin Lutz was a druggist who owned the building in which Peters kept his shop. Theodore Scheffer was a Harrisburg printer who, like Peters, was born near Dresden in Saxony.[4] As a youth, he had served as an apprentice in Peters's firm. In the years following Peters's death, he built up the business until it be-

---

*According to the *Pennsylvanische Staats Zeitung* for March 24, 1847, Peters died during the night of March 22. His *first* viewing was held on the twenty-fourth at 3:00 P.M. in the home of Martin Lutz. Peters was buried later in the afternoon. His will was not discovered and probated until the next day (Dauphin County, *Will Book F*, vol. 1, p. 50).

Harrisburg

came one of the largest and most influential German printing houses in the state.

From Recipe Snippings to Best Seller

It was not until August of 1848 that Lutz and Scheffer were able to settle with Peters's other heirs and consolidate their control of the company. On August 1, 1848, they announced in the Harrisburg *Keystone* that they would continue to print all of the books published by Peters and, presumably, finish the many projects he had started. We must assume, then, that *Die geschickte Hausfrau* appeared sometime after August of 1848.

Lutz and Scheffer may have wanted to get the cookbook out in time for Christmas of that year, since it was sold initially as a gift book at a price of ten cents a copy. Perhaps it was only coincidental, but this edition of *Die geschickte Hausfrau* was bound in deep green paper with a border design overprinted in red, giving it a somewhat festive, Christmas appearance. Other than this, little else is known about the early stages of *Die geschickte Hausfrau*.

As a collection of recipes, *Die geschickte Hausfrau* is fairly straightforward. And since editorializing and recipe tampering are almost totally absent, it is not difficult to follow the trail of Peters's culinary banditry and pinpoint his sources of inspiration. This in itself tells us something about Peters's view of cookery and about the audience for whom he wrote.

The inventories of Peters's bookshop and private library, taken after his death in 1847, reveal much about his interest in culinary subjects. He owned a copy of William Kitchiner's *Cook's Oracle* (probably the New York edition of 1825), Louis Ude's *The French Cook* (Philadelphia, 1828), and several other works on what might be considered period *haute cuisine*. None of these books provided material for *Die geschickte Hausfrau*. To understand this work, we must turn to books of a more popular nature.

Of the 141 recipes in the original *Geschickte Hausfrau*, 28 can be traced directly to *The Kitchen Companion*, an 1844 Philadelphia cooking manual of similar chapbook character and format. Other recipes can be traced to Mary Randolph's *Virginia House-Wife* (Washington, D.C., 1824) and to Thomas Cooper's *Treatise of Domestic Medicine* (Reading, Pa., 1824), which is usually classified as a cookbook because most of it is devoted to cookery. Mary Randolph's cookbook was known and used by some Pennsylvania Germans, which is not surprising considering that part of the Pennsylvania-German settlement area included the Valley of Virginia. But of the three works just mentioned, Cooper's is the least known and most unusual. In connection with *Die geschickte Hausfrau*, it deserves some explanation.

Advertisements in the *Pennsylvanische Staats Zeitung*, a Pennsylvania-German newspaper printed in Harrisburg, make it clear that Peters was selling *The Virginia House-Wife*, several other American cookbooks, and a number of cookbooks imported from Germany. He also sold copies of Cooper's treatise, both the Reading reprint of 1824—sold as a separate work—and A. F. M. Willich's *Domestic Encyclopedia*, in which the treatise first appeared as an appendix to the third edition of 1821. Cooper edited that edition of the *Encyclopedia* while he was professor of chemistry and mineralogy at the University of Pennsylvania. By his own admission, he garnered his recipes from Beauvillier's *L'art du cuisinier*; Menon's *Cuisinière bourgeoise* (a French work known in Philadelphia since the 1790s); and from Maria Rundell's *New System of Domestic Cookery*, an English work reprinted in Philadelphia in 1807, 1808, and 1810. Cooper's claims aside, most of the recipes in his treatise appear to come from Mrs. Rundell rather than from the French cookbooks. Since material from Mrs. Rundell's popular work also appeared in *The Virginia House-Wife* and *The Kitchen Companion*, one could argue that her influence on *Die geschickte Hausfrau*, while not direct, was nonetheless pervasive.

This is one reason why, at first glance, the recipes in *Die geschickte Hausfrau* seem overwhelmingly "English" or, more accurately, mainstream Anglo-American in character. The twist is that they have been given an entirely different context in a Pennsylvania-German cookbook. Whatever their origin, in practice, different customs prevailed.

As we shall see later in this book, we cannot presume that Pennsylvania-German cooks—or most American cooks for that matter—used recipes literally as printed. Many times I have watched Pennsylvania-German women, now in their eighties and nineties, read spotty old recipes and from them make seemingly impossible dishes with perfect ease. Rather than follow the recipes verbatim, they brought into use a body of knowledge that was not in print. This in itself may explain why many errors in the original *Geschickte Hausfrau* were simply overlooked as inconsequential—the cooks knew better anyway.

When using printed recipes, Pennsylvania-German cooks would interpret cream as sour cream unless otherwise specified. Butter was always sour cream butter (almost universal in rural Pennsylvania before the appearance of commercial creameries). Cloves were exchanged for cassia, particularly in pickles—an old peculiarity of the Philadelphia region. Corn meal always meant *roasted* corn meal. Whiskey, even brandy, was taken to mean rye. Butter in pastry dough became leaf lard (pork lard rendered from the loins only). Meat pies required rye pastry. And wheat flour was always regarded as a legitimate thickener in sauces and gravies, whether called for or not—a taste preference doubtless carried over from South German cookery.

From an ethnological standpoint, there was not much in *The Kitchen Companion*, *The Virginia House-Wife*, or Cooper's *Treatise* to appeal to the sensibilities of a Pennsylvania-German cook, provided, of course, that she could, or wanted to, read English. And while there was no question that *Die geschickte Hausfrau* served a purpose in assimilating many general American dishes into the cookery of the Pennsylvania Germans simply by making recipes for them available in German, the final product was not total Americanization but something quite different, in fact, quite the opposite. For the cookbook marked the beginning of a search for a culinary identity, for something that was not German in the Old World sense, but something that was uniquely *Pennsylfaanisch*.

Cultural Tastes Versus Social Realities

Until 1848, the average Pennsylvania-German housewife did not have a great selection of native cookbooks reflecting her particular cultural tastes and point of view. Certainly, before this time, there were a number of Pennsylvania-German books and periodicals that included domestic recipes. Johann Krauss's *Oeconomisches Haus- und Kunstbuch* (Economical Domestic Receipt Book: Allentown, 1819) and Samuel and Solomon Siegfried's *41 bewährte Recepte* (41 Proven Recipes: Millgrove, Pa., 1834) both included a handful of kitchen recipes, although most of the material in these works was clearly intended for men.

Then, of course, there was George Girardey's *Höchst nützliches Handbuch über Kochkunst*, already mentioned. While brain dumplings or pig's feet in mustard sauce were frequent enough on the well-stocked tables of German Pennsylvania, with this cookbook one usually needed a brace of chafing dishes to get from point A to point B. It was not really a practical cookbook for the rural household—least of all for rural Ohio or Pennsylvania, although there was certainly a wide range of recipes, from authentic peasant dishes to the most refined sort of Philadelphia *haute cuisine*. Indeed, Girardey's cookery might be characterized as period Philadelphia high-style cookery done up in German, for the overall appeal of his recipes was limited to the circumstances and economics of German-speaking caterers and the most urbanized element of Pennsylvania-German society. It was certainly not a middle-class cooking manual by any stretch of the imagination. How many American housewives of the 1840s would be willing to fuss with a béchamel sauce or mutton tongue *à la Liégeoise*?

Before 1848, the only steady source of middle-class German-language cookbooks was Europe. In most cases, these books were not completely suited to the special needs of the Pennsylvania Dutch, but a few of the titles are worth mentioning anyway, particularly those that exerted some measure of influence on culinary thinking here.

Thus far, the earliest-known imported work with any reference to cookery surfacing from a Pennsylvania-German kitchen is the *Allgemeines oeconomisches Lexicon* (General Practical Encyclopedia: Leipzig, 1731). It contains general descriptions of many dishes and their preparation, as well as considerable material on culinary herbs and spices. There are not many actual working recipes, for after all, this is only a household reference book, not a culinary manual. Yet it is typical of the sort of literary sources once found in the eighteenth-century Pennsylvania-German household, more common, in fact, than cookbooks, because a large portion of the female population at the time could neither read nor write. Most eighteenth-century German cookbooks seem to have fallen into the hands of confectioners and professional cooks.

Among these was Marcus Loofft's *Nieder-Sächsisches Koch-Buch* (Lower Saxony Cookbook: Lübeck, 1778).[5] Loofft's book was known and used in Pennsylvania—his taffy recipe may be the source for Pennsylvania-German *Moschi*—but his full importance in terms of continuing culinary influence cannot be assessed until more eighteenth-century Pennsylvania-German manuscript cookbooks come to light.

Not until after the Revolutionary War, when more Pennsylvania-German girls were sent to school, did the cookbook come into its own. Naturally, Pennsylvania-German women sought out cookbooks that represented a cookery most familiar to them. One of the most popular of the imported cookbooks was Friederike Löffler's *Oekonomisches Handbuch für Frauenzimmer* (Stuttgart, 1791), and small wonder, considering that her cookbook stayed in print in Germany until 1930. Friederike Löffler was to the Pennsylvania-German housewife what Maria Rundell and her *New System of Domestic Cookery* was to the Anglo-American cook. In general, Löffler's cookery was South German, but her particular emphasis was on her native Swabia. Doubtless she had great appeal in Pennsylvania, since roughly one-third of the Pennsylvania Dutch were of Swabian extraction.

Friederike Luise Herbord was born at Kürnach-bei-Bretten (Baden-

Friederike Löffler's *Vollständiges Kochbuch*, with the engraved title page by Hugo Sebald.

Württemberg) in 1744, the daughter of a druggist.[6] Her early life is not too well documented, but we do know that in 1779, at the age of thirty-five, she had an affair with a soldier, became pregnant, and had to scramble to the altar. Her wooer, Johann Friedrich Löffler, was a trumpeter and drummer for the Horse Guards of the Duke of Württemberg—presumably a dashing candidate for a husband. For most of her life Frau Löffler was employed by the state as a *Beschließerin*, one of those ambiguous German terms for "kitchen personnel." She never became a royal cook or master chef, because in Germany those positions were professionally organized trades and not open to women. Regardless, she was an excellent cook and under ducal privilege, published her cookbook in 1791. Overnight, she became famous, and when she died in 1805, her book was already entering its fifth edition. According to the records of the J. F. Steinkopf publishing house, which first printed the book and which is still in existence, her cookbook went through at least thirty-eight editions.

Löffler's recipes crop up constantly in Pennsylvania-German sources. They were published regularly in the old Reading *Adler* and other Pennsylvania-German newspapers. Her recipes appear in manuscript cookbooks and have come down to us through oral tradition. In short, when a Pennsylvania-German housewife was not sure how a certain "folk" dish should be made, she probably consulted Löffler.

By the 1820s, copies of Löffler's cookbook were being imported and sold regularly, but the market does not seem to have been satisfied.[7] Demand for her cookbook grew so much during the following decades that Franz Loës, an editor for *Die freie Presse* (a Philadelphia newspaper), and Hugo Sebald, an illustrator, collaborated to publish an "Americanized" edition of her cookbook under the title *Vollständiges Kochbuch für die deutsch-amerikanische Küche* (Complete Cookbook for the German-American Kitchen). The book was published without date or copyright about 1856. A later edition was published by F. W. Thomas of Philadelphia. Both editions were widely advertised in Pennsylvania. The *Republikaner von Berks*, for example, carried an advertisement in its issue of August 15, 1872, and excerpts from the cookbook appeared in other newspapers as late as the First World War.

That Löffler's influence was enormous is undeniable. That she should finally emerge in print from a Pennsylvania press a few years after the appearance of *Die geschickte Hausfrau* may have been the result of the influx of so many new German immigrants into Pennsylvania after 1848. But the most intriguing implication of her role in Pennsylvania-German culinary literature is that Löffler (particularly in the Americanized editions), Girardey, and *Die geschickte Hausfrau* do not seem to overlap: They represent three separate intellectual currents in a much larger and more complex culinary picture.

Certainly, *Die geschickte Hausfrau* represents the thinking of the oldest and most Americanized generation of Pennsylvania-Germans—

the so-called "silent majority" of the times. By the 1840s, there was a general readiness to break a historic dependence on Germany for intellectual nourishment. This shift in thinking crystalized after the German Revolution of 1848, with the realization that the oppressive political system in Germany was corrupt and was dumping thousands of refugees, or *Deitschlenner*, as the Pennsylvania Dutch commonly called them, on Pennsylvania. Older elements of the Pennsylvania-German community became locked in a bitter struggle with these new Germans. It was a struggle for political identity that also had very definite ethnic and nationalistic overtones. The total absence of the term "German" or "German-American" in the title of *Die geschickte Hausfrau* was probably intentional, as doubtless was its presence in Franz Loës's edition of Löffler, serving as a reminder that Löffler belonged to a larger group than just the Pennsylvania Dutch.

J. C. Myers, a Virginian of Pennsylvania-German background who visited Harrisburg in July of 1848 (in time to see Governor Shunk on his deathbed), noted in his *Sketches* (1849) that there was a huge commotion in the Pennsylvania-German community over the "multitude of aliens" who were recently given the right to vote.[8] The *Deitschlenner* were accused of taking control of the churches, publishing houses, and newspapers, which they had, in fact, done. And since they were not large landholders and were often extremely liberal politically, the *Deitschlenner* were seen as a threat to the very institutions that held the Pennsylvania Germans together as a distinctive community.

Nativism and the Know-Nothing party, Locofoco factions, and ugly antiforeign sentiments were all displayed prominently in the state capital. The Pennsylvania Dutch, fearful that they would be swallowed up in the new wave of immigration, fell victims to an identity crisis of major proportions; they knew they were not Germans, even though they spoke a German-based language. This nativist thinking is in essence what made *Die geschickte Hausfrau* so tailored to the times. It appeared at absolutely the right moment. Between 1848 and 1854, the cookbook ran through six distinct editions with many intermediate printings. In short, it became a best seller overnight and remained in print for thirty-five years.

Only a book appealing to the broadest spectrum of Pennsylvania-German society could claim such a success. That there were no recipes for rasped rolls, terrapin, shad roe with oranges, vanilla ice cream, or any of the other dishes then so popular among Pennsylvania's upper classes certainly attested to the middle-class American character of the cookbook. That there were no traditional recipes of the sort widely adapted from Löffler suggested that the Dutch were still unsure about who they were and what actually constituted their culture. In terms of cookery, the nostalgia and ethnic symbolism connected with certain dishes had not yet developed—that came during the Civil War. For the time being, the Dutch had to look elsewhere for the kind of identification they needed. It came in the form of *Die geschickte Hausfrau* and its offshoot Aunt Pall.

Enter Aunt Pall: Cook and Commentator

"Pall" is Pennsylvania Dutch for Mary. It is a nickname that, in the context of *Die geschickte Hausfrau*, is meant to imply a whole range of familiarities and characterizations as humorous as they are lovable.

Aunt Pall appeared on the scene about 1850. The exact date of her "birth" is unknown because she may have started her career in any one of several local Pennsylvania-German newspapers. In all probability, however, her character took shape under the pen of Jacob Maximilian Beck, an émigré of the 1848 revolutions, a talented *Deitschlenner* whom Lutz and Scheffer brought into the firm to edit their new agricultural journal called *Der amerikanische Bauer* (The American Farmer).[9] The *Bauer* was written for German-speaking Americans all over the country. It began publication in the fall of 1850, thus more or less initiating the official existence of Aunt Pall, who faithfully wrote letters to "Mister Beck" in Pennsylvania Dutch.

Pall was probably modeled on *der Alte vom Berge* ("The Old Mountain Sage"), a fictitious Pennsylvania Dutchman who wrote letters to the editor of the *Philadelphier Demokrat*, a liberal German newspaper whose politics coincided with Jacob Beck's. *Der Alte* was actually Ludwig Wollenweber, editor of the *Demokrat*, who subsequently collected many of his letters and published them in 1869 under the title of *Gemälde aus dem pennsylvanischen Volksleben* (Pictures from Pennsylvania-German Folklife). Aunt Pall's letters have never been collected.

As a folk figure, Aunt Pall was thoroughly vernacular. She was cast in the role of a big-hearted but outspoken cook who waged an endless campaign of complaining letters. Her correspondence usually contained culinary advice and almost always appeared with a handful of recipes reprinted from *Die geschickte Hausfrau*. But Pall also attracted attention for other reasons, because she inevitably expounded on her philosophies of life, the low status of women, and the ignorance of the male sex: "Do you believe that I really care anything about men? No indeedy! Not for the whole world!"[10] Remarks like that drew avid fan mail, which was sometimes published, as well as scorching criticism, which she countered in one of her letters by commenting: "When anyone tries to cross me, I stick my fingers in my ears and keep shouting what I think as loud as I can until I shout them down."[11] Pall believed staunchly in women's rights, but her outspoken independence was also a spoof of the suffragettes. Taken a step further, Pall was also a spoof of the Pennsylvania Dutch themselves.

Most importantly, by writing her letters in Pennsylvania-German dialect, the language of the hearthside, Pall was able to communicate directly with her Pennsylvania-Dutch readers under the guise of an ethnic underdog with a salty sense of humor. It was this image of cultural inferiority in an aggressive Anglo-American world—of self-worthlessness impressed upon them by less tolerant English-speaking neighbors—that struck a deep chord in the minds of Aunt Pall's readers. They loved her. Aunt Pall was made to order. Like them, she reveled in her misery. Like the complaining aunt or grandmother everyone knew, Pall was the kind of scrappy old widow who could cook a perfect dinner for twenty and describe in detail, before she finished serving, everything that had gone wrong in the kitchen. Aunt Pall was a true anti-heroine.

Her popularity among the Sauerkraut Yankees seems to have been instant and universal. Her dialect letters were quickly reprinted in numerous German-language newspapers. The *Libanon Demokrat*, for example, carried Pall's letters in weekly installments on the front page. In this way, Aunt Pall received an informal syndication that went far beyond the national readership of *Der amerikanische Bauer*. While Lutz and Scheffer made no direct reference to Pall in later editions of *Die geschickte Hausfrau*, the association was clear enough. Her image became so firmly planted in the popular imagination that Lutz and Scheffer did not *need* to publicize their cookbook. As her role evolved around *Die geschickte Hausfrau*, Pall fell into place as its symbol and its transmitter. The *Geschickte Hausfrau* became *geschickte Pall*.

As a result of this huge popularity, Lutz and Scheffer reedited the 1850 edition of *Die geschickte Hausfrau*; they changed the subtitle slightly, corrected many of the textual errors, introduced neater typography, and replaced a recipe at the end. With this new face, *Die geschickte Hausfrau* ran through several consecutive printings, until it was further corrected in 1851 and given a more decorative cover in 1852. In 1853 the cookbook was thoroughly reedited, many of the dialect words were standardized, the subtitle was changed back to its original wording, and L. Johnson and Company of Philadelphia was contracted to make stereotype plates. After 1853, this stereotyped edition was issued many times, often without date, so that it is now difficult to determine the exact order of publication.

Certainly Gustav S. Peters never dreamed his little cookbook would reach the heights of popularity it experienced during the 1850s. Much of its success was due to timing and to the larger unforeseen events that rapidly changed the mood of the nation. Although the popularity of *Die geschickte Hausfrau* declined considerably by the end of the Civil War, as other cultural symbols began to evolve for the Dutch, it did remain in print until Theodore F. Scheffer's death in 1883. Thus, for almost thirty-five years, Aunt Pall reigned as queen of the Sauerkraut Yankees. Copies of her cookbook found their way into every corner of Pennsylvania and into every far-flung German-American settlement in the United States and Canada. Now, however, existing copies of *Die geschickte Hausfrau* are extremely scarce. As a paperback designed to fit into every Aunt Pall's apron pocket, it was literally thumbed to shreds.

2

Meats and Hearthside Savories

*Fuffzich Brodwarscht in dar Pann
siss genunk fer eenzicher Mann!*

Translation

Fifty sausages in the pan;
That's enough for any man!

OLD FOLK SAYING

The central characteristic of classical Pennsylvania-German cookery was the interplay of sweet flavors against salty ones. The combination of fruit and salty meat in such Pennsylvania-German dishes as *Schnitz un Gnepp* (a stew of dried apples, smoked ham, and dumplings) or its older cousin *Gumbis* (apples, ham, bacon, and onions), for which George Girardey published a recipe, were typical of this classic arrangement of flavors.[12]

Both of these dishes have a long history in South German cookery. *Gumbis*, a dialect corruption of the Latin *compositum* (a mixture), may trace to the ancient monastery cookery of central Switzerland. It is considered a traditional dish in Canton Zürich, where it is better known by the name of *Gumbistöpfel* ("pot" Gumbis).[13] *Schnitz un Gnepp*, its variation, is well known as *Schnitz un Drunder* in Canton Aargau and some of the other neighboring cantons.[14] It is known as *Schnitz un Gnepp* in Swabia and the Rhineland, two areas to which many Pennsylvania Germans trace their ancestry.[15] Doubtless, this type of fruit and meat cookery was brought to Pennsylvania from Europe in the early eighteenth century; it was not invented here, as many people think. It did undergo considerable alteration once it reached Pennsylvania, however, partly because of the sorts of meats available to cooks on this side of the Atlantic. Furthermore, Pennsylvania-German fruit and meat cookery was shaped by the emphasis Pennsylvania Germans placed on the combination of dishes during the course of eating.

On the peasant level, a dish like *Schnitz un Gnepp* combined all the basic elements of a meal. The dried apples provided acidic contrast to the meat, the dumplings provided a form of cereal starch (instead of adding groats or rice, for example), and the liquid provided the basic sweet and salty gravy.

In middle-class Pennsylvania-German households, such one-pot meals were disassembled and the various components were served individually. The liquid became a soup, served first, as in Girardey's ap-

ple soup (recipe 63)—with or without the wine; the apples, chopped
and cooked with sauerkraut (recipe 128), celery, and onions, would
appear as a side dish; the dumplings (originally a substitute for meat
anyway) became an unsweetened flour pudding (recipe 67), perhaps
with the addition of raisins or some other dried fruit. And the ham
hock, which supplied *Schnitz un Gnepp* with its meat and much of its
flavor, became a pork roast (recipe 9) with a gravy of its own. We have
just created the basic two-course meal—a soup course and a meat
course—as it was known in eighteenth-century Pennsylvania.

In old Pennsylvania High German, as well as in dialect, the most
common word for course was *Gang*, a word that implied the motion
of going through something. This, of course, was exactly what one did
when one progressed through a meal. *Gang* had a more specific meaning as well, for it could also be a "remove." The remove was a dish
brought on to replace an earlier dish on the table. It was the main feature of the second course—usually a roast of some kind—and was
brought on to replace the soup tureen after the first course was over.

The roast was always the centerpiece of the Pennsylvania-German
meal; it was also the centerpiece of the table, unencumbered by flowers. There was no room for table decorations, because there was usually a large platter in the middle of the table to serve as a hot plate for
main dishes. The decorations went on the roast. Furthermore, there
was no clutter of candlesticks, because people ate dinner in the
middle of the day—supper, of course, was another matter. But generally, in the Pennsylvania-German two-course meal, the remove differed
from colonial English custom in that it was usually pork rather than
beef and rarely ever mutton. Yet it could be a haunch of venison (recipe 10), baked fish, or, for that matter, a goose (recipe 30) if the occasion required.

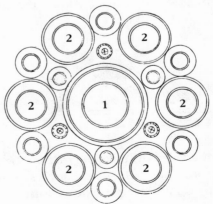

Arrangement of platter (1) and side dishes (2) according to formal upper-
class practice for a circular dining table. Vinegar and oil cruets, three of
each, stand symmetrically arranged around the platter. Such formal dinner arrangements were more typical of entertaining in towns than in the
countryside.

The roast would be surrounded by a number of lesser dishes arranged symmetrically on the table. One can imagine how attractive that would have looked on the Meissen services advertised for sale by Carl Heinitsch in the *Neue unpartheyische Lancaster Zeitung* for September 7, 1791. Whether served on Meissen, pewter, plain Queen's ware, or "Delft" (cheap and very popular among the Pennsylvania Germans), each side dish was designed to complement the roast in some way with an interplay of sweet and salty flavors. The number of these complementing dishes and the elaborateness of their preparation depended on the economic circumstances and taste preferences of the household.

As a rule, two-course meals were prepared only on special occasions, for in practice, even among the wealthy, many families reverted to one-course "peasant" meals when not entertaining. By modern standards of consumption, the simplicity of their general eating habits might very well be called Spartan. But dietary caution was thrown to the wind when it came to meat, because one rule remained invariable: The Pennsylvania Germans ate meat in some form at least three times a day. They considered it a necessity.

It is a state of mind best expressed in the Pennsylvania-Dutch saying:

> *Besser en Laus im Graut*
> *ass wie gaar ken Fleesch!*

> Better a louse in the kraut
> than no meat at all!

When Gottlieb Mittelberger visited the colonies in the 1750s, he was astounded at the wealth of foodstuffs consumed by the Germans. Unquestionably, they ate better than their cousins back home, better even than the Frieslanders and Pomeranians, who were legendary in Germany for their prodigious meat appetites. Mittelberger wrote: "I don't think that there is any country in which more meat is eaten and consumed than in Pennsylvania."[16] Mittelberger may have overstated his case, but there was a glut of meat, that much was true, and it continued unabated into the nineteenth century.

Johannes Klein, an immigrant from Birkenau in Hessia, wrote home in 1831 and described the Pennsylvania Dutch of Franklin County: "If they don't have meat three times a day, they can't stand it. Meat eating here is really astounding. My neighbor, a shoemaker, devoured four hogs in three months and has to earn it all by shoemaking."[17]

The important point in both of these observations made almost a century apart is that the meat consumed in such enormous quantities was pork.

In German-speaking Europe, pork was the most favored meat

among the farming classes, because hogs were not difficult to raise and did not require pastureland, which belonged almost exclusively to the nobility.[18] Furthermore, unlike mutton, pork could be put to a vast number of uses, from sausages to pot puddings. Very little of the animal was wasted, so in terms of economic return, it was by far the most practical source of meat for a small farmer. Because the Pennsylvania Germans were basically gardener-farmers rather than cattle and sheep raisers as were the peoples of the British Isles, they continued the tradition of pork raising in America. Pennsylvania-German cookery was based on pork. If the Pennsylvania Germans had not continued pork raising in the New World, their traditional cookery would have vanished in the first generation or would have taken on a completely different form.

As it happened, traditional Pennsylvania-German cookery existed side by side with the English. But since farms were much larger in Pennsylvania and less specialized than in Germany, the Pennsylvania Dutch were able to diversify and add cattle and sheep to their livestock herds. Cattle were mostly viewed as a form of economic return, so the animals were usually sold to drovers who took them to market in Philadelphia or Baltimore. In terms of the amount of beef produced, only a small proportion of it found its way onto Pennsylvania-German tables. But as market patterns shifted with the building of the railroads in the 1830s and 1840s, Pennsylvania Germans were less able to compete against large-scale cattle producers elsewhere. Thus, more and more beef was consumed locally. This had a direct effect on the composition of the Pennsylvania-German meal.

When beef is substituted for the main dish in the two-course meal, the side dishes and gravies change accordingly to take on greater character of their own. Unlike pork, beef is best plain and does not absolutely require the sharp acidic contrast of fruit or vinegar to enhance its flavor. This is one reason why the Pennsylvania Germans took up Anglo-American side dishes when they took up beef eating. With a few exceptions, the very nature of the meat prompted the abandonment of traditional taste combinations—a pattern that accelerated as the nineteenth century progressed.

The beef recipes in *Die geschickte Hausfrau* represent a transi-

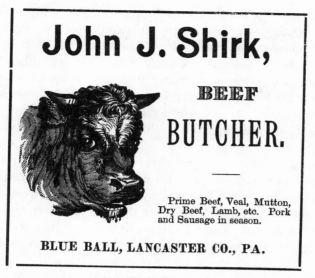

Beef butchering was once a specialized branch of butchering among the Pennsylvania Germans. To supplement their trade, beef butchers handled other meats, such as mutton and veal, and in this case, even pork. (From a Lancaster County broadside, 1870s)

tional phase in the Pennsylvania-German diet, for by the 1840s, there were certainly many Pennsylvania Germans who had given up pork, at least partially, if not altogether. The recipes for marinated beef (recipe 11) and tongue (recipe 23) are two beef dishes that might be characterized as adaptations of the basic sweet-and-salty taste system favored by the Pennsylvania Dutch. In both cases, vinegar is employed to enhance the meat, and in the tongue recipe, which calls for raspberry vinegar, we have the classic interplay of fruit and meat flavors.

The greater availability and relative cheapness of beef and veal in Pennsylvania had another major effect on Pennsylvania-German cookery: It encouraged a shift in emphasis away from sausages in favor of English-style meat pies, particularly mince meat pie (recipe 74). By the nineteenth century, mince meat pie often took the place of sausage as a side dish in a two-course meal, as well as serving as a sausage substitute at breakfast or supper. Mince meat itself could be preserved more easily than delicate sausages like *Blutwurst* (blood sausage), and the interplay of vinegar, molasses, and meat was consistent with traditional Pennsylvania-German taste. Thus, mince meat pie was looked upon not only as a Christmas food, but also as a general cold-weather dish.

As for the mutton and lamb recipes in *Die geschickte Hausfrau*, the consumption of mutton and lamb was so low among the Pennsylvania Dutch that it is surprising to find recipes for them in the cookbook. Even the English-speaking Pennsylvanians ate less lamb and mutton than their New England cousins. As James Lemon has pointed out in his 1972 study of southeastern Pennsylvania agriculture, many factors contributed to this interesting difference in diet.[19] Pennsylvania's hot, humid summers were not friendly to the breeds of sheep available to the English colonists in the eighteenth century, although Mittelberger states that they were better than the sheep in Germany. But more important, Pennsylvania agriculture was based on intensive farming, which made large-scale sheep raising unprofitable.

In addition to this, mutton could not be utilized like pork in traditional Pennsylvania-German cookery. Pennsylvania-German cooks had no repertoire of mutton recipes to rely on, except to treat it like venison, which was one common solution. Very sweet contrasting flavors usually enhance mutton. The Pennsylvania Germans were not accustomed to highly sweetened foods like the fruit and herb jellies used by the English to complement their mutton dishes. Jellies served no condiment purpose on the Pennsylvania-German table until people began to eat white bread in imitation of upper-class Anglo-Americans, and this did not begin on a large scale until after the Civil War. Today, sweet jellies and pickles have been tacked onto the Pennsylvania-German meal to compensate for the smaller amount of meat served, even to the extent that in some households (and many restaurants) the meat has become little more than a garnish.

In this chapter, recipes 1–5, 10, 15, 21, 22, 23, and 24 may be traced to *The Kitchen Companion*. Recipes 1–19 were later reprinted in the third volume of *Der amerikanische Bauer* in the same order that they appeared in *Die geschickte Hausfrau*. Recipe 23, for tongue, also appeared in the *American Pocket Farrier* (Philadelphia, 1845).

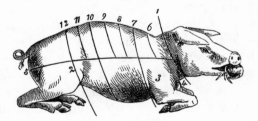

1. To Roast a Suckling Pig
(Ein Spanferkel zu braten)

Crumble the soft part of 2 loaves of bread; add 1 pound of butter, a sufficient quantity of salt, pepper, and sage; stuff the piglet with this mixture and sew it up. Roast it 2½ hours, basting it frequently with salt and water. Take care that the meat does not scorch.

Suckling pigs were regarded with particular awe by the Pennsylvania Dutch. Their presence on the menu was usually reserved for special occasions of festive, community-wide importance, such as militia musters, fairs, and Second Christmas—the great market-fair celebrated by the Dutch each December 26. The roasting was done in the market square or in a field nearby, and literally everyone was involved, from the first slaughter to the last bite.

For the more genteel, at-home banquet, George Girardey's *Handbuch über Kochkunst* suggested a rich forcemeat stuffing of minced ham and calf's liver seasoned with salt, pepper, powdered cloves, chopped sage, and sweet basil.[20] Purists will remind us that to be utterly true to traditional Pennsylvania-German taste, the piglet should come to the table on a pewter platter surrounded by sauerkraut, celery, sliced cucumbers, or a combination of all three.

The ideal piglet for roasting should be about three weeks old and weigh close to twelve pounds. It *must* be freshly killed or the skin will not be crisp, and crisp skin was one thing the Pennsylvania Germans liked about roast suckling pig.

To achieve crispness, the piglet was placed on a spit about fourteen to eighteen inches from a bright fire and turned slowly over a dripping pan. The drippings were used for basting and for gravies.

How did one know when the piglet was done? "When the eyes drop out, it is half done," one old housewife told me. On that note, take up a decanter of Madeira and gain strength to wait out the remaining hour and a half.

Incidentally, when the Pennsylvania Germans call their pigs, they cry: "*Wutz, Wutz, Wutz!*" Thus, a piglet becomes a *Wutzli*.

2. Sauce for the Above
(Brühe zu dem Obigen)

Simmer the entrails and feet [of the piglet] with salt and pepper until tender. Then chop the liver fine and combine 3 ounces of [melted] butter with 2 or 3 tablespoons of flour. Whisk this [together] into a sauce, and bring it to a boil again. If the piglet is carved [before serving], then one may also add the brain to the sauce.

The Pennsylvania-German dialect word for sauce is *Brieh*, from German *Brühe*. Like our English word for sauce, derived from Latin *salsa*, *Brieh* originally meant a salted liquid, that is, the salted drippings or juices of the meat.[21] Now, *Brieh* can mean simply the juices of the meat (without salt or herbs), or for that matter, the liquid part of anything. *Au jus*, for example, may be rendered into Pennsylvania Dutch as *mit Brieh*, or *mit Kraftbrieh*, the latter term being a little more specific than the first.

The most typical thickener for Pennsylvania-German *Brieh* was roux, called *gereeschtes Mehl* in dialect. Roux was made with flour cooked in butter or lard in a number of ways, depending on the consistency and flavor desired. The least-cooked roux was white; the middling or blond varieties were actually the color of straw; and the truly brown versions could range anywhere from tan to dark walnut. Sometimes the flour was scorched in a pan before cooking it in the butter. In other cases, as in the recipe above, it was simply combined with butter and another ingredient (such as minced liver), cooked until relatively thick, and then thinned with meat stock. In the recipe above, the broth from the cooked entrails and feet is intended to supply the necessary stock, even though the drippings from the piglet itself might also be used. English-speaking Pennsylvanians, however, would have preferred to use hot milk or cream instead of stock. This was one of the basic differences between Pennsylvania-German and Anglo-Pennsylvanian sauce cookery. In addition, while their English-speaking neighbors were likely to choose sage for savory sauces, the Pennsylvania Germans generally chose marjoram or rosemary.

Since suckling pig was such a special dish for the Pennsylvania Dutch, great attention was paid to the *Brieb* served with it. Some of the sauces were lavish. One of the most elegant was made with herring—now about as rare as suckling pig itself. A more countrified sauce, and one that probably appeared with more frequency on Pennsylvania-German tables, was made by cooking dried cherries or dried peaches in the sauce above and dispensing with some of the more "organic" ingredients. Actually, considering that the piglet would have been served on a wreath of sauerkraut (recipe 128), and probably also with a number of cabbage side dishes, the rich gravy called for in the recipe may not seem so formidable.

3. Roast Mutton
(Hammelsbraten)

A leg of mutton may be stuffed with bread, butter, salt, pepper, and sage, and should roast for 2 or 3 hours. If it is not stuffed, it will require less time to roast. A shank or leg requires a longer time to roast than the breast. Serve with potatoes, beans, pickles, mashed turnips, and stewed onions.

Technically, mutton is called *Schof-Fleesch* in Pennsylvania Dutch, but *Hammelfleesch* will do just as well. Thus, roast shank of mutton becomes *gereescht Schofschenkel* or *gereescht Hammelfleesch*. When it was eaten by the Pennsylvania Germans, mutton generally was boiled rather than roasted, and was usually overcooked. Elizabeth Drinker noted rather disparagingly in her journal for August 28, 1771, that she was served boiled mutton and old kidney beans for dinner at the home of Peter Pennypacker near Adamstown in Lancaster County.[22] Meager as the mutton may have seemed to her, Peter may have been trying to please his English-speaking guests.

Some Pennsylvania Germans who had mutton to dispose of let it hang as long as possible before cooking, longer in fact than most of us today would consider safe. However, after curing ten to fourteen days, such mutton could pass for venison. Some of the "foul venison" complained of in early travel accounts may never have had antlers.

Prior to the Civil War, mutton was used in the Dunkard (Church of the Brethren) love feasts because it symbolized the Paschal Lamb. Actually, other meats were allowed. The minutes for the Brethren Annual Conference of 1827 stated that "mutton is recommended as a most agreeable meat for the Lord's Supper, but forebearance is to be exercised if some congregations use other meat."[23] Evidently, religious scruples were not always strong enough to overcome the gamy taste of mutton.

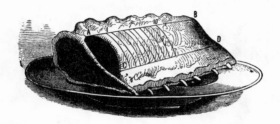

4. Roast Beef
(Rindsbraten)

The usual rules for roasting beef are to maintain a good, brisk fire, to baste the roast frequently, and to season it well. Twenty minutes for each pound is sufficient [time] for roasting.

In 1783, Johann David Schoepf noted in his *Travels in the Confederation* that the Pennsylvania-German farmer raised enough beef to overstock the market. A lot of that beef was driven to Annapolis, Baltimore, or Philadelphia, long before the cattle industry took shape in the West. In any case, the Pennsylvania-German love affair with beef was more a banking matter than a culinary one, for beef on the hoof was looked upon principally as cash.

In eighteenth-century German cookbooks, recipes for roast beef are almost always crowned with the phrase *auf englische Art* (in the English manner), which tells us immediately how very foreign this type of roast was to German culture. Marcus Loofft (1778), who simply calls his recipe *Rindfleisch auf Englisch* (Beef "in the English"), serves his beef with a *Sauce-Hachee* (hash gravy), that is, a gravy made with chopped ham, morels, mushrooms, anchovies, parsley, and butter.[24] Doubtless, the German officers who fought here in the Revolutionary War knew all about this, but for the common man, this sort of cookery was simply out of reach.

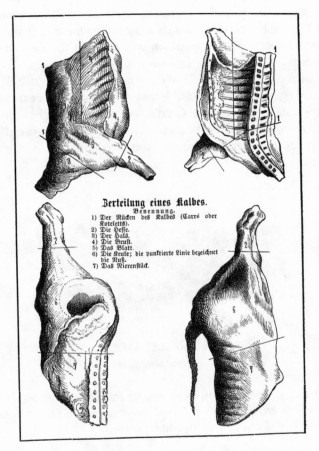

Berteilung eines Kalbes.
Benennung.
1) Der Rücken des Kalbes (Carré oder Koteletts).
2) Die Hesse.
3) Der Hals.
4) Die Brust.
5) Das Blatt.
6) Die Keule; die punktierte Linie bezeichnet die Nuß.
7) Das Nierenstück.

Various cuts of veal used by the Pennsylvania Germans

5. To Roast Veal
(Kalbfleisch zu braten)

Season it well, set it over a quick fire, and place paper over the meat so that it does not scorch. Baste it often, and cook it until sufficiently done.

———————————————◆◆◆———————————————

Roast veal is mentioned so often in early Pennsylvania diaries and kitchen accounts that it must be considered a typical cheap dinner for the period. In contrast to mutton, which was largely a spring meat, veal was eaten year-round, although most slaughtering seems to have been done in June and September. In Pennsylvania, the leftovers were ground for veal sausages called *weiße Würste* (or in dialect, *Weiss-warscht*), which were somewhat like the *Weißwurst* now available in German delicatessens except that they also contained a liberal quantity of bread and rabbit meat, that is, when rabbit was deemed "in season."[25]

The original recipe in *The Kitchen Companion* suggested that if veal were a fillet, "it should be stuffed with bread, butter, salt, and pepper."[26] George Girardey, however, suggested a more old-fashioned Pennsylvania-German method using minced tongue and ham, parsley, chervil, cloves, egg yolks, brandy, salt, and pepper, all of which was pounded into a paste in a mortar. Thus stuffed, the fillet was placed in an earthenware casserole with bacon, tiny carrots, sliced onion, stock, and white wine or mild vinegar. Although he called it *Kalbsbruste nach deutscher Art*, the recipe was rather standard for fillets, briskets, and even leftovers from boiled calf's head.[27]

Incidentally, the paper referred to in the recipe is a heavy white paper called "cooking parchment," which is still manufactured in this country and can be purchased at some supermarkets. It is quite different from modern writing paper, which is not a good substitute, since it contains chemicals that may be detrimental to the health.

6. Stewed Beef
(Gedämpftes Rindfleisch)

Fry the meat until it begins to brown, then put it in a pot with 2 quarts of water to each 8 pounds of meat. [Add] a gill of vinegar, 3 tablespoons of catsup, a little salt, red pepper, marjoram, onions, and cloves—cover it and let it simmer slowly until it is completely done. [Set aside] the meat, keeping it warm while you skim the stock. Thicken the stock with flour, and pour it over the meat.

This is Pennsylvania-German *Schmorbrode*, usually stewed beef or veal. From *Schmorbrode* comes *G'schmortes*, a stew. In German-American cookbooks, it was known as *Schmorbraten* and remained popular throughout the nineteenth century. In Henrietta Davidis's *Praktisches Kochbuch für die Deutschen in Amerika* (Practical Cookbook for German-Americans), adapted for German-American kitchens in 1897, *Schmorbraten* was called *boeuf à la mode*, its most common name in Anglo-American cookbooks.[28] However, unlike most *boeuf à la mode* recipes, the recipe here replaces wine with vinegar, a popular variation in temperance-minded households.

Strictly speaking, beef stewed in wine is *boeuf à la mode*; beef stewed without wine is stewed beef. But even that distinction broke down by the nineteenth century, at least in general American cookery. On a popular level, *boeuf à la mode* became almost *any* sort of stewed beef. Recipes varied so greatly that they became totally unrecognizable from the appealing French original that had risen to fashion in the seventeenth century.

Yet of all the beef preparations, the *à la mode* technique was one of the most popular among the Pennsylvania Germans. Stewing was one of their culinary strengths, and a number of traditional dishes were prepared in a similar way. Furthermore, since the attractiveness of the dish lay in its gravy, Dutch cooks could adjust the recipe to suit their own taste preferences without really destroying the structure of the dish.

One variation was to add sour cream to the gravy. If cooked with raspberry vinegar or even herb-flavored vinegar instead of plain cider vinegar, or with one of the sweetish local wines the Pennsylvania Germans made with Isabella grapes (see chapter 9), the personality of the stew could be thoroughly altered. In any case, Friederike Löffler published a recipe for *boeuf à la mode* with sour cream and wine in her *Oekonomisches Handbuch für Frauenzimmer* (1795 edition).[29] This, at least, provides some literary evidence for what was once general practice in Pennsylvania and may even supply a clue as to where Pennsylvania-German cooks got the idea. One thing is certain, the dish à la Löffler entered rural Pennsylvania via the German community in Philadelphia.

Even if one treats the recipe in *Die geschickte Hausfrau* simply as a stew, forgetting all the allusions to *à la mode* cookery, the basic dish has many recommendations, not the least being that it goes well with rye bread and Yuengling beer—reward enough for a hard day's work in the field.

7. Beef Steaks
(Beef-Steaks)

Beef steaks should be ½ to ¾ of an inch thick. Rub the meat with salt and pepper and lay it on a hot gridiron, which should be larded beforehand. Maintain a bright fire; turn the meat over often. Should the meat juices drip into the flames, quickly take the gridiron away from the fire because the smoke will give the meat a bad flavor. The steaks will be ready to serve in 12 to 15 minutes.

This is one of those upper-class foods that has filtered down to other classes over the past two centuries. Just the same, beef steaks are today what they always have been: a form of fast food, hence their popularity with restaurateurs.

Although most Pennsylvania Germans would call them *Bief-schteeks* and let it go at that, the story of the steak in rural Pennsylvania has a peculiar twist. Unlike roast beef, steak was something many Pennsylvania Germans borrowed from the English with a vengeance.

Since steaks could be cooked in a matter of minutes, they were usually served for breakfast or supper. Breakfast for the Pennsylvania Dutch occurred early, between 6:00 and 7:00 A.M., and supper, a light meal like the modern lunch, could occur any time between 5:00 and 7:00 P.M., sometimes even later. During the 1770s, Heinrich Müller, owner of an inn across the road from Ephrata Cloister in Lancaster County, often served a supper of beef steaks and hot chocolate to his guests before they prepared for bed. Such evening repasts were still common in the 1840s.

The proper cooking of beef steaks has always been a subject of heated discussion among gourmets and hearty eaters alike. The *Germantown Telegraph* of November 5, 1851, had this to say:

> The best pieces for steak are the *sirloin* and *rump*. The top of the round, next to the aitch bone, is very juicy, and by pounding it with a mallet may be as tender as the rump. The steaks should be cut nearly an inch thick. It is not necessary to grease the gridiron before putting on the steak, indeed, the flavor of the meat is much impaired by so doing.

This, a direct contradiction to the advice in *Die geschickte Hausfrau*! At any rate, after some experimentation, I found that larding the gridiron attracted ashes from the coals. This, I suppose, is what "impairs" the flavor of the steak. Today, we do not mind the charcoal flavor imparted by the smoke complained of in the recipe. In 1848, however, this flavor was thought to spoil the meat, which only goes to show how much American tastes have changed in the past one hundred years.

8. Beef Steak, French Style
(Beef-Steak, französische Mode)

Cut the steaks ¾ of an inch thick. Remove the skin and bone; rub salt and pepper into the meat. Pour drawn butter and minced onions over them. Let them stand ¾ of an hour in a covered pan, then fry over a quick fire. Fry cold boiled potatoes and lay them around the steaks, pouring over this the juices [left in the pan].

———————————————————

On the subject of beef steaks, which he calls *Rindstecks*, Girardey offers ample advice and enough recipes to placate the most wolfish of gourmands. For beef steaks with potatoes—his answer to beef steaks the French way—he suggests quartering the potatoes before frying and serving the dish with tomato sauce rather than the brown sauce suggested above. But then he offers many other variations as well, some calling for Madeira wine, others for oysters.

Although much less exotic, the recipe in *Die geschickte Hausfrau* can be traced to colonial cookbooks and ultimately to Europe. Richard Briggs, cook at the Temple Coffee House in London, called this dish "Beef-steaks the French Way" in his cookbook reprinted in Philadelphia in 1792. There is a basic similarity between the way his recipe and this recipe were prepared. By the mid-nineteenth century, beef steaks the French way had become an old-fashioned standby in almost every American cookbook. Today, it has become the ubiquitous steak and French fries.

9. Roast Pork
(Schweine-Braten)

If the pork is a shank, or any other cut on which there is skin, then after it is washed, take a sharp knife and score the skin in a criss-cross pattern. Rub the skin thoroughly with salt, pepper, and powdered sage before you set the meat over the fire. Butter the skin so that it becomes crisp, and baste the roast frequently with the drippings. It should be done in 2½ hours, and can be served with apple sauce.

———————————————————

Seibrode! What could be more traditionally Pennsylvania German than roast pork? Twice as much pork as beef was consumed in Pennsylvania-German households during the 1840s, yet some would not touch it. The followers of Conrad Beissel, the mystical founder of Ephrata Cloister in the 1730s, would not eat pork or eat from utensils in which pork had been cooked. Fortunately for the butchers, these celibates were by far an exception.

Those Pennsylvania Germans who truly savored roast pork but hated the grease prepared a unique and delicious dish called *saurer Seibrode*, or marinated pork roast. This variation of *Sauerbraten* was made by placing the roast in vinegar for several days and flavoring it with chopped onions, sage, thyme, sweet basil, and juniper berries. The roast was then steamed in a pot until tender and coated with a mixture of crumbs, dark sugar, and cloves. The meat was set in a hot oven until the crumbs formed a sweet, brittle crust, then the roast was ready to serve with traditional molded sauerkraut and strong salt pickles.

Sauerkraut and strong pickles were naturally (and chemically) necessary accoutrements to Pennsylvania-German roast pork, plain or marinated. Taste preferences aside, these side dishes were necessary a century ago, because butchers were not as meticulous about removing the fatty parts of animals, and there is considerable evidence that Pennsylvanians once preferred their meats much fattier than we do today.

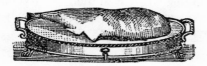

10. Venison
(Wildpret)

A haunch of buck must roast 3½ to 3¾ hours. Sprinkle a little salt on it and spread a sheet of white, buttered paper over the fat. Then spread luting paste* on heavy paper and cover the haunch with it. Tie it all up with fine packthread and set the meat some distance from a bright fire. Baste it often with the drippings. Ten minutes before it is to be served, remove the paper and the luting paste, and set the meat closer to the flame. Butter it and sprinkle generously with flour.

Venison has always been the aristocrat of meats on the Pennsylvania-German table. Usually marinated in wine or vinegar a day or two before cooking, it was often served with stewed fruit, sour cream sauce, or poached pears, but whatever the recipe, venison was king among the Pennsylvania Dutch. It still is.

This rather straightforward recipe may be found in H. L. Barnum's *Family Receipts* (Cincinnati, 1831).[30] Barnum probably took it from the *Domestic Encyclopedia* or more directly from Mrs. Rundell. That

*A mixture of flour and water, about six to seven tablespoons of water to one cup of flour. Before the Civil War, it was generally made with rye flour. It was not meant to be eaten.

this recipe should appear over and over in early American culinary literature is itself a remarkable testimony to its popularity. Actually, it is nothing but a plainer version of what the English cook Charles Francatelli called haunch of venison *à l'anglaise*, which can be traced to eighteenth-century British and French cookbooks.[31]

Its inclusion in *Die geschickte Hausfrau* makes perfect sense when we realize that it strikes a middle path between two very opposite schools of venison cookery among the Pennsylvania Dutch: the utterly unadorned "camp-fire" cookery of the folk level, which many purists preferred; and the elegant preparations, which nearly hid the fact that the meat was venison. George Girardey's easy but rich chafing dish recipe was typical of this second line of thinking, influenced, naturally, by Philadelphia's high-style chefs.

Girardey's Sautéed Venison

Slice the meat in thin strips. Beat them [until tender] and sprinkle with a little salt and pepper. Then sauté slowly in a generous amount of butter. Serve with sauce *à la Robert*.[32]

Sauce *à la Robert* is an old French recipe, long popular in Germany. Its Pennsylvania-German equivalent was made with onions fried in butter, meat stock, vinegar or dry white wine, flour, salt, and pepper. This sauce mixture was reduced until thick, then, just before serving, a generous helping of strong mustard was added.[33] In English cookbooks, sauce *à la Robert* was usually served with pork, particularly with pork cutlets, which now seems to be general practice in this country as well.

Purists may snub their noses at Girardey's recipe even though it is infinitely easier to prepare than the stodgy haunch in *Die geschickte Hausfrau*. Pennsylvania-Dutch purists demand cooking tricks learned from the Indians, but I dare suggest that they will never develop a taste for skunkweed, the venison spice par excellence with Pennsylvania's pre-Columbian cooks.

11. Marinated Pot Roast
(Sauerer Rindsbraten)

Choose a piece from the shank in which there are no bones. Beat [it until tender], rub salt into it, and set it in good vinegar with bay leaves, cloves, ginger and some juniper berries. Let this marinate about 8 to 10 days, during which time it should be turned occasionally. When one wishes to cook the meat, lay it on a slab of bacon in a pot, and add a large crust of stale bread, as well as the above-mentioned herbs and spices. Pour a mixture of half vinegar and half water over this, cover the pot tightly, and let the meat steam slowly. Should the liquid boil down too much, add a little hot water or a glass of wine, and if too thin, [add] a little browned flour.

Also called "German pot roast," this is a superb species of roast known by several names among the Pennsylvania Dutch, including *Sauerbrode* and *Sauer-Toppbrode*. There are many delightful variations of this basic recipe, some calling for red wine instead of vinegar, different spices, and so forth. But this particular recipe was thought typical enough to be included in Hark and Barba's *Pennsylvania German Cookery*, and with good reason. It can be reproduced very easily by starting with a four-pound pot roast, and pouring the vinegar hot over the meat, enough to cover it, in a deep bowl or porcelainized pot. The meat need stand in the vinegar only two to three days. Ten days causes it to disintegrate if the vinegar is strong.

Edith M. Thomas published a similar and equally delicious recipe, which she called *Sauergebratens*, in her classic study of Pennsylvania-German folk cookery, *Mary at the Farm* (Norristown, 1915). She aptly described the popularity of this dish.

> The writer knew an old gentleman who had moved to the city from a "Bucks County farm" when a boy, who said that he'd walk five miles any day for a dish of the above [*Sauergebratens*] as his mother had prepared it in former times.[34]

12. Roast Veal
(Kalbs-Braten)

Veal must be roasted until well browned, but at first should not be placed too near the fire. Baste a shoulder frequently until it is done, then butter it and sprinkle flour over it. Make a sauce for it with drawn butter and some thin slices of lemon.

13. Stuffing for Roast Veal
(Gestopftes für Kalbs-Braten)

Mince 4 ounces of leaf lard, a little parsley, and lemon rind. Add pepper, grated nutmeg, salt, and bread crumbs, and mix it all together with 2 eggs.

This recipe has appeared in other nineteenth-century cookbooks as a stuffing for mutton or lamb, with the addition of chopped celery and onion.

14. Stewed Veal
(Gekochtes Kalbfleisch)

The veal should be chopped into small pieces and, with pepper, salt, spices, and a little piece of butter, brought to a boil over the fire until tender. This should take 1½ hours. Then fry fine bread crumbs in butter and pour the veal stock over them. Cool the meat in cold water, then let it cook again for some time in the [thickened] stock until done.

Could this be the once-popular Philadelphia boardinghouse dish that doused the hunger of many Pennsylvania-Dutch scullery maids? Veal being cheap, stale bread being common, and the procedure being simple, it is no wonder that this hearty stew was eaten so often by hardworking people. It was the poor man's version of stewed beef (recipe 6) and a good way to get rid of "monkey veal," that unpleasant but very cheap species of meat that came from calves slaughtered too young.

15. Boiled Calf's Head
(Kalbs-Kopf)

Soak the head 2 hours, clean it well, split it in half, take out the brain, and boil with a clean cloth wrapped around it. Then boil the brain with a little parsley and chop it up fine. Sauté it in a pan with a little butter, salt, and pepper. Boil the skin and tongue, set them in the middle of a platter with the brains around them, and serve with the head.

In his diary for May 28, 1828, James Allport described a Pennsylvania meal where calf's head was served.

Dinner consisted of (first course) R. Beef Calf's head (boil'd) Bacon & Asparagus, meat patis & potatoes. Second course wild Ducks & Sea Kale followed by Jelly & Rhubarb Tart, currant pudding, Coffe Cream etc., Desert Figs, Apples, Almonds, Raisins, Sponge Cake, Ginger Bread etc.— took tea, played Billiards, etc., spent the evening in a very pleasant manner.[35]

However idiosyncratic the diarist's spelling and punctuation, we can easily perceive the general tone of the menu. Here, the basic two-course dinner has been expanded into five, and this, no doubt, so impressed James Allport that he felt compelled to write it all down. Such elaborate country repasts were unusual, this one doubtless even more so: Served at the home of Hardman Philips of Philipsburg (Centre County), dinner came to the table at the décolleté hour of 4:00 P.M., then considered *very late*. Yet the Philips dinner is representative of the kinds of meals Pennsylvania's rural gentry could muster when they wanted to, and not at all out of keeping with the sort of elaborate meals suggested in period Anglo-American cookbooks. The calf's head, however, is what interests us.

The calf's head returns to the kitchen untouched.

It is served here as part of the first remove, largely as a decorative balance for the roast, along with four side dishes—meat patties, asparagus, bacon, and potatoes. (Note the even number of plates on the table.) In all likelihood, the calf's head was there more for its impressiveness than for eating. It was one of those fashionable dishes that helped make a table look festive, particularly if the head were decorated with pastry leaves, olives, capers, and the like. That it was largely decorative is confirmed by the fact that many period diaries remark what a pity it was to see it returned to the kitchen cold and untouched. But it was not wasted; it was reboiled for soup (recipe 61).

The Pennsylvania-German custom for serving whole calf's head differed from that of the Anglo-Americans. When calf's head came to the table, it did not come as a secondary roast, but as the main feature of the meal. The Dutch were less inclined to serve decorative showpieces than something that could be more easily and more fillingly eaten. Rather than roast beef and calf's head, two roasts—perhaps pork and veal—would be their choice. Convert the calf's head into head cheese and serve that as a side dish—a simple and less wasteful solution. Furthermore, the Dutch liked souses of this sort with their roasts, and the brains could be used for dumplings, always acceptable in Pennsylvania.

When calf's head appeared in place of a roast on the table, it was usually because the calf's head had been improved with the addition of other things. Ann Hark and Preston Barba published an excellent recipe for calf's head and oysters in *Pennsylvania German Cookery*; the addition of oysters raised the character of the dish into something quite ethereal. The marriage of oysters and veal, incidentally, was another one of the classic features of old Pennsylvania-Dutch cookery.

16. Veal Cutlets
(Kalbsschnitten)

Cut the meat in slices half an inch thick and set them over a quick fire. When nearly done, put a little flour in the skillet, pour some boiling water over it, and add pepper, butter, and salt.

Shallot

The reason for adding the flour and water to the skillet was to make a sauce for the cutlets with their own *Brieh*. Some Pennsylvania-Dutch cooks added nutmeg, parsley, thyme, two or three shallots, two tablespoons of butter, a cup of veal stock, a dash of lemon juice, and enough flour to thicken it. While this is considerably more elaborate, it is just as authentic. In fact, the variations were truly infinite, as the following recipe will demonstrate.

17. Veal Cutlets Another Style
(Kalbs-Schnitten auf eine andere Art)

Moisten the meat with egg whites, sprinkle it with a mixture of parsley and fine bread crumbs, a little salt and pepper, then fry the cutlets. [When done], set the cutlets [aside] in a warming dish. Put a little flour and butter in the skillet and brown it. Add some catsup and pour this over the meat.

18. Baked Calf's Liver
(Gebratene Kalbs-Leber)

Wash and dry the liver, then cut a long slit in each piece and stuff them with bread crumbs, herbs, a nice piece of fatty pork, onions, salt, pepper, a little piece of butter, and an egg. Then rub the liver with lard and bake it. When done, make a nice brown sauce for it, and serve with red currant jelly.

Calf's liver, like lungs, was an extremely popular dish among the Pennsylvania Germans, and there were many different ways to prepare it. George Girardey suggested baking the liver in a casserole with bacon and onions and serving it with a highly spiced sauce. The recipe given above, however, is probably one of the most adaptable, for it was modernized and published in Hark's and Barba's *Pennsylvania German Cookery* (Allentown, 1950). The brown sauce called for is one of the noteworthy features of this recipe.

Pennsylvania-German brown sauce was made with roux. Generally, the flour was allowed to cook until it turned a deep brown color, then stock and meat glaze were added to give it greater flavor and a base. Brown sauce was so widely preferred that it served as an ingredient in a great variety of dishes, from soups to casseroles, from stuffings to vegetable purees. At its best, it could be elegant; at its worst, well, it could taste a lot like ashes and grease. And doubtless, in the real world of cookery where few cooks are perfect, there were many gradations in between.

The use of roux-based brown sauces is also an integral part of the regional folk cookeries of South Germany. It appears there under a variety of names, such as *gewöhnliche Butter-Sauce* (Common Butter Sauce) in Friederike Löffler's cookbook.[36] She recommends brown sauce specifically for cooked cabbage or boiled endive. Löffler's basic recipe was evidently popular in Pennsylvania, and even Girardey's recipe for brown sauce is based on it.[37]

19. Boiled Ham
(Abgekochter Schinken)

If the ham is too dry, soak it in water about 14 to 15 hours before cooking. Put it in a large pan or pot with cold water. Let it simmer gently for 3 or 4 hours, and then boil it until done, which should occur in 1½ hours. When the ham is ready to serve, cut the rind off carefully, and replace it as soon as the ham is cold. Ham acquires a better flavor if it is not sliced until after it has cooled.

There were several traditional ways for serving boiled ham. Perhaps one of the most popular was to lay it sliced over boiled spinach and hard-boiled eggs, with a thin sauce made from the ham stock and butter.

20. To Bake Ham
(Schinken zu braten)

Cut the ham through the middle and cover the pot, since the meat will be much tenderer if the steam is retained. When almost done, take the lid off so that the steam can escape.

Dutch oven

This recipe is actually just a helpful hint. The idea was to bake the ham in a "Dutch" oven, a heavy iron kettle that had many uses in the nineteenth century. One could even bake bread in it. The name, however, has nothing to do with the Pennsylvania Dutch, who call this implement a *Backtopp*, or "baking pot." But among Anglo-Americans, the term "Dutch oven" was also applied to the bonnet or reflector ovens that were placed in front of the fireplace and used mostly for baking or roasting. The Dutch called these ovens *Blechoffe* (tin ovens), so in Deitsch, at least, there was no confusion of terminology.

21. Tripe
(Kuttelfleck)

Boil the tripe, then put it in salted water. Pour freshly salted water over it each day until it is to be used. Dip the tripe in a batter and fry it like pig's feet; or boil it in fresh saltwater with a sliced onion and some sprigs of parsley. Then pour drawn butter over it.

Tripe is a folk delicacy that has become grossly neglected in this country. A century ago it was prepared in a great number of ways, from sousing or frying in butter, to pickling in sauerkraut and grated horseradish. In fact, Girardey published nine recipes for tripe, which he served in a variety of ingenious ways with liberal helpings of fish, cream, or oyster sauce. Fortunately, excellent tripe is still available in Pennsylvania, where it goes into a number of well-known dishes, not the least being Philadelphia Pepperpot. In Pepperpot, it serves as a substitute for the entrails of sea turtle—the original recipe ingredient.

22. Pig's Feet Soused
(Gepökelte Schweins-Füsse)

Clean the pig's feet well, remove the skin, then simmer the feet gently until they are tender. Cut up the feet and put them with the ears in salted vinegar with a little mace. Cover the crock carefully and set it away. When you use the feet, first dry each piece with a cloth before dipping in the beaten yoke of an egg and then in fine bread crumbs; fry nicely in butter and lard. One can also eat the feet directly from the vinegar.

For those who enjoy trotters, this recipe will be fun to experiment with. The crock, however, must be *unglazed*, or one may also enjoy lead poisoning.

23. An Excellent Recipe for Prepared Tongue, to be Eaten Cold
(Vortreffliches Rezept, Zungen herzurichten, die kalt genossen werden)

Pickle the tongue in salt, saltpeter, brown sugar,* pepper, cloves, finely ground mace, and allspice for 8 days. Then take it out of the brine, place it in a small pan, and put some butter on it. Cover it with a brown crust† and bake it slowly until so tender that a straw can go through it easily.

Cold meats, such as tongue, were usually eaten at breakfast or supper, or as a garnish or side dish at dinner. Tongue was often added to meat pies, ollapodrida (an early eighteenth-century form of pepperpot called *Ohlie* by the Pennsylvania Dutch), and such light dishes as meat salads and omelettes. In the second half of the nineteenth century, when picnics at camp meetings and chautauquas became more common among the Pennsylvania Germans, tongue was tucked into the picnic basket and sliced for sandwiches, or simply served as a cold salad with raspberry vinegar as its only dressing.

Since this combination may strike some people as peculiar (it is really quite delicious), I provide a translation of Löffler's recipe for the

---

*Please refer to the discussion of sugars on pages 154–56. What is intended here is Muscovado sugar, which may be reproduced by mixing one tablespoon of unsulfured molasses to each cup of dark brown sugar.

†This is luting paste made with rye flour: six to seven tablespoons of water to each cup of flour. This crust was not meant to be eaten.

same, as published in the *Vollständiges Kochbuch für die deutsch-amerikanische Küche* (Philadelphia, ca. 1856).[38]

Another Style of Fresh Beef Tongue, with Raspberry Vinegar

Boil the tongue in the usual manner. Fry until straw color a cooking spoon full of flour in six ounces of butter, then add a pint of raspberry vinegar. If there is already sugar in the vinegar, then add no more; but if the vinegar is without it, then sweeten it to taste. After the tongue is cooked and skinned, cut it in four pieces lengthwise, lay them on a platter, and pour the vinegar dressing over them. One can also make a sauce for tongue with fresh cherries or cherry juice, but if this should prove too sweet, add some vinegar to it.

---

24. Sausages
(Bratwürste)

Mince 6 pounds of lean and 2 pounds of fat pork, [mix, and add] 4 tablespoons of salt, 6 of finely chopped sage, 5 of black pepper, 2 of cloves, and a little rosemary. Unless the meat is to be stuffed in intestines, keep it in a tightly sealed crock. When needed, roll it in balls, dust it with flour, and fry.

This recipe is probably one of Anglo-American origin, for it is similar to "Common Sausages" in Hannah Glasse's *Art of Cookery* (London, 1796).[39] But it also bears close resemblance to the typical nineteenth-century breakfast sausages of Germany. Indeed, a recipe for nearly the same thing appeared in Anna Fürst's *Vollständiges Kochbuch für alle Stände* (Complete Cookbook for All Social Classes: Stuttgart, 1846), a work imported and sold during the 1850s by John Weik, a German bookseller in Philadelphia.[40] The Germans, however, invariably put their *Bratwurst* in intestines.

In Pennsylvania, *Bratwurst*, or in dialect *Brodwarscht*, could be either: stuffed in skins or loose. In any case, it was the so-called "father" in the sausage trinity of Pennsylvania-German cookery. The other two, in their correct spiritual order, were *Summerwarscht* (summer sausage) and *Panhas* (scrapple). Of the three, summer sausage, as its name implies, was the standard hot-weather sausage. Today it is erroneously called bologna or sweet bologna, although it has absolutely no resemblance to the mortadella sausage of Bologna, Italy. *Summerwarscht* is made mostly with beef, it is often sweetened with honey,

Sausage shop

and it is well smoked. It is a German sausage still made by some farmers in the Palatinate, from whence the Pennsylvania species originates.

That *Brodwarscht*, *Summerwarscht*, and *Panhas* should be the most popular sausages among the Pennsylvania Germans is readily explained. They were the easiest to make at home, and they could be preserved with less difficulty under conditions of no refrigeration. Novelty sausages, such as *Blutwarscht* (blood sausage) and sausages made with veal or rabbit, were more often the province of the local butcher shop than of home cookery.

As in Germany, sausage making was a specialized trade in early Pennsylvania. We know this because it is possible to find newspaper references to sausage makers even in the eighteenth century. Philip Weiss, a sausage maker on Sixth Street between Arch and Race, is mentioned in the *Wöchentliche philadelphische Staatsbote* for May 16, 1775. Unfortunately for the curiosity of posterity, there is no list of the types of sausages he made. But doubtless, in perusing the pages of Marcus Knackwurst's *Wurstologia* ("Sausage-ology": Schweinsfurt, 1662), we would spot many a *Warscht* familiar to Pennsylvania-German settlers. Knackwurst's name is obviously a nom de plume, but the object of his entertaining satire was real enough: to bring about a "Sausage Reformation," that is, to separate "orthodox" from "heretical" sausagery.

Sausage making at home was far less prone to theological complications, for families generally made no more than the three types of sausage already mentioned. *Lewwerwarscht* (liver sausage) might be the one exception, but it was never made in large quantities, and by its very nature, had to be eaten soon after it was made. Liver sausage does not keep. For this reason, the Dutch considered it a "fresh" sausage.

The *Brodwarscht* described in recipe 24 was also called "fresh" sausage, unless it was smoked. Fresh sausage was preserved from spoiling by storing it in crocks sealed with lard. The crocks were then set in the cellar, and the sausage could be dipped out as needed.

As a folk food, *Brodwarscht* was probably the most universally consumed of all Pennsylvania-German sausages. Its popularity cut across economic boundaries because of its quick and easy method of preparation. Furthermore, inventive Dutchmen were always coming up with new devices for making the work of chopping the meat even easier. In 1818, David Beissel of Harrisburg invented a chopper that became popular with farmers for many years.[41] It also chopped the cost of making sausage to rock bottom. So naturally, in less affluent Pennsylvania-German homes, *Brodwarscht*, like scrapple, was treated as a standard substitute for roasts in the basic two-course meal.

25. Scrapple
(Panbas)

Take a pig's haslet and as much offal,* lean and fat pork as you wish, to make scrapple; boil them well together in a small quantity of water until they are tender; chop them fine, after taking them out of the liquor; season, as sausage; then skim off the fat that has arisen where the meat was boiled, to make all soft, throw away the rest of the water, and put this altogether in the pot; thickening it with ½ buckwheat and ½ Indian. Let it boil up, then pour out in pans to cool. Slice and fry it in sausage fat, after the sausage is done.

Recipes for scrapple dating from the eighteenth century are extremely rare in Pennsylvania. The reason for this is that scrapple making was standard knowledge, something most country people learned to do even as children. Furthermore, scrapples were not the sorts of foods that found their way into polite cookery books of the period. Pennsylvania scrapple recipes do not begin to appear in printed sources until the second quarter of the nineteenth century, mostly as instructions to outsiders who wanted to know more about this local specialty.

Since its audience was Pennsylvania German, the original editions of *Die geschickte Hausfrau* did not include a recipe for scrapple. Yet pot puddings of this type were such an important aspect of Pennsyl-

---

* The haslet is a collective term for the heart, liver, and other edible organs; the offal are those entrails normally thrown away.

vania-German culture that it seemed appropriate to include an example in *Sauerkraut Yankees*, particularly since scrapple has already been mentioned several times. Thus, the recipe here has been taken from *The Economical Cook and House-Book* (Philadelphia, 1855), a cookbook written by the Orthodox Quaker Elizabeth Nicholson.[42]

Nicholson's recipe is one of the most traditional that has come down to us and probably dates from the middle of the eighteenth century, judging from its terminology and the way it is put together. It should be apparent that the main purpose of her scrapple making was to utilize leftovers from butchering. It was just one simple way to avoid waste by extending meat leftovers with some form of cereal, usually buckwheat.

The dish as it is known in Pennsylvania can be traced to the Lower Rhineland of Germany. In Westphalia, it is considered a regional specialty. It is still made there and is known by the name *Panhas* or *Pannas*.[43] The dish was evidently brought to Pennsylvania in the 1680s by the Crefelders who settled at Germantown, hence its historic association with Philadelphia. The dish and its Lower Rhineland name were subsequently assimilated into Pennsylvania-German culture. For *Panhas* as such is not known in the Palatinate or in the other areas of South Germany from which most of the Pennsylvania Germans originated.

In eastern Holland (in areas near the German border), the dish is known as *balkenbrij*, from *balken* (rafter) + *brij* (pudding).[44] The name refers to the fact that the scrapple, once made, was knotted up in a clean piece of cloth and hung from the rafters in a cool place. In Gelderland, a mixed spice called *rommelkruid* (licorice, sugar, and red sandalwood) was added to give the scrapple an unusual flavor and a pink color. In Westphalia, however, scrapple is usually black after cooking because of the addition of pork blood in the basic recipe and the exclusive use of buckwheat meal, which is dark to begin with.

In Pennsylvania, the pork blood was eliminated, and the buckwheat was cut with an equal quantity of roasted cornmeal—the "Indian" meal in Nicholson's recipe. Otherwise, Pennsylvania-German scrapple and Westphalian scrapple are very much alike.

As for the term *Panhas*, there are many variant spellings. In his Pennsylvania-German dialect dictionary (1924), Marcus Lambert provided a speculative etymology for the term, but his explanation is incorrect.[45] The word is found in several Lower Rhineland dialects and stems from a combination of two root words: *pann* + *harst*, meaning pan-roasted or pan-fried meat. Contrary to Lambert's explanation, *harst* has nothing to do with rabbits; it is Low German for "roast meat."

In Pennsylvania, *Panhas* and scrapple are different terms for the same dish. Today there is no implied difference in ingredients or procedure. Furthermore, as it is used in Pennsylvania speech, the term scrapple is evidently a local corruption of *schrapel*, a scrap or scraping, as defined in Henry Hexham's *English and Netherduytch Dictionarie* (Rotterdam, 1648).[46] Like *Panhas*, *schrapel* is also a word of Lower Rhineland origin, although its exact lineage in connection with the dish has not received much attention from food scholars in Europe. We do know for certain, though, that if buckwheat is taken out of the recipe and some other grain is substituted, then by traditional definition, the dish ceases to be *Panhas* or authentic "Philadelphia" scrapple. Buckwheat determines the flavor and to some extent the consistency of the dish. Its presence is absolutely crucial.

26. To Cure Beef and Pork
(Rind- und Schweine-Fleisch einzupöckeln)

To each gallon of water, add 1½ pounds of salt, ½ pound of sugar, and ½ ounce of saltpeter. In these proportions, any quantity of this pickle can be made as desired. Boil these ingredients together until the dregs of the salt and sugar have risen and are skimmed off. Then pour the liquid into a large tub to cool, and when completely cold, pour it over the meat, which must cure in this mixture from 4 to 5 weeks. The meat must be completely covered by the brine, and cannot be put in it until 2 days after butchering, during which time it must be sprinkled with a little saltpeter. This pickle is always preferred over others like it.

The last line in this recipe was evidently no exaggeration, for it is still being made in some Pennsylvania households. John Marquart reprinted this classic in his *600 Miscellaneous Valuable Receipts* (1860),[47] and it remained a favorite for at least another generation, since it was found in the manuscript cookbook (ca. 1880) of Mrs. George Leber, a Pennsylvania German from York County. Fifty years later, the recipe was published in the *Pennsylvania State Grange Cook Book* (Harrisburg, 1932),[48] having been submitted by Mrs. Benjamin Stubles, yet another Pennsylvania German.

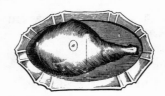

27. To Cure Ham
(Schinken einzumachen)

A cure for hams that resemble the celebrated Westphalian hams in flavor may be made in the following manner. Cover a tender ham with dry salt. Let it stand 24 hours so that the blood is completely drawn out. Then dry it off thoroughly and lay it in the following brine: dissolve 1 pound of brown sugar, ¼ pound of saltpeter, ½ pint of bay salt, and 3 pints of table salt in an iron pan over a fire. Stir these ingredients constantly until they have reached a moderate temperature. Cure the ham in this brine for 3 weeks, turning it occasionally, then hang it up to dry in the chimney, and smoke it with a wood fire. The smoke of oak wood, or sawdust and shavings, gives it a fine flavor.

The Pennsylvania Dutch call ham *Schunkefleesch*. In spite of its inelegant dialect name, Pennsylvania-German ham is still well-known for its fine taste and texture, even when it is not imitating the costly Westphalian variety.

Recipes for imitating Westphalian ham were standard articles in seventeenth- and eighteenth-century cookbooks, which is why this recipe seems a bit old fashioned and even unnecessary. It was unnecessary because there was no need to imitate. Any number of Pennsylvania Germans came from Westphalia and knew how to make *Schunkefleesch* every bit as tasty as the Old World variety. That is no well-kept secret. Some of the earliest farmhouses in Germantown and Montgomery County, where most of these people settled, reproduced many of the features of the traditional Westphalian tripartite farmhouse. It was a farmhouse divided into three units: a living area, a threshing area, and a stable, all under one roof. This is relevant in a discussion of making hams the true Westphalian way.

Farmhouse, built in 1580, at Langlingen in the Lower Rhineland

Josef Schepers mentions old Westphalian curing and smoking techniques in his *Haus und Hof westfälischer Bauern* (The House and Farm of the Westphalian Farmer: Münster, 1973). One common technique was to hang the hams from the rafters of the *Deele*, a high-ceilinged area inhabited by the farmer and his family (see illus.). Since the traditional *Deele* featured an open hearth without a chimney, smoke simply rose and collected under the roof. In that high, sooty, dark netherworld of smoke, hung row upon row of hams.

Another method of later medieval origin is described in Richard Bradley's *General Treatise of Husbandry and Gardening* (London, 1726). One of Bradley's friends traveled to Westphalia and sent back a description of the attic "smoke closets" used by some farmers for curing ham and bacon.[49] Called *Rauchkammer* in Pennsylvania Dutch, these closets were also known and used throughout the German areas of Pennsylvania in the eighteenth and early nineteenth centuries. Some old Pennsylvania-German farmhouses still have extant smoke closets in their attics, but most Pennsylvania farmers no longer know how to use them.

The smoke closet is not limited to Westphalia. It just happened that Bradley's friend saw one there. Actually, it is found throughout German-speaking Europe, and the construction is almost invariably the same, no different in principle from those in Pennsylvania.[50] Built in the attic next to the chimney stack, the closet pulled a draft through a hole in the chimney so that smoke produced downstairs during cooking or heating could be utilized upstairs. To prevent fires, it was lined entirely with a thick coat of plaster, and iron hooks were installed for hanging the meats from hickory rods. The smoke closet was so popular in Pennsylvania that it was even built in the attics of summer kitchens, a kind of transitional phase between the traditional attic *Rauchkammer* and the freestanding smokehouse that became more popular among the Pennsylvania Germans after the adoption of coal-burning stoves.[51] The *Rauchkammer* does not work where coal is burned because coal fumes cannot be used for smoking meats.

28. Excellent Brine for Curing Meat
(Vortreffliche Fleisch-Pöckel)

Mix 5 pounds of brown sugar, 5 pounds of bay salt, 5 pounds of ordinary salt, 1 pound of saltpeter, 5 ounces of finely ground paprika, 3 ounces of powdered black pepper, and 1 ounce of grated nutmeg with 5 gallons of boiling water. This pickle will give the meat not only a fine red color, but a delightful taste as well.

This is just one of several "excellent" pickles for curing Pennsyl-

Keine Wage mehr,

oder das

Gewicht des Rindviehes

und der

Schweine

mittelst nachstehenden Tabellen zu bestimmen.

Bearbeitet von

Henry Günther.

Doylestown.

Gedruckt bei Oliver P. Zink.

1851.

Henry Günther's *No More Weighing* was a Pennsylvania-German pocket calculator for estimating the weight of live cattle and hogs before butchering.

vania-German ham. A similar period recipe, and perhaps the ultimate source of this one, can be traced to Bensalem Township in Bucks County.[52] That recipe gained wide circulation in Pennsylvania. The only difference between it and this recipe is that the older version also added summer savory, sweet marjoram, and allspice.

Hams cured in pickles such as these required from two to six weeks, depending on their size and the weather—cold weather meant longer pickling. The hams were then wiped dry and smoked with the shank end down to prevent the juices from dripping away. Some farmers coated their hams with honey before sending them to the *Rauchkammer*, thinking that this improved the flavor of the meat. Small hams could be smoked in two weeks, while larger ones required four weeks or more.

Most slaughtering was done in the fall or early winter and again in January or February. It was once a necessity because farmers were not able to fodder all their livestock over the winter.

Among the Pennsylvania Germans, butchering reached its greatest social significance with pork. Nearly every Pennsylvania-Dutch farmer kept at least a pair of hogs to be fattened up for Christmas. In late November, these hogs were slaughtered and converted into sausage and pudding. The hams, shoulders, and sides were pickled, as in the recipe here, and then smoked. This furnished the family with meat well into the following summer.

After slaughtering, it was always customary to send portions of the spareribs, pudding, and sausage to neighbors and friends, and they were expected to return the courtesy. These culinary gifts, particularly the sausages, were known as a *Metzelsupp*, or "butcher's stew."[53] The name originated in the gift of a soup or stew made from the leftovers of butchering. This soup was shared among all those who had helped with the slaughter. By the 1840s, the soup custom began dying out, but its connection with a gift of meats persisted, probably because the *Metzelsupp* was a standard feature of the Pennsylvania-German Christmas. It was considered so basic that to omit it would be a serious insult to the neighborhood.

Although primarily for men, the traditional *Metzelsupp* banquet in December was a natural spin-off of the soup-sharing custom. The actual soup disappeared, but it was replaced with a relatively standard menu of fried sausage, pudding, sauerkraut, pork roast, pig's feet, and tails, all washed down with a steady stream of beer or wine. By 1900, however, as people raised fewer and fewer hogs at home, the *Metzelsupp* tradition—even as a Christmas custom—became a thing of the past. Alas, Christmas has become a little less colorful.

3

What the Dutch Call "Gefliggel"

Ich koch was ich kann;
Was mei Sau net fresst,
Sel gewwich meim Mann!

Translation

I cook whatever I can;
What my hog won't touch,
I feed to my old man!

OLD FOLK SAYING

The ubiquitous barnyard hen, the duck, the wild turkey, the canvasback, the grouse, the goose, yes, even an occasional swan slumped to its fate beneath the Dutchman's ax. During the nineteenth century, at least, the list of culinary victims was as extraordinary as it was long. The selection in *Die geschickte Hausfrau* was ample enough, but if seven recipes seems unusually skimpy by present-day standards, then remember that cooking fowl was never a complicated science for country housewives. Turning the spit was one of the first things young girls learned to do in the kitchen. It was hardly necessary to tell mama how to roast.

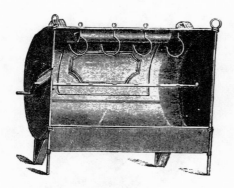

Bonnet or reflector oven for roasting fowl

There is another point to keep in mind. Since roast meat was considered the centerpiece of the meal, fowl were usually relegated to the secondary position of a side dish, as in fricasseed chicken (recipe 32) or roast pigeons (recipe 31), the latter always considered *light* eating. Being a side dish also meant that there was less emphasis on elaborate methods of dressing the birds, for nothing was to detract from the great roast of pork. Of course, the reverse was true when the roast was turkey (recipe 29) or goose (recipe 30). In such cases, the side dishes would also be reversed, that is, there would be some form of pork—pig's feet and sausages, for example—and perhaps even a small dish of *Sauerbraten*, all intended to form a contrast of flavors.

In the case of the dinner given by Hardman Philips (page 35), the fowl were relegated to a third course, or "second" remove, replacing the roast and calf's head in the middle of the table. In most Pennsyl-

51

vania-German households, such course arrangements beyond the basic two-course meal were usually dispensed with. There was no shortage of servants in those days, but servants and family normally ate together at the same table, so a question of logistics always arose when it came to carrying plates. In large households, as in my great-great grandmother's where forty to fifty persons were common for a Sunday dinner, the men and boys generally ate first—a custom that persists in some homes even today. They were joined by guests who had a distance to travel. Otherwise, the second seating was for the women. While the hired help cleaned up in the kitchen afterwards, zithers and accordions would be brought into the dining room, and the women would sing hymns and old ballads over pie and coffee.

In this section, recipes 29, 30, 31, and 32 were originally adapted from *The Kitchen Companion* (Philadelphia, 1844).

DAR WELSCHHAHN.

Goppel! Goppel! Goppel! Dar Welschhahn schreit laut, Ess mich zu' Grischdaag mit Sauerkraut!

Old children's book. Translation: "Gobble, gobble, gobble," the turkey cries out, "eat me for Christmas with sauerkraut."

29. To Roast a Turkey Cock
(Einen Welschhahn zu braten)

Stuff the turkey with fine bread crumbs, a pound of butter, salt, pepper, and 2 minced onions. Sew it up and sprinkle salt, pepper, and flour over it. In 2½ hours it should finish roasting, unless it is a very large bird.

The giblets, liver, etc., should be boiled with salt, pepper, and a little onion for a gravy, which is thickened with butter and flour.

Chickens are roasted in this same manner. One hour is sufficient for an ordinary hen. Baste it frequently in the drippings. A little finely chopped salt pork improves the flavor of the stuffing.

The virtues of American turkey are well known. The French gourmand Brillat-Savarin devoted a flattering discourse to it and even joined in a turkey shoot near Hartford, Connecticut, in 1794.[54]

It was universally agreed, even among the French, that the best-tasting American turkeys were the wild ones native to our forests. Unfortunately, they were not easy to domesticate, at least for purposes of the table, for the secret of their flavor was acorns. Yet even as late as 1900, it was common practice among enterprising Pennsylvania farmers to keep a few wild turkeys on hand, either hatched from eggs found in the woods, or raised from chicks brought in from the wild. Those that did make it to maturity (the survival rate was never very good) were eaten with great relish. Nothing was wasted; even the craws were used. Stuffed with a delicious forcemeat, for which George Girardey has preserved the recipe, they became the once-famous Pennsylvania-German *Rundwarscht* (round sausage), a delicacy that has regrettably faded from rural markets.[55]

In 1848, the Pennsylvania turkey population was rather mixed, with wild turkeys eating in the same barnyard with the white domesticated turkeys. The white turkeys, originally from Mexico, were raised at first only by gentlemen farmers, who took more care about size than flavor, as the following notice in the January 8, 1851, *Germantown Telegraph* illustrates:

> The largest turkey ever seen in the Philadelphia market was exhibited the day before Christmas, by James C. Cornell, Esq., President of the Bucks County Agricultural Society. It was of his own raising, and weighed *thirty pounds*! It attracted much attention, and sold for $15., or fifty cents per lb. This was not only the heaviest turkey, but sold for the highest price ever obtained in the city for a similar fowl.

We may assume from this report that the eighteenth-century accounts of thirty- and forty-pound wild turkeys may have been somewhat overstated, or else wild turkeys of today are mere runts compared with their ancestors. Whatever the case, that monster turkey sold the day before Christmas may not have been on its way to Christmas dinner, traditionally goose in Pennsylvania, but to New Year's Day dinner, one of the few holidays condoned even by the Quakers.[56]

Turkey with sauerkraut was once the most traditional Christmas-Day meal for Pennsylvania Germans. This custom still prevails in the region extending southwest from Harrisburg to York and down into the Pennsylvania-German counties of Maryland.

Roast turkeys were also popular at Pennsylvania-German weddings, although turkey roasts were specifically condemned in Friedrich Schwarzentruber's *Ernste Betrachtung* (1937), a tract for the Amish sect. Schwarzentruber condemned turkey roasts as being too worldly, as was anything else connected with "wedding grandeur and all unnecessary entertainment."[57] Most Pennsylvania Germans, however, were not afraid of fun.

But fun did not include the traditional New England Thanksgiving dinner with its turkey and other accoutrements. That was not fully accepted into local custom until almost this century, as the Lancaster County Quaker Phebe Earle Gibbons observed in her *"Pennsylvania Dutch" and Other Essays* (1882):

> Thanksgiving is beginning to be observed here, but the New Englander would miss the family gatherings, the roast turkeys, the pumpkin-pies. Possibly we go to church in the morning, and sit quiet for the rest of the day; and as for pumpkin-pies, we do not greatly fancy them. Raisin-pie or mince-pie we can enjoy.[58]

30. To Roast a Goose
(Eine Gans zu braten)

Mince 6 onions, season them highly with pepper, salt, and sage. Stuff the goose with this mixture,* sprinkle salt and pepper over it, and baste it often in the drippings. Two hours are sufficient for a goose, 1 hour for ducks. For a sauce, cook the giblets 3 hours with pepper, salt, and onions.

No cookbook would dare claim to be Pennsylvania Dutch without a recipe for roast goose. Like pork, goose played a fundamental role in the diet of the Pennsylvania Germans, so naturally, geese were raised everywhere. They were boiled to make *Zittergans*, a goose aspic; the giblets, feet, and neck provided the basis for a delicious soup stock; the livers (those wonderful livers!) were transformed into *Gans-*

---

*Peters omitted a sentence in translation from *The Kitchen Companion*. The stuffing should also include bread, butter, or mashed potatoes.

lewwerboi, a cold pie of goose-liver paté, generally served at Christmas. Goose grease was used as medicine, and in the spring, the eggs were eaten as a great delicacy. The feathers, of course, went into eiderdowns and quilts or were made into pens used for drawing Fraktur art. Few animals, except perhaps the hog, were put to as many uses by the Pennsylvania Germans as the goose.

Roast goose was served mostly on special occasions, such as St. Martin's Day (November 11) or Christmas. St. Martin's Day, called *Mordidaag* in dialect, was not a religious holiday for the Pennsylvania Germans, but its widespread observation was a carryover from the medieval church.

There are many legends surrounding St. Martin and the reasons he is considered the patron saint of geese. The most common story is that he was so modest he hid among a flock of geese rather than become the Bishop of Tours. The geese gave him away, and so to commemorate their watchfulness (or betrayal!), they are eaten. Actually, *Mordidaag* was important to the Pennsylvania Germans because it was one of the first butchering days on the folk calendar, a day of sumptuous eating and entertaining, and of course, such occasions called for goose. Regardless of the day or the occasion, it was always considered a great compliment to be invited to a dinner where goose was served.

As for methods of preparation, goose was served in a great many ways, but the most typical among the Pennsylvania Germans was to stuff it with apples and chestnuts, mashed potatoes, or even sauerkraut and chestnuts. One old family recipe called for a fruit stuffing that included dried apples, peaches, and apricots, pork sausage, and Madeira wine. The crushed petals of damask roses were added to give it a certain mysterious "bouquet" that was enhanced at the table if the wine were particularly well chosen.

31. Roast Pigeons
(*Gebratene Tauben*)

Pigeons should be stuffed with chopped parsley, and well seasoned. Serve them with parsley and butter, and green peas or asparagus.

There is a classic Pennsylvania-German saying: *Gebrodne Dauwe flieje em net ins Maul nei*, "roast pigeons do not fly into one's mouth." It means that one must work for something in order to enjoy it, and I suppose that applies to more than just pigeons. In any case, there is no distinction between doves and pigeons in Pennsylvania-German dialect. One is wild, the other is a nuisance, but both are good to eat.

Admittedly, we would never suspect this from the sparse recipe in *Die geschickte Hausfrau*, but its inclusion should not be passed over without comment, for pigeon cookery was once one of southeastern Pennsylvania's great native arts. Historically, Philadelphia has taken much of the credit for the preparation of squab and wild pigeon; in fact, the pigeons came from the outlying counties, and there was never a shortage of good pigeon cooks in Pennsylvania's smaller country towns.

According to the reminiscences of Henry D. Paxon (1917), Bucks County in particular developed a seasonal pigeon industry.[59] Its farmers sent wagonloads of passenger pigeons into the Philadelphia market each fall until about 1875, when the wild pigeons began to disappear; the last one seen in Pennsylvania was shot in Monroe County in 1895.

During the eighteenth and early nineteenth centuries, pigeon, especially pigeon pie, was one of the most popular breakfast and supper foods, next to cornmeal mush. It was also standard tavern and restaurant fare, so cheap, incidentally, that pigeon pie might be considered early Pennsylvania's equivalent of the TV dinner.

George Girardey published a recipe for pigeon pie more typical of middle-class rural kitchens than the one in *Die geschickte Hausfrau*. I include it here, because even today every Pennsylvania-German farmer with a barn or stable knows where to find the very best squab.[60]

George Girardey's Baked Squab

Brown some flour in butter and add a little sugar, thinly sliced ham, a glassful of meat stock, and a dash of salt and pepper. Then add the pigeons and 1 pint of [fresh] peas. Let this bake 1 hour.

This recipe may be reproduced either in a covered baking dish (earthenware or heavy iron) or in a crust. When using a crust, the center of the upper crust should be peaked up considerably higher than the edges for an authentic appearance. This may be accomplished with three large pigeons or five small ones laid in the middle of the pie and stacked pyramid fashion before the top crust is put on. In the seventeenth and eighteenth centuries, the crust was usually a luting paste of whole wheat flour and was not meant to be eaten. It was often highly decorated with figures and leaves, but for practical purposes, it was simply intended as a form in which to bake the meat.

32. Fricasseed Chicken
(Fricassirte Hühner)

Boil the chickens in a little water, let them cool, and cut them up. Meanwhile, add the giblets, a little lemon rind, pepper, nutmeg, herbs, and an onion to the broth in which the chickens were boiled. Boil this well and press it through a sieve. Then simmer the chicken in this until done. Remove the chicken from the broth and keep it warm. Thicken the broth with flour and butter, grate a little nutmeg into it, and [season with] salt. Bring this to a boil again, whisk in the yolk of an egg, and add half a pint of [sour] cream, which should not be allowed to boil.

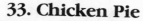

Fricassee warmer

Originally a French court dish in the fifteenth century, fricasseed chicken became a gentleman's dish by the seventeenth century and middle-class fare by the end of the eighteenth. The recipe here is not too different from a typical fricassee of the 1600s, which means we may assume that fricassees were indeed old fashioned even by 1848.

A proper fricassee consisted of meat—usually chicken, veal, or rabbit—chopped into pieces and fried, then simmered. Beyond that, the definition became a bit hazy, because fricassee meant different things to different people.

A proper Pennsylvania-German fricassee should include eggs, lemon (for flavoring only), and a healthy quantity of sour cream—sour cream was always used unless sweet cream was specifically called for. Fricasseed chicken was the sort of inexpensive, uncomplicated dish a woman could prepare on blue Monday, when most of her energies had to be given over to the week's laundry.

Sarah Tyson Rorer, once called the "Queen" of nineteenth-century American cookery (and a Pennsylvania German by birth), quipped that washday fare always came to the table "impregnated with soapsuds."[61] Perhaps Pennsylvania-German fricassees suffered likewise. In upper-class Pennsylvania homes, where help was plentiful and soapiness no problem, chicken fricassees entered the dining room in a chafing dish, as a third course after beef or pork.

33. Chicken Pie
(Hühner mit einer Decke)

Cut up 2 young hens, place them in a deep pot lined with pastry dough and thin slices of salt pork or ham. Pour cold water or a cold, weak meat stock over the chicken. For a small chicken pie, use 2 ounces of butter, a little flour, cover with a light pastry dough, and let it bake 1 hour in the oven.

The Pennsylvania Dutch know this more commonly as *Hinkelboi*, not "chicken in a blanket" as the original German reads. Although *Hinkelboi* is in some ways similar to a Pennsylvania-German chicken *Botboi* (pot pie), and may even taste like one, it must not be confused with the true *Botboi*, a folk stew thickened with large flat noodles, rather than encased in a crust. In fact, many Pennsylvania Dutch call the noodles the *Botboi*, as well as the dish itself. Nevertheless, both *Hinkelboi* and chicken *Botboi* have a common ancestor. The meat pie, after all, is nothing more than a stew or casserole in a crust, hence the infinite variations.

We tend to associate meat pies with English cookery, but they were also known in Germany. Originally, German meat pies were made of fish for consumption during times of religious fasting, but gradually beef and pork pies also gained in popularity.[62] However, not having their own term for meat pies, the Germans borrowed *pastete* from the French as early as the fourteenth century. Thus chicken pie became *Hühner-Pastete*.

Technically, a proper *Pastete* must have an upper crust, otherwise, to the Pennsylvania Germans, it would fall into the category of a tart or *Kuche*, like pumpkin pie. To safeguard the distinction, many Pennsylvania Germans use the term *Boi*, from English pie, for any sort of meat pie, hence *Hinkelboi*.

As a food, meat pies were enormously popular with the Pennsylvania Germans because they made use of leftovers or poorer grades of meat. They could be baked ahead and reheated or warmed over the next day. They were an ideal meal for travelers and were often served to workhands during their breaks in the fields.

34. Roast Duck
(Gebratene Enten)

Ducks can be roasted immediately after they are butchered. Stuff them with bread crumbs; season them with sage, butter, salt, and pepper, and set them over a quick fire. The gizzards and livers can be boiled, finely chopped, and added to the sauce.

Like goose, duck was often served on festive occasions stuffed with mashed potatoes, with apples and grapes, or served with boiled turnips. The sauces were almost innumerable. One early Germantown recipe for duck, dating from about 1720, called for carrots, turnips, onions, cumin, coriander, wine, and honey, among other things.[63] It was probably a bit cloying for modern palates, but the combination of duck and turnips, at least, was almost universally popular among the Pennsylvania Germans. Also popular were duck sauces made with saffron or marjoram.

35. To Tenderize Old Chickens Quickly
(Alte Hühner bald mürbe zu machen)

Light some brandy 3 times,* pour it over the chickens and cover. Then pour hot butter in the [cavities of] the chickens and the brandy taste will completely disappear. Rub the chickens with spices and marinate them 2 days in vinegar so that they will taste like wild fowl.

Recipes like this were common in old cookbooks, because in practice, chickens were not eaten young, particularly in the country. Chickens were more important for their eggs, which the housewife could sell for extra income—one of the few outside sources of income available to her. Chickens were not usually butchered until they "burned out"—until they were no longer good for laying. So this is the sort of

---

* That is, light it and blow it out three times in succession. This was thought to be a quick way to reduce the alcohol.

recipe Aunt Pall would use for the hen with one leg that had outwitted the ax for three or four years, perhaps longer. Who would dare send it to market?

One of the good traits of the Pennsylvania-German farmer was that he was more likely to sell his best produce than to keep it for himself. So if the best chickens met their fate in some burgher's kitchen, the *Vater* had to settle for the one-legged runt. He hardly suffered, though, because with this recipe his wife could conjure up a feast. With burnt brandy and a little ingenuity, she could transform that tough old bird into a well-seasoned "pheasant."

4

Fish and Shellfish

Ich winsch Dir en goldner Disch,
Uf jedem Eck en gebratner Fisch,
In der Mitt en Bottel Wei,
Un des soll unser Neijohr sei!

Translation

A golden plate for you I wish,
On every corner a roasted fish,
And in the middle a bottle of cheer,
And that is how we'll greet the year!

FROM AN OLD NEW YEAR'S GREETING

Even though they lived more than one hundred miles from the sea, the Pennsylvania Germans were not denied its bounties. Indeed, their location encouraged fish cookery, because the Delaware, Schuylkill, and Susquehanna Rivers were once major inland waterways. Crabs, clams, and oysters were commonly packed alive in barrels and sent upriver. The trip was often only a matter of hours. Throughout the late eighteenth and early nineteenth centuries, "oyster saloons," as seafood inns were called, proliferated even in such landlocked places as Chambersburg, where one justice of the peace operated a seafood eatery in his log office.

During this period, crayfish were so popular that in his *Haus- und Kunst-Buch* (1818) Jacob Biernauer published a recipe with directions for serving them *schön roth*—a nice red—and looking very much alive.[64] Incidentally, this was one of the earliest published Pennsylvania-German recipes for crayfish, a food item that has completely disappeared from the Pennsylvania-Dutch table.

Throughout the eighteenth century, many Pennsylvania Germans went to the October and May markets in Philadelphia. These were semiannual festivals that gave the country people an opportunity to close business transactions, hear the latest news from abroad, and, of course, to savor the best catches seafood vendors had to offer. Unfortunately, Pennsylvania fairs became scenes of violence and widespread drunkenness. Following the scandal of the Robert Dunn murder at the 1815 Fall Fair in York, the legislature passed an act forbidding market fairs altogether. Fall fairs disappeared, but country people continued to flow into the towns each spring, so spring fair activity was transferred in practice to Whit-Monday, the day after Pentecost.[65]

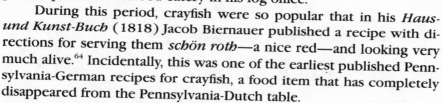

This reorganization of the folk calendar naturally had repercussions on local eating patterns, but even more influential was the growth of canals and railroads, which made the transportation of both fresh and saltwater fish easier and cheaper.

By the 1840s, canals and railroads had penetrated many of the smallest upstate communities, and fish of all kinds could be found on local menus and in local newspaper advertisements. Fesig and Rhode, a Pennsylvania-German grocery store in Reading, advertised mackerel

Das unentbehrliche

Haus- und Kunst-Buch,

Für den Bauer und Stadtmann.

Enthaltend

Die ausgesuchtesten und sichersten

Haus-Mittel,

So wie auch

Die unerhörtesten und geprüftesten

Kunst-Stücke,

Die noch niemals zuvor im Druck erschienen
sind.

Von Jacob Biernauer.

Gedruckt, für das allgemeine Beste
1818.

Title page of Jacob Biernauer's *Indispensible Domestic Receipt Book*

by the half and the quarter barrel in the Reading *Adler* of May 27, 1851. Mackerel, like many other large sea fish, were often sold salted or smoked.

Then there were the hucksters. Even as late as my grandmother's childhood—the early 1900s—fresh shad, cod, mackerel, oysters, and clams were hawked from farm to farm by hucksters driving wagons specially fitted out with ice and barrels of seaweed to keep their products fresh. These peddlers carried "fish horns," which they blasted from time to time to attract attention; then they would run off into a musical jingle about fish. Most of these charming fish chants have never been recorded for posterity, but here is a typical one:

> Shad, shad, best to be had.
> Fresh on ice. The price is nice.
> Shad, shad, I'll sing no louder!
> Shad, shad, for pots of chowder!

Naturally, there were dialect versions of this chant, because Susquehanna Soup, also commonly called "Shad Chowder," was one of the great inventions of Pennsylvania-German cookery. Alas, the world at large has not yet discovered it.

36. Fish
(Fische)

Fish should be well cleaned and cooked thoroughly, otherwise, they will be unpalatable and also very unhealthy.

37. To Poach Salmon, Bass, and Other Large Fish
(Salm, See-Bass, und andere grosse Fische zu sieden)

Place the fish in cold water. When the water comes to a boil, skim it carefully, add salt and some vinegar, and let it simmer until the meat falls easily from the bones. Then pour a sauce of butter and vinegar over it.

For rural cooks who were not accustomed to the adroit handling of *au bleu* cookery, poaching in vinegar and water was by far the most successful way to treat fish. From a technical standpoint, Pennsylvania-German housewives well understood the art of boiling dumplings and puddings, so poached fish was more in keeping with that line of knowledge. Certainly for larger fish it was the most popular mode of preparation.

As an alternative to vinegar, a number of cooks used wine. George Girardey never skimped on it. Since his poaching recipes are generally more elaborate than the one above, it might be instructive to sample his recipe for salmon.[66]

George Girardey's Poached Salmon

Take a moderately large salmon and cook it in claret with sliced carrots and onions, four cloves, four bay leaves, a handful of parsley, a little thyme, and salt and pepper. Let it simmer very slowly. Serve without a sauce, and decorate with some sprigs of parsley. If one strains the stock, it goes very well as a sauce over boiled noodles or potatoes.

Salmon, being pleasantly pink to begin with, may be considered an unusual victim of claret, for we are left with a rather grapey-looking fish.

38. To Fry Trout and Other Small Fish
(Forellen und andere kleine Fische zu backen)

After the fish are cleaned, dry them on a board and sprinkle with a little flour. Fry until golden brown and pour [a sauce of] drawn butter, parsley, and fine, fried bread crumbs over them. Eels look particularly nice on the table when they are dipped in egg and bread crumbs and thus fried.

Early Pennsylvania-German settlers commonly erected weirs on many of the streams and rivers in the southeastern part of the state in order to catch shad, herring, salmon, and rockfish. At one time, these fish went up the rivers in great schools to spawn. The weirs along the Schuylkill were so numerous that they impeded navigation, and in 1761 the colonial assembly was obliged to pass a law against them.[67] This did not stop the farmers from fishing, but it did put an end to the unnecessary slaughter of fish.

After the Revolutionary War, pole fishing came into its own in Pennsylvania. By the 1840s, it was one of the most popular Pennsylvania-German sports. In the summer, Ascension Day was specially set aside as a time for fishing. A great many people, even among the Plain Sects, took off from farm chores to go fishing for eel and trout. Like their German cousins, the Pennsylvania Dutch have always been particularly fond of trout. In colonial times, the Sun Inn in Bethlehem, once managed by the Moravians, was famous for its trout. This tradition is not dead, and while it might be possible to publish 100 Pennsylvania-German trout recipes, my guess is that 100 would only scratch the surface!

The Sun Inn, later known as the Sun Hotel

39. Cod Fish
(Stock-Fisch)

Fresh cod fish is best boiled or baked. Salted cod must soak in warm water until the skin comes off easily, then put it in fresh water. Place it over a moderate fire, and let it simmer slowly 3 or 4 hours. When done, pour drawn butter over it.

Judging from newspaper advertisements, much of the cod eaten in Pennsylvania during the nineteenth century came from New England. Pennsylvania-Dutch merchants called it "Yankee" to distinguish it from other types of cod then available. This included the most sought after and the most expensive cod imported from Germany or Holland, which was available from German import shops in Philadelphia and in large Pennsylvania-German towns, such as Reading, York, and Allentown.

Domestic or imported, cod played an important role in the cookery of many Pennsylvania-German households. Cooked with sauerkraut or in pea soup, it was an important substitute for meat in the fasting dishes of Pennsylvania-German Catholics who settled at Bally, Conewago, Lebanon, and elsewhere in southeastern Pennsylvania. References to their eighteenth-century fish and sauerkraut meals have come to light in these areas.[68] Friederike Löffler provides us with a typical way of preparing it in the late 1700s.[69]

Fish turner

Friederike Löffler's Sauerkraut with Cod

While cooking your sauerkraut, soak 3 or 4 small pieces of dried cod in hot water, and pick out the bones. Clean a fresh herring and chop it fine with one onion. In five ounces of butter, fry a handful of flour until straw color. Then simmer the herring and onion in the butter. When somewhat reduced, remove everything from the pan and place a piece of cod on the bottom. Cover with a layer of the herring, onion, and butter mixture and continue in this fashion until all the ingredients are in. Then pour over this a half ladle * of broth, cover, place the pan in hot ashes, and keep hot until served.

On a large platter, make a layer of cooked sauerkraut, then a layer of the cod mixture, and continue until there is enough on the plate for serving. No meat is eaten with this dish.

---

* Löffler used standard French cooking equipment in most of her recipes, but her measurements are not always clear.

40. Fried Clams
(Gebackene Muscheln)

Place the clams in a colander so that they can drain, then roll them in flour mixed with a little salt, and fry them in butter. When serving, squeeze lemon juice on them.

This same recipe was used for river mussels, which were once plentiful in the Delaware and Susquehanna.

River mussel

41. Fried Oysters
(Geröstete Austern)

For frying, large oysters are best. Cook them slowly in their own juices for 2 minutes, then let them drain until dry. Dip them in egg yolk and fine bread crumbs, and season with nutmeg, red pepper, and salt. Then fry until golden brown. When serving fried oysters, pour a little drawn butter over them, mixed with their own juices.

Drawn butter was often dispensed with and replaced by *schwartze Butterbrieh*, or "black butter." This was essentially the same as French *beurre noir*, butter that was fried until black over a slow fire. A *Schpritz* of herb vinegar was sometimes added and, if Pennsylvania-Dutch cooks thought they could get away with it, a dash or two of flour as well.

42. Fried Oysters
(Gebackene Austern)

Oysters may be dipped in a batter of wine, eggs, and sifted flour, seasoned with nutmeg, and then fried in hot butter.

Odd though it may seem to us today, fried oysters were once popular for winter breakfast. They were piled high beside cold chicken, fried mush, scrapple, crumb cakes, and fruit pies, and if hot pepper vinegar were not enough to help digest them, many were the kitchens that started off the day with a shot of Schnapps!

A whole lore was built up around oysters, more so, in fact, than the folklore surrounding many other foods. This happened because the Dutch were very much in awe of oysters' alleged aphrodisiac qualities. They often referred to them obliquely as *Ditze*. It was for this same reason that oyster suppers, once popular entertainments among

Oyster wagon of the 1840s

Pennsylvania-German teenagers, were so much frowned upon by Amish and Mennonite church fathers. Oysters, not the frolicking, were often blamed for the downfall of many a young girl; as one religious tract put it, they led to a "sensual and wanton heart."[70] Thus the common phrase: *Wammer Eischdere esst, fall net in die Schaal!*—"If you eat oysters, don't get caught!"

5

A "Karrich" of Vittles and Herbs

Wann's net fer unsere Bauere waer,
Was waer dann unser Marrick?
Mer hett yoh nix zu fresse meh—
Un sell waer drumm so arrick!

Translation

If it weren't for our farmers,
    What markets would be had?
We wouldn't have a thing to eat
    and wouldn't that be bad!

FROM AN OLD SONG

From the very earliest period of settlement, the Pennsylvania Germans were intensive gardeners. This is evidenced not only in the thorough way they cleared and manured their lands, but also in ample references to kitchen gardens and vegetable produce in eighteenth-century documents. Many wills, for example, specified the type and amounts of produce a widow was entitled to take from the gardens. Many period travel accounts discussed in minute detail the varieties of vegetables the Pennsylvania Germans grew and how they differed from those of the English.

In spite of the abundance of fresh vegetables, the primary interest of the rural cook was not in their tenderness, but in how well they would keep. Since most period vegetables—string beans, for example—were hybridized for pickling or drying, they tended to be tough unless cooked for some time. This explains, in part, why nineteenth-century cooks boiled their vegetables longer than we do today, and why certain vegetables appear in *Die geschickte Hausfrau* and others do not—broccoli is noticeably missing.

In general, vegetables were used as side dishes, extenders in soups and stews, and as garnishes for the meat course. Sometimes opposing flavors such as the sweetness of parsnips (recipe 47) were played against the salty flavor of meat. In other cases, vegetable side dishes echoed the flavor combinations of the gravy in the main dish. The hot and sour dressing served on cauliflower (recipe 44) might serve as a reminder of the flavors in sour marinated pot roast (recipe 11), and surely, the effect would be heightened with a balancing dish of stewed fruit.

In less affluent households where a true European type of folk

73

cookery persisted even into the late nineteenth century, vegetable side dishes reverted to the pot and came to the table as extenders in meat dishes, particularly stews. Where meat was scarce or unaffordable, vegetables took the place of the meat altogether. The cauliflower recipe, for example, could be served as a meal in itself. Cabbage salad (recipe 54) was often treated this way, and the same could be said of squash (recipe 53). A simple baked casserole of squash, chopped onions, and dill seed—well dotted with butter—was a favorite one-meal dish during the humid months of summer.

The humid months of summer were also busy months for gardening, one of the domains of the Pennsylvania-German housewife. With the help of her children, a kitchen maid, or even a hired hand or two, she was able to reap the rewards of Pennsylvania's fertile soil. The fertility of Pennsylvania's gardens was the subject of envy and admiration in nineteenth-century farm journals across the country, and Quaker and German botanists busied themselves developing new strains of vegetables and fruits for the *Hausfraa* to plant. Today the farms are gradually falling victim to the bulldozer, but a hint of the former bounty remains. In fact, I am told that it is still possible to find an occasional *Hockschterfraa* selling her fresh herbs and vegetables from door to door. If she is the enterprising sort, she will even arrive in her *Karrich*, which is Dutch for a cart. This is a great pun for Pennsylvania Germans, since a *Karrich* is also a church.

43. Vegetables
(Gemüse)

Vegetables must be fresh and cooked until completely soft. Clean thoroughly to rid them of insects. Boil the vegetables quickly in a good quantity of water, and if boiling continues uninterrupted, they should be ready as soon as they sink to the bottom of the pot.

The original German literally advises us to boil the vegetables until they are soft "through and through." This is why root vegetables always stood up better than green ones in many Pennsylvania-Dutch kitchens.

44. Cauliflower
(Blumen-Kohl)

Remove the outer leaves, leaving only the flowers. Boil 15 to 20 minutes, depending on size. Test the stem with a fork, and if it is soft, then it is done and must be taken out directly. Let it drain until dry, and pour a butter sauce over it.

Cauliflower was known in Germany as early as the sixteenth century, so it was already well established in the diet of the first Pennsylvania-German settlers when they arrived here in the late 1600s. The Pennsylvania-Dutch name for it is *Blummegraut*, or "flowering" cabbage.

Some Pennsylvania-Dutch housewives were fond of dipping small cauliflower stems into a brandied batter and frying them like fritters. Others served boiled cauliflower as a side dish with roast pork, pigeon, or chicken. Traditionally, boiled cauliflower was served with a sour dressing. The method of preparing the dressing varied somewhat from present-day practice in that sugar was rarely used, but its basic structure has not changed in German folk cookery for several centuries.

The old Pennsylvania-Dutch farmer's market at York

One of the most charming descriptions of this cauliflower dressing has come down to us in a Rhineland cookbook called *Die cölner Köchinn* (The Cologne Cook: Cologne, 1806), a work with a good many recipes familiar to Pennsylvania-German housewives. That recipe may be translated as follows:[71]

Cauliflower with a Hot Sour Dressing

After the cauliflower is picked and washed clean, dip it briefly in boiling water. Pour the water off and put the cauliflower in a shallow pot. To this add strong meat stock, butter, mace, pepper, and salt. Let this cook together [until done.] [In a separate pan,] make a dressing with egg yolks, butter, pepper, nutmeg, and a mixture of half vinegar and half water. Stir this continuously over the fire. Drain the cauliflower and lay it on a platter, then pour the dressing over it.

The reason for dipping the cauliflower in the boiling water was simple: It was one way of removing some of the bitterness, but it also killed the aphids that normally infested the plant in the days before potent chemical sprays.

45. Celery
(Cellerie)

Celery improves the flavor of salads, soups, and sauces, and [when] boiled, tastes very good with stewed meat. Wash 6 or 8 celery stalks, strip off the outer leaves, cut the stalks into pieces 3 or 4 inches long, and boil them until soft in half a pint of veal stock. Add 2 full spoons of cream and 1 ounce of butter rolled in flour. Season with pepper, salt, and nutmeg. And let it all simmer together.

Sellerich, as the Dutch call it, was raised in Pennsylvania almost from the earliest period of settlement. It was one of the most popular winter vegetables because it could be dug up in the fall and "planted" in barrels of earth or damp sand in the cellar, where it could be kept for many weeks.

This handy recipe, once popular throughout the country during the nineteenth century, originally appeared as "stewed" celery in *The Kitchen Companion*. Today we would call it creamed celery.

46. Carrots
(Gelbe Rüben)

Small, young carrots should cook in 1/2 hour. Large, old carrots will require 2 hours or more. Young carrots should be boiled with meat, in which case, pour butter over them.

Carrots, or *Geelriewe* in dialect—literally, "yellow turnips"— were important to the Pennsylvania Germans for an unusual reason: They were looked upon as an herb. They were used as medicine for consumptive persons. They were fed to cows to yellow the cream, or the juice was added to the cream before it was churned for butter, a little trick that made the butter even yellower. As a vegetable for the table, however, carrots were not considered worth the trouble. They were flavoring only.

Perhaps so few people bothered to grow them because carrots did not unite well with pork or the other meats the Dutch ate. But few people did, and that seems to have been the case even in the eighteenth century, a hint that carrots may not have entered German folk cookery until relatively late. This peculiarity of local taste is not too far behind us, for there are older Pennsylvania Germans today who can recall carrotless childhoods.

This attitude toward carrots is born out in Pennsylvania-German culinary literature and nowhere more strikingly than in George Girardey's *Handbuch über Kochkunst*. In his section on vegetables, Girardey published forty-six recipes. Only one was for carrots. The reason surfaces in the last line of his recipe:[72]

George Girardey's Sautéed Carrots

Fry a little flour in butter. Add some sugar, meat broth, julienned carrots, salt, pepper, and nutmeg. Sauté the carrots in the sauce until soft, then serve hot. If the carrots are small and young, they may be used whole as above, but generally, turnips are to be preferred.

---

47. Parsnips
(Pastenaten)

Clean and serve parsnips like carrots. Let them boil 1 to 2 hours, depending on their size and freshness. Parsnips are [also] sometimes served mashed with butter, pepper, salt, and milk. They can be eaten by themselves, or with cured beef, pork, or salted fish. Drawn butter and vinegar make a delicate sauce for them.

Parsnips, like turnips, have been an integral part of the German farmer's diet since the early Middle Ages. In cookery, they were treated much like potatoes, which have now largely replaced them. In Pennsylvania, parsnips remained an important part of folk cookery even after the assimilation of potatoes in the eighteenth century, perhaps because they were easier to store and less susceptible to disease and insects.

Aside from serving parsnips mashed, as this recipe suggests, they were also grated, mixed with flour and egg, seasoned, and made into patties called *Baschtnade-Kichelche*, or *Baschtnade-Kichli*, depend-

ing on which part of the state one came from. These *Kichli* were then fried until deep yellow and served with sour cream.

48. Red Beets
(Rothe Rüben)

Beets should not be sliced or skinned until after they are cooked. Boil them briskly 1 hour until done. In the winter, they may need to be cooked 3 hours until done. Then cut them in thin slices, lay them in spiced vinegar, and after several days, they will be ready to use.

—————————————◆·◆·◆—————————————

Beet salad, pickled beets, beet pies—the list of Pennsylvania-German beet recipes is almost endless. The recipe here, actually for pickled beets, was usually improved to suit Pennsylvania-Dutch taste by adding whole hard-boiled eggs. The eggs, which absorb the red color of the beets, are highly decorative when sliced and thus may be used as garnishing for other dishes.

It may be interesting to note that the standard German word for beets is *Mangold*, but that the Pennsylvania Dutch call them *Rotriewe*, or "red turnips." Pennsylvania-Dutch classification of root vegetables is based on the old assumption that most rooty things are a variety of turnip, hence "yellow turnips" for carrots and "red turnips" for beets. It is a vestige of medieval thought that is still with us.

49. Asparagus
(Spargel)

Tie the asparagus in little bundles. Put them in a sauce pan with a spoonful of salt and boil 12 to 20 minutes. As soon as they are soft, take them out, lay them on sippets of fried bread and pour drawn butter over them.

—————————————◆·◆·◆—————————————

Here is a vegetable with a colorful Pennsylvania-German name. Since its introduction into Germany in 1565, the Germans have called asparagus *Spargel*, which is a corruption of the same Latin word used in English. The Pennsylvania Dutch, however, having little use for Latin, called it *Mickegraut*, or "fly plant." This was because in the days before screens people hung mature asparagus plants in their houses and stores to keep out flies.

Naturally, the Pennsylvania Germans also *ate* asparagus, mountains of it, every spring. It was added to chicken soup. It was cooked, chopped, stirred into omelettes, and served hot on buttered toast—a popular supper dish in the 1820s and 1830s. It was also boiled and used in salads with shredded ham and hard-boiled eggs. And, of course, it was very good served as directed in the recipe above.

50. Green Peas
(Grüne Erbsen)

Boil peas quickly in a small quantity of water, to which a spoonful of salt and a piece of sugar have been added. Stir in some butter and a little pepper. In 15 to 20 minutes the peas will be ready [to serve].

———————————————————

During the Middle Ages, the poor in Germany used ground, dried peas for making bread, but it was not until the eighteenth century that green peas became generally popular. Today, one of the many things visitors notice in the spring are the long rows of peas sprouting up by kitchen doors all over German Pennsylvania, which attests to the universal popularity of peas among the Pennsylvania Dutch. They call them *Blickarbse* when they are unshelled and *Arbse* when they are ready for boiling. Sugar peas, another favorite, are called *Zuckerarbse*. The word *Arbs*, which is much closer to medieval German *Arbas* than to modern German, is really a corruption of the Latin *ervum*. It is an archaic and rather poetic Pennsylvania-Dutch way of saying just plain peas.

51. Tomatoes
(Tomatoes)

Peel the tomatoes and put them in a pot with a little salted water, and let them cook ½ hour. Then serve them on fried bread in a deep bowl. Or, put the tomatoes peeled [on a layer of] fine bread crumbs and ground crackers in a deep pan. [Add another] layer of bread and crackers, then another layer of tomatoes. Between each layer, add butter and a little salt and pepper. Let this cook ¾ hour.

The second suggestion in this recipe, which should have a layer of crumbs on top, makes a rather conventional casserole, but then we must remember that in 1848, tomato cookery was still in its infancy in Pennsylvania.

Thomas Jefferson is said to have introduced the tomato to this country in 1781, but there is evidence suggesting that tomatoes were at least known to many other Americans well before then.

James Mease wrote in his edition of Willich's *Domestic Encyclopaedia* (Philadelphia, 1804) that "the cultivation of this excellent vegetable is rapidly extending in Pennsylvania, where a few years ago, it was scarcely known. The apples stewed make an excellent sauce for fish, and a fine catsup, which is used by the French in a variety of dishes."[73] Like many of his contemporaries, Mease called tomatoes "love apples." Writing many years later in his *Family Kitchen Gardener*, Robert Buist, a Philadelphia nurseryman, commented on the popularity of tomatoes.[74]

In taking a retrospect of the past eighteen years, there is no vegetable in the catalogue that has obtained such popularity in so short a period as the one now under consideration. In 1828–9 it was almost detested; in ten years more, every variety of pill and panacea was "extract of tomato." It now occupies as great a surface of ground as cabbage, and is cultivated the length and breadth of the country. As a culinary dish it is on every table from July to October. . . . It is brought to the table in an infinite variety of forms, being stewed and seasoned, stuffed and fried, roasted and raw, and nearly every form palatable to all. It is also made into pickles, catsup and salted in barrels for Winter use, so that with a few years more experience, we may expect to see it as an every-day dish from January to January.

That was in 1847.

Tomatoes still do not play as important a role in Pennsylvania-German cookery as they do in Creole cookery, particularly in sauces, but the Pennsylvania Dutch have perfected a few tomato recipes worth mentioning. Among these are tomato "figs" (sun-dried pear tomatoes), yellow tomato pie, green tomato mincemeat pie, tomato "butter," and tomato compote (tomatoes stewed with lemon and sugar and served cold, like fruit).

52. Spinach
(Spinat)

Spinach should be picked, washed clean, and cooked in boiling salt water until tender. Then pour off the water, press and chop the spinach fine. Hard-boiled eggs, sippets of buttered bread or fried bread may be arranged around it and thus brought to the table.

Spinach soup, creamed spinach, spinach dumplings, these are just a few of the many ways spinach is prepared by the Pennsylvania Germans, who would call the recipe above *Schpinatmus* because it has the consistency of mush. Some cooks might add two tablespoons of bread crumbs, two tablespoons of sweet cream, butter, salt, pepper, and a beaten egg. This was stirred into the spinach and served hot with vinegar on fried bread, garnished with slices of hard-boiled egg.

53. Squash
(Kürbiss)

First, skin the squash, cut it in inch-thick pieces, and boil until soft. Then mash with a spoon. Cook it again a little longer, and when done, press it through a sieve. Then add some salt and a little butter.

Squash strainer

In 1835, nurseryman Thomas Bridgeman wrote in his *Young Gardener's Assistant* that squash was a "good substitute for Turnips, which cannot be raised in perfection in hot weather."[75] He later suggested that after cooking, squash be pressed dry "and thus prepared for the table in the same manner as Turnips."[76] It seems that this method of preparation was by far the most common among early American settlers, including the Pennsylvania Germans. Rather than cook this New World vegetable the way the Indians did—stewed, for example—European settlers simply treated squash like something they knew, much the same way the Germans treated beets and carrots when they were first introduced in the Old World. The recipe for pureed squash in *Die geschickte Hausfrau* is a classic example of food acculturation on the folk level. That is why it is also one of the most traditional ways of preparing squash in Pennsylvania.

The kinds of squash available in 1848 were very much like the squash known today. Some of the common commercial varieties were Early Bush Scallop, Green Striped Bush, Early Crookneck, Large Cushaw, Vegetable Marrow, Winter Crookneck (technically a pumpkin), Lima Coconut, and Acorn Squash, also called California Squash after its place of origin.

Cymling

Among the Pennsylvania Germans, the Bush Scallop, sometimes called a cymling; Early Crookneck; and the Winter Crookneck, which is commonly called the gooseneck pumpkin, were the most popular. Of the three, the Winter Crookneck was definitely known to have been grown locally by the Indians, and in some ways, its preparation differed from that of the other varieties. It is discussed more fully under recipe 88 for pumpkin pie.

54. A Good Cabbage Salad
(Guter Kraut-Sallat)

Wash a nice, fresh head of white cabbage and cut out the heart. Then shred it fine on a cabbage plane, put it in a deep porcelain bowl, and pour the following mixture over it. Take 1 gill or ½ water glass of good fruit vinegar, ¾ pound of butter cut into 4 pieces and rolled in flour, 1 small salt spoon of salt, and about as much red pepper. Mix this together well and let it come to a boil in a sauce pan. Beat the yolks of 3 eggs, and as soon as the above mixture begins to boil, take it from the fire and stir in the beaten eggs. Then pour all of this hot over the shredded cabbage and mix it together thoroughly with a spoon.

The hot salad has a long history in Middle European cookery. The 1806 recipe for cauliflower with a hot dressing is one variety we have already sampled (recipe 44), but the most commonly used vegetables were cabbages or greens. The concept of combining vegetables and hot dressings appears to be a peasant adaptation of the olive oil and vinegar salad that sifted northward from Italy during the Middle Ages.[77] Since German country cooks generally could not afford olive oil, hot lard or butter was substituted. Eventually, eggs were added to provide a more stable liaison—this was certainly true of upper-class versions of the dressing even in the sixteenth century. Unlike the lard and vinegar dressings, the cooked dressings with egg could be reserved and served cold.

In Pennsylvania, there was no standard type of hot dressing. Bacon lard and vinegar dressings on dandelion or purslane were the oldest and most primitive, but dressings using eggs were also known. It was common practice in some households, however, to substitute flour for the eggs. The resulting dressing was not as creamy as the egg dressings, and if cooked too much, the flour tended to separate. But if used quickly, it was deemed quite acceptable in rural cookery, more so in that it saved eggs.

The eggless dressings might be called "late winter dressings," because in the days before heated chicken houses, chickens laid fewer eggs or none at all when cold weather arrived. Thus, there was a predictable time when eggs would be scarce and substitutions were necessary. One of the most crucial of these periods was that of the "six-weeks want"—February to the middle of March.[78]

It was during the six-weeks want, when only the longest-keeping vegetables were left in the cellar and garden vegetables were not yet planted, that the hot salad made with wild greens, beet tops (from the cellar), or potatoes became a vital part of the Pennsylvania-German diet. Cooks could improve the salads with chopped bacon or diced ham. As a meal in themselves, hot salads might be served on a large platter surrounded by fried sausages and apples.

We learn in Christian Becker's *Sprachlehrer* (Easton, Pa., 1808) that when salads were eaten as meals in themselves—typical inn fare— they were often served with cheese and warm beer or wine.[79] The most popular cheeses for salads were *Schtinkkees* ("stink" cheese), a Pennsylvania-Dutch version of ripe Limburger; *Schweizerkees*, a domestic Emmenthaler; and *Westfeelischerkees*, which resembled Münster. *Schapzeegerkees*, a pungent green cheese flavored with clover leaves, was sometimes grated over salads to heighten the flavor. It does much to improve the recipe in *Die geschickte Hausfrau*.

Of all the Pennsylvania-German foods outsiders disliked most, hot salads seem to have ranked at the top. As Thomas Hill, a New Jersey farmer, remarked in 1799: "Salad with milk, oil, vinegar, bonny clabber and bread; good God! How can they work so hard on such food!"[80]

55. To Preserve Parsley
(Petersilien aufzubewahren)

To preserve parsley for seasoning soups, etc., gather it on a dry day, lay it directly on a tin pan, and set the pan near a hot fire. The parsley will soon become crumbly or dry, whereupon it should be rubbed fine and placed in bottles.

The Pennsylvania-Dutch word for parsley is *Peeterli. Peeterli* was used in practically everything, including witchcraft. One reason so many Dutch dried their parsley for winter use rather than putting pots of it near a sunny windowsill indoors was undoubtedly that a pot of parsley in the house was considered a very bad omen indeed. The herb was seen as a precursor of death and funerals, so a gift of potted parsley was certainly no gift to a Pennsylvania Dutchman.

Contrary to what some writers on Pennsylvania-German foods have stated, herbs and spices played a fundamental role in the cookery of the Pennsylvania Dutch, at least until the advent of temperance and the philosophies of homeopathic medicine, which advocated the elimination of spiced foods. Many Pennsylvania-German cooks were converted to that fanatical blandness of taste that our great-great-grandmothers thought so pious and healthful. At one time, however, the list of culinary herbs was long and colorful.

Even the most cursory glance at Franz Daniel Pastorius's "Medicus dilectus oder Artzney-Büchlein" (The Beloved Doctor, or Small

Book of Medicine: Germantown, 1695); Christopher Sauer's *Kurtzgefasstes Kräuterbuch* (The Concise Herbal), issued at Germantown in a series of installments between 1762 and 1778; and the *Vortreffliches Kräuterbuch* (The Excellent Herbal), printed in Hanover in 1809, will produce a surprising roster of culinary herbs, not to mention the thirteen most common kitchen herbs discussed by Girardey in his *Handbuch über Kochkunst*. For the Pennsylvania Dutch, herbs were an intrinsic part of daily life and an essential ingredient in their cookery.

Some of the most popular kitchen herbs and spices, with their Pennsylvania-Dutch names, are listed below.

Anise	*Anis*
Basil	*Basel* or *Versammlingsgraut*
Calendula	*Ringelros*
Caraway	*Kimmel*
Cassia	*Kaschia* or *Zimmtbliet*
Chervil	*Kerbelgraut*
Chives	*Schnittloch*
Cinnamon	*Zimmet* or *Zimmt*
Cloves	*Negelin* or *Nelke*
Coriander	*Korianner*
Cumin	*Kimmel* or *Weisser Kimmel*
Cress	*Gartengress* or *Gordegress*
Dill	*Dill*
Fennel	*Fenichel*
Garlic	*Gnovlich*
Loveage	*Liebschteckel*
Mace	*Muschgatbliet*
Marjoram	*Marun* or *Marrijanner*
Mustard	*Senf*
Nutmeg	*Muschgatniss*
Parsley	*Peeterli*
Purslane	*Seibatsel*
Rosemary	*Roschmarei*
Saffron	*Saffran* or *Safferich*
Sage	*Salwei*
Sorrel	*Sauerampel*
Savory	*Bohnegreidel*
Tarragon	*Schtragon*
Thyme	*Gwendel*

Most of these herbs are mentioned in various recipes throughout *Die geschickte Hausfrau* or in the accompanying commentaries. Many Pennsylvania-German cooks, however, liked to combine the fresh herbs and make soup with them. *Ringelros-Sippli*, a charming little broth flavored with calendula petals, was once a popular "cup soup" in the summer. In the spring, when not many vegetables were available, spring herbs formed a major component in soups.

Just to illustrate how these various herbs could be used together, the following recipe is translated from the scrapbook of Solomon Gery of Harlem, Berks County.[81] Although the scrapbook dates from 1868–72, Gery's recipe is typical of the Pennsylvania herb soups made in the eighteenth and early nineteenth centuries. Structurally, it is similar to an herb soup that appeared in Marcus Loofft's *Nieder-Sächsisches Koch-Buch* (Lübeck, 1778). Loofft's recipe, however, called for chervil, sorrel, spinach, tarragon, and purslane, and specified fried flour instead of bread crumbs.[82]

Solomon Gery's Herb Soup

Pick fresh chervil, cress, parsley, carrots, and leeks. Wash them well and chop fine. Place ¼ lb. of butter in a soup pot and braize the herbs gently in the butter. Gradually add meat stock and bread crumbs* until the soup becomes thick. The soup should cook gently for two hours and become very high flavored. Before serving, beat eggs into it or add small pieces of roast beef.

It is interesting to note that carrots are treated here as an herb. This is consistent with the old Pennsylvania-German practice of planting carrots in the herb garden and using them as flavoring agents in soups rather than as table vegetables.

56. To Make Good Mustard
(Guten Senf zu machen)

Senf

Boil 1 quart of vinegar, dissolve 3 ounces of salt in it, and pour it over 2 ounces of grated horseradish in a stone crock, which must [then] be covered. Let this stand 24 hours before straining it through a cloth. Gradually stir in a pound of the best powdered mustard, and store this in a bottle with a wide neck. After using, always seal the bottle carefully.

—◆—

Salt, pepper, vinegar, and mustard were four classic accoutrements to the Pennsylvania-German table. As a contrast to tomato catsup (recipe 126), mustard sauce, as this is more properly called, was a very old Pennsylvania-Dutch condiment. Even in the eighteenth cen-

---

*For ordinary soups, the most commonly used breadcrumbs were those of rye bread. It was customary to fry the crumbs in butter before adding them to the soup.

tury, imported German mustard was available in nearly every Pennsylvania-German shop, but those who could not afford it made their own. Whether bought or homemade, mustard was popular on pork, bacon, and sausage. It was even served on potatoes, as illustrated in the following recipe translated from Johann Evangelist Fürst's *Der verständige Bauer, Simon Strüf* (Simon Strüf, the Prudent Farmer), a Bavarian work on farm economy that was imported and sold in Pennsylvania during the 1820s.[83]

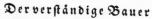

Although now quite rare, *Simon Strüf* was once popular reading among the Pennsylvania Dutch. Copies of the book were sold by Gustav Peters.

Johann Fürst's Potatoes with Mustard

Wash and peel the potatoes. Cut them into round slices, but not too thin, and rinse them again in fresh water. With finely chopped parsley root and onions, set the potatoes [in some water] over the fire and let them cook until soft, but not until they begin to fall apart. Drain off the water. Melt some butter in a shallow pan, pour the potatoes in, and let them simmer a little in the butter. Stir in two spoonsful of powdered mustard and just enough hot meat broth to equal [but not cover] the potatoes. Season with salt. If this should make too much liquid, bring to a boil and reduce. Pour the potatoes and mustard into a deep serving dish. In a sauce pan, sauté chopped parsley and onion in butter for a few minutes, but not over a very hot fire. Pour this evenly over the potatoes and serve.

Johann Fürst was the father of Anna Fürst, whose *Vollständiges Kochbuch für alle Stände* (Complete Cookbook for All Social Classes) was imported and sold in Philadelphia, Allentown, and Reading during the 1850s. She capitalized on the popularity of *Simon Strüf* by assuming the pen name of Marianne Strüf.

6

Soups, Broths, and Stews

Wann ich in mei' Kichli geh
Fer mei' Sippli koche,
Hockt des bucklich Mennli do,
Un fangt a' zu boche.

Translation

Whenever I enter my kitchen
a little broth to warm,
there sits a hump-backed gnome
who begins to taunt and storm.

OLD CHILDREN'S RHYME

Of all the kitchen utensils, the *Kochkessel*, or stewpot, was probably the one fraught with the most symbolism and meaning for the Pennsylvania Dutch. It was associated with all things motherly and good, as much a part of Aunt Pall as her apron and her Bible. It was one of the first words a child learned in days when cradles stood near the hearth. And without a doubt, of all the kitchen utensils, it was also one of the busiest. As the everready stockpot, as the practical catchall for leftovers, the stewpot was an institution in German Pennsylvania.

No well-managed house was ever short of broth, be it vegetable, fish, poultry, or meat. Any extra juices, any liquids in which food had been boiled, were poured off and saved. The Pennsylvania Dutch developed soupmaking to such a high art that complete cookbooks could be written about their soups alone; there was literally an appropriate soup for every day of the year, including a variety of hot and cold fruit soups.

This penchant for soup had its roots in South Germany, but the Pennsylvania Dutch took it one step further, particularly in the symbolism associated with religious meals in which soup was the central feature. Soup then became the symbol of community, of religious fellowship, and even communion. One of the most unusual mutton dishes in Pennsylvania-German cookery was the mutton soup (recipe 58) served at the Dunkard *Liebesmahl*, or "love feast," a deeply moving reenactment of the Last Supper.[84] Likewise, bean soup was traditional among the Amish after Sunday meeting. It was a way of melding, through the communal soup bowl, all the spiritual aspects of the day with the basic human condition of life and friends and family.

The Pennsylvania Germans developed a distinct hierarchy of

soups. They differentiated between light brothy soups called *Sipple*, or "little soups"; "cup soups" (*Koppsuppe*)—such as rolls broken up in coffee; and the thicker, more chowderlike *Suppe*, which could serve as meals in themselves. Stews, or *G'schmorte* (also pronounced *Schmorte*), were generally characterized by the lack of broth, in which case there was simply a rich *Brieh*, or gravy. *G'schmortes* (singular) derives from the German verb *schmoren*, which means to stew or cook slowly for a long period of time.

In arranging the courses for a basic two-course meal, it was the soup that came first, without variation. My grandfather once told me that soup came first because the sun rises before it sets. The logic of that Pennsylvania-Dutch saying I will not attempt to explain, but it says it all. Fish or shellfish soups might be followed by fowl or by a hot salad instead of a roast. A fruit soup might come before pudding. But one thing never changed: Soup came first. So when the household reverted to folk cookery or a one-pot meal, it was usually soup of some sort that appeared.

Noodle cutter

The Pennsylvania Dutch have always liked to thicken their soups with some form of starch. The most common thickeners were mashed potatoes, flour, rice, noodles, fried bread, dumplings, and *Riwwels*. *Riwwels* may require some explanation.

Riwwels are large crumbs made by rubbing egg yolk and flour between the fingers. Those made simply by rolling the fingers were known as "round" *Riwwels* (*runde Riwwle*), even though they were slightly elongated in shape. Another variety was made by dropping round *Riwwels* on a plate and pinching them together with the fingertips. These were called "formed" *Riwwels,* or *Riwwel* "peas" (*Riwwel-arbse*), and were often fried before the cook dropped them into the soup. A third variety was made by pressing *Riwwels* flat either on a plate or between the fingers to form "flake" *Riwwels* (*Riwwelflocke*). These were sometimes used for making *Riwwel* cakes, a species of crumb cake. Making *Riwwels* was busywork, so it usually became a task for the young girls in the family. It required patience and untiring hands.

Riwwel is sometimes written in English as rivvel; it appears in a number of cookbooks spelled this way. But the origin of the word is German, stemming from the verb *reiben*, to rub. In some South German dialects, *Riwwels* are called *Reible*, which is closer to the German spelling. But in Pennsylvania, *Riwwels* are *Riwwels*, minidumplings plain and simple.

Another popular additive to soups in the nineteenth century

were morels. The morels used by the Pennsylvania Germans were a species of black mushroom found near springs in the cow pastures of Pennsylvania and Maryland.[85] An abundance of cow dung and mucky ground was a guarantee for a steady crop of morels. They were gathered in April and May and sold fresh, or dried and packed in tins. Today, native morels are a forgotten delicacy whose absence leaves many old soup recipes languishing.

Morel

Many Pennsylvania-German women grew a variety of herbs especially for soups, while others found an ample selection of exotic spices in the old German apothecary shops that once were so common in larger Pennsylvania-German towns. Herbs and spices were important because the varieties and quantities and their use were what often distinguished the cookery of one Pennsylvania-German locality from another.

A soup cooked *nach lengeschder Art* (Lancaster style) was literally yellow with saffron. Lancaster, Lebanon, and York counties were once centers of saffron growing, so naturally saffron became a significant ingredient in the food of these areas. The "saffron belt" Dutch were so fond of the crocus that they applied it to everything, not always with good results. It was a common joke among the other Pennsylvania Germans to call these saffron lovers *Geeldeitsch*, or "Yellow Dutch." Today *Geeldeitsch* cookery is happily not so heavy handed.

As for the technology of soup making, every Dutch *Hausfraa* knew that soup cookery in a large *Kochkessel* over an open fire was a science unto itself, which required a number of utensils now extinct in the modern kitchen. A *Kesselgalje*, or crane (literally, a kettle "gallows"), attached to the chimney wall, allowed the cook to swing her soup in or out of the fireplace. Most of the earliest Pennsylvania-German cranes were made of wood, *not* iron. Hanging from the crane were either adjustable chains or a *Feierhohl*, a trammel. The trammel looked something like a saw and permitted the cook to raise or lower her kettle over the coals, depending upon how quickly she wanted her soup to boil. Also necessary was a *Schepper* (dipper) and a *Schaumleffel* (skimmer). Skimmers were used primarily to remove the *Heidel*, the excess fat or skin that formed on the surface of soups. Skimmers were absolutely necessary a century ago, because meat in those days was cooked with much more fat on it than today. Thus, there was much more grease.

Schepper

Pennsylvania-German soups were normally simmered in covered pots; otherwise, fireplace fumes would penetrate the stock and ruin the flavor. Tasting was accomplished by swinging the crane out over the hearth, then removing the lid. Soups intended for use at a later time were taken away from the heat and cooled in a partially covered earthenware pot.

In this chapter, beef soup (recipe 60) and calf's-head soup (recipe 61) may be traced to *The Kitchen Companion*.

57. Chicken Soup
(Hühner-Suppe)

Chicken bones, as they come from the table, as well as the heads and feet, can make a nice bowl of soup, particularly when the chickens are boiled and the stock is saved for soup. Boil the bones until they are completely white. Chicken soup may be made richer if a piece of lean beef, a veal bone, and 3 or 4 mutton bones are added.

Although this is called *Hühner-Suppe* in the original German, the Pennsylvania Dutch would probably call it *Hinkelsupp* in dialect. Admittedly, the recipe is extremely plain, but plain chicken soup was only a beginning. In his *Nieder-Sächsisches Koch-Buch* (1778), Marcus Loofft assumed that ordinary German chicken soup would always include meat dumplings of some kind, and if the dumplings were improved with a sprinkling of raisins in them, so much the better.[86]

58. Mutton Soup
(Hammelfleisch-Suppe)

Cut as much meat as is needed in thin strips from the neck or loin of a lamb. Put it in a pot of cold water with 1 or 2 onions and a little salt. Let this boil slowly ¾ hour, and skim it well when it boils. Turnips and potatoes can also be cooked in the stock, or cook the potatoes separately and mash them.

Hammelsupp made the old way was very much like gravy, ideal for pouring over buttered noodles or dumplings. *Hammel-Sippli*, or mutton broth, could also be made with this recipe, except that the turnips and potatoes would then be eliminated. It was the *Sippli*, not the *Supp*, that was served at Dunkard love feasts before the Civil War. The meat was served separately with a variety of breads and pies, and unsweetened coffee.

A Dunkard Love Feast

Although the recipe is called "mutton" soup in the original German, the directions actually call for lamb, which means that the recipe has been tampered with. There is a world of difference between mutton and lamb, and years ago mutton, not lamb, would have been used for souping. Meat from a leg of lamb works very well as a substitute; it is also much less expensive than loin. But for the absolute authenticity and cheapness, use the rib chops of mutton. That is what was meant by the "neck."

59. Veal Soup
(*Kalbfleisch-Suppe*)

For a 6-pound veal knuckle, take ½ pound of pork cut into small slices and lay it on the bottom of the cooking pot. Place the veal knuckle over this. Add about 1½ pints of cold water for each pound of veal. After the broth boils and is skimmed, add onions, celery, carrots, and sage as well as a little black pepper, spices, and cloves. If the soup needs thickening, stir in a few spoonfuls of flour. The soup should simmer at least 6 hours.

Called *Kalbfleeschsupp* in dialect, this was nothing more than a Pennsylvania-Dutch *pot-au-feu*, a stock in which to float dumplings.

The most typical dumplings for veal soup were meat dumplings, and Pennsylvania-German recipes for them abound. To illustrate the way dumplings were made in the 1840s and 1850s, the following recipe is translated from the scrapbook (begun in 1832) of Johannes Reisner, a farmer from Berks County. The original recipe—gratefully specific—appears to have been cut out of an issue of the Reading *Adler*, a popular source of local recipes in the nineteenth century.[87]

Dumpling
shovel

Meat Dumplings

Take ¼ pound of lean beef or pork, mince this very fine and work it into a dough using ½ ounce of (white) breadcrumbs, 1 egg yolk, and 1 teaspoon of butter. This should yield about 14 small dumplings. The dumplings should be done after boiling about 10 minutes in the soup. This dumpling mixture can also be used as filling in fowl.

---

60. Beef Soup
(Rindfleisch-Suppe)

Put 4 pounds of lean, fresh beef in 3 or 4 quarts of cold water and a little salt over a hot fire. Let this simmer slowly 6 hours, then add as much chopped carrot, celery, and parsley as you like. The soup will be even more delicious if a piece of leftover cold roast beef is cooked with it. Cut bread into small pieces, fry, and pour the soup over them.

The Pennsylvania Dutch have another name for this soup: *Feiwarflichesupp*. *Feiwarfliche* means something diced, and in this case, the "dice" are the ingredients. It was also jokingly called "gamble soup," because no one was certain what the handy housewife had put in it.

61. Calf's-Head Soup
(Kalbskopf-Suppe)

Parboil a calf's head, remove the skin, chop the meat into small pieces, take out the black part of the eyes, skin the tongue, and cut it up fine. Put all of this into 3 quarts of good meat stock, season it with red pepper, mace, and salt, and add the rind of ½ a lemon and about a dozen meatballs. Boil this 1½ hours, then dissolve 2 spoonfuls of flour in a little cold water. Pour ½ a pint of soup into it, and then stir it all back into the pot. Squeeze the juice of ½ a lemon into the soup, add the yolks of 8 hard-boiled eggs, and let it cook together a few minutes longer.

Some Pennsylvania Dutch call this *Schnaebbersupp*, or "snapper" soup. By the end of the eighteenth century, it had become a farmer's version of the real turtle soup served by West Indian planters.

In Philadelphia, the gentry considered turtle soup a native dish, and in the summer months especially, great sea turtles were auctioned off at dockside to caterers and owners of hotels and oyster cellars throughout the city. Baron von Closen tried the soup at the home of Governor Reed in 1781 and noted that the Reeds served their ninety-pound turtle, using its immense shell as a tureen.[88] For those curious to know how this was done, I would suggest reading "To dress a turtle the West-India way," in Richard Briggs's *The New Art of Cookery* (Philadelphia, 1792).[89] Suffice to say, the meat balls, the lemon, and the hard-boiled eggs in calf's-head soup were all intended to create an illusion of turtle meat, turtle flavor, and turtle eggs.

Most Pennsylvania Germans lived too far inland to find West Indian turtles in their markets, and even if they had, I suspect that the expense would have eliminated most cooks from the start. As it happened, calf's-head soup, the cheaper substitute, became more popular and was a regular standby at a number of well-known Pennsylvania-German inns. It was also served in large families, because in those days veal was inexpensive and the soup went far.

Calf's-head or mock turtle soup was also popular in Germany, no doubt owing to the Hanoverians, who made many English things fashionable, including plum pudding. By the 1850s, this species of calf's-head soup could be found in almost every German cookbook. Anna Bergner, for example, called it "Turtle Soup without Turtle" in her once-popular *Pfälzer Kochbuch*, published in 1858 in Mannheim.[90]

62. Rice Soup
(Reis-Suppe)

To 1 pound of rice, add 2 quarts of water, a little pepper and potherbs. Let this simmer in a well-covered pot. Then add 2 pounds of beef, a little cinnamon, and let it cook until done.

Surviving eighteenth-century transport agreements from Rotterdam to Philadelphia have shown that Pennsylvania-German immigrants often spelled out in contract form what food they were to receive during the voyage to America. The Germans, it seems, were accustomed to fresh rather than salted provisions. Among the bills of fare was this staple dish for one person: "one pound of beef cooked with rice," often served three times a week. It was popular because it was thick and filling. The recipe in *Die geschickte Hausfrau* is essentially the same recipe (but double the quantity) as that used by innumerable Germans en route to America. It continued to be popular in the nineteenth century because it was one of those inexpensive dishes that could serve as a one-course meal when there were many mouths to feed. Indeed, this particular recipe proved so popular that it was republished verbatim in the 1856 *Neuer gemeinnütziger pennsylvanischer Calender*, a Lancaster County almanac with a large agricultural audience.

Although fruit soups did not appear in the original editions of *Die geschickte Hausfrau*, two have been added here, because fruit soups were an important element in the Pennsylvania-German menu in the eighteenth and nineteenth centuries.

In general, fruit soups were treated as light, one-meal soups, usually served for supper, or in very hot weather, as the dinner itself. In such cases, it was not unusual to put dumplings in the soup—bacon dumplings in the apple soup are excellent. Where wine was unavailable or abjured, cider was often substituted.

63. Apple Soup
(Aepfelsuppe)

Peel and core 12 good apples, then cook them until soft in a quart of water with a small piece of cinnamon and half a lemon. Then add a bottle of wine and a little sugar, and let this cook together a few minutes. Beat the yolks of 3 eggs in a little wine, and whisk this into the soup thoroughly. Serve the soup over slices of bread fried in butter.

———————————◆◆◆———————————

This typical winter soup is reproduced from the 1842 edition of George Girardey's *Höchst nützliches Handbuch über Kochkunst*.[91] By a "bottle of wine" he evidently meant two pints, because the apple broth and wine should be in equal proportions. A red wine would engulf the flavors of the other ingredients. The amount of sugar depended on the sweetness of the apples and personal preference. But the soup had a fruitier taste if the cores and peelings were first boiled and then strained from the quart of water the recipe specified.

64. Huckleberry Soup
(Heidelbeeresuppe)

Remove the stems from about 2 pints of huckleberries, wash the berries, and put them in a pan with a very small amount of water over a low fire—the berries will produce enough liquid for soup themselves. Let them simmer until soft. Then, to each pint of berries, add a pint of white wine. Season the soup with the grated rind of 1 lemon, a little powdered cinnamon and cloves, and sugar to taste. Let this cook together briefly, then serve over coarsely chopped bread or rusks. [For a smoother soup,] one can remove the berry skins by straining the cooked berries through a sieve before adding the lemon and spices.

———————————◆◆◆———————————

This once-popular midsummer recipe was published in the *Vollständiges Kochbuch für die deutsch-amerikanische Küche*, the Loës and Sebald edition of Friederike Löffler's Swabian cookbook.[92] Excellent cold or hot, huckleberry soup was generally served with a garnish of whipped or sour cream. If made without the lemon and cinnamon, diced potatoes were sometimes added, though personally I think blue potatoes look odd.

7

Puddings, Pies and Other Sweets

Wer will gude Kuche backe
Der muss hawwe siwwe Sache:
Butter un Schmalz,
Zucker un Salz,
Millich un Mehl,
un Safferich macht
die Kuche gehl.

Literal Translation

To bake good cakes,
Take seven things:
Butter and lard,
Sugar and salt,
Milk and flour,
And saffron,
To make the cakes
Yellow.

OLD CHILDREN'S "PATTY-CAKE" RHYME

This is properly a dessert chapter, for nearly all of the recipes may be considered "treats" or *Leckerbisse*, as the Dutch called them. First among the treats were puddings.

Boiled, or "Dumpling" Puddings

Until the turn of this century, boiled puddings of all varieties appeared regularly on Pennsylvania-German tables. Of the dessert species, some of the favorites were lemon pudding, rice pudding (recipe 65), bread pudding (recipe 66), suet pudding, and, in hot weather, fruit puddings, such as cherry, blackberry, or raspberry. In rural areas, even in well-to-do families, boiled "dessert" puddings usually served as a complete meal rather than a third or fourth course as in the case of the Hardman Philips dinner (page 35). Furthermore, when these puddings were served in place of a roast or some other main dish, they were invariably made without sugar. The practice of serving unsweetened pudding as a main course was common in seventeenth-century England but became increasingly old fashioned toward the end of the eighteenth century. In Pennsylvania, this practice lingered a century longer.

Throughout southeastern Pennsylvania, all types of boiled puddings were called "dumplings" in common speech, even among the Quakers and other non-German groups. The Pennsylvania Dutch rarely used their own dialect term *Budding*, except in poetry or a literary context. As a result, there were a large number of words in common usage. Some Pennsylvania Germans called pudding *Gnepp*, while others called it *Gnoddel*.

In its technical meaning, a *Gnepp* is a "knob" or pudding ball—small and usually formed with two spoons. A *Gnoddel* is much larger, for in its original sense, it is formed with the hands and ought to be about the size of a baseball. Pennsylvania-German boiled puddings were larger than this, because the most commonly used pudding bag was an old, well-washed, five-pound flour sack.

Since "dumpling puddings" were generally cut up at the table and served in small portions, individuals could sweeten the pudding to taste with a sauce or, more commonly, by sprinkling sugar over it. This meant that boiled puddings were eaten in bowls of milk or cream.

It was a characteristic of southeastern Pennsylvania cookery to substitute vanilla for the sugar in plum, flour, and batter puddings.

THE

KITCHEN COMPANION,

AND

HOUSE-KEEPER'S

OWN BOOK,

CONTAINING ALL THE MODERN, AND MOST APPROVED METHODS IN

COOKERY, PASTRY, & CONFECTIONARY,

WITH AN EXCELLENT COLLECTION OF

VALUABLE RECIPES,

TO WHICH IS ADDED, THE

WHOLE ART OF CARVING, ILLUSTRATED.

PHILADELPHIA:

PUBLISHED BY TURNER & FISHER,

No. 15 NORTH SIXTH STREET;

74 CHATHAM STREET, NEW YORK.

1844.

Since vanilla is not documented locally until about 1800, this taste preference may have been entirely a development of the nineteenth century.

This adjustment does not usually appear in nationally marketed cookbooks of the period. However, in Hannah Bouvier Peterson's *National Cook Book* (Philadelphia, 1855), there is specific mention of vanilla as an alternative flavoring in plum pudding.[93] A great many of her other boiled pudding recipes either omit sugar or use it only to sprinkle over the pudding after it is done.

In local cookbooks, the omission of sugar is common. The plum pudding recipe omits sugar in J. Thomas Huey's *Household Treasure* (Philadelphia, 1871), a cookbook published largely for Irish Philadelphians.[94] The same is true of the plum pudding recipe in I. H. Mayer's *Domestic Economy* (Lancaster, Pa., 1893).[95] This last cookbook was definitely written for a rural audience. Likewise, sugar is omitted from some of the recipes in *Die geschickte Hausfrau*, or added "to taste."

This should not be surprising in view of the fact that the first five recipes, 65–69, can be traced to *The Kitchen Companion* and therefore reflect regional preferences. These same five recipes also appeared (in the very same order) in Esther Allen Howland's *New England Economical Housekeeper* (Worcester, Mass., 1844). How irritating it must have been for New England housewives to find the sugar missing!

65. Plain Rice Pudding
(Einfacher Reis-Pudding)

Boil 3 cups of rice in 2 quarts of milk until soft, then add 2 quarts of cold milk. Beat 8 eggs to a froth. [Add] ¼ pound of butter, 2 [grated] nutmegs, and sugar to taste. Let this bake 2 hours.

This is doubtless a recipe of English origin, for it is the sort of rice pudding that was once served for Sunday dinner in rural Britain. The English cook Mary Smith published a similar recipe called "Common Rice Pudding" in her *Complete House-keeper* (New Castle, 1786).[96] Richard Briggs gave us his version, which he recommended for busy "sea-faring men" in his *New Art of Cookery* (1792).[97] Maria Rundell's *New System of Domestic Cookery*, reprinted in Philadelphia in 1807, included a similar "Plain Rice Pudding."[98] And finally, Amelia Simmons, who lifted a great many of her recipes from English sources, published yet another version in her *American Cookery* (1796).[99]

Whatever its genealogy, one thing is certain. When brown sugar was added to this recipe, it became "Farmer's Rice Pudding." When cinnamon, lemon rind, and cream were added, and the pudding was baked in a deep pie dish lined with puff pastry, it became the "Dutch

Rice Pudding" once so popular in Victorian Philadelphia. As for the "Dutch" part of it, perhaps. It was popular among the Pennsylvania Germans, doubtless because it had a counterpart in the Old World, not because they invented it.

After all, rice pudding was well known in Middle Europe long before the Germans settled in Pennsylvania. *Ein gut Gebackens von Reis* (a nice baked pudding of rice) appeared in Master Sebastian's classic *Koch- und Kellermeisterey*, published in Frankfurt in 1581, but that was by no means the earliest German reference.[100] In the oldest surviving German cookbook, the great codex known as *Daz buoch von guoter spîze* (Book of Goodly Fare), written sometime between 1345 and 1354, there are several rice recipes. In that period, rice was definitely an expensive alternative for meatless days, a luxury food for the court and nobility. Yet it was probably this very aspect of luxury in the Middle Ages that gave rice and rice puddings such a special place in later traditional cookery.

Günter Wiegelmann has noted in his *Alltags- und Festspeisen* (Everyday and Festival Foods: Marburg, 1967) that rice pudding played a colorful role in the folk cookery of rural Germany.[101] As a symbol of wealth and good luck—harking back to its status as a luxury food in the Middle Ages—rice pudding was often served at wedding banquets. Since rice also had ulterior associations with fertility, this connection with the rite of marriage was fully consistent with the folk perspective of things. More interesting, however, is the fact that rice pudding also had these *same* associations for the Pennsylvania Germans, particularly in the eighteenth century. But here and there, the practice lingered even longer, for there are accounts of great rice puddings at wedding dinners as late as 1920. The bride and groom were required to share the first bite. No one could go home until everyone had a portion and the whole pudding was eaten—one good way to insure a long evening of jollification.

66. Bread Pudding
(Brod-Pudding)

Cut 1 loaf of bread in fine pieces, sprinkle it with a little salt, pour 2 quarts of boiling milk over it, and let the bread soak well. Then mash it, add 6 [beaten] eggs, 1 pound of butter, some cinnamon or nutmeg, and sugar. Let it bake 1½ hours.

The primary advantage of bread pudding was that it used up stale or unwanted bread and made a palatable dish of it. Plain bread puddings were considered a staple food in rural diet, and more often than not, the Pennsylvania Germans made these puddings with dark bread rather than white. Bread pudding made with rye bread was particularly common, and because of the nature of rye bread, sugar and sweet spices were usually omitted. They might be replaced, however, with chopped onion, chopped bacon, marjoram, or sage.

Among the Pennsylvania Germans, puddings were baked by setting a tin or earthenware pudding mold in a pan of water and letting it steam gently, or by pouring the batter into a deep earthenware pot and baking it at a low temperature in the outdoor bake oven.

67. Flour Pudding
(Mehl-Pudding)

Beat 12 eggs, add 2 quarts of milk, a little water, and make a batter of this with wheat flour. Next, pour it into a cloth or bag and boil 4 hours. Two pounds of dried currants can also be added.

Wheat

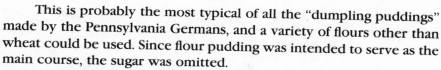

This is probably the most typical of all the "dumpling puddings" made by the Pennsylvania Germans, and a variety of flours other than wheat could be used. Since flour pudding was intended to serve as the main course, the sugar was omitted.

The cloth or bag referred to in the recipe was the so-called "pudding bag," an important article in the nineteenth-century kitchen. Although most cooks used old flour bags, there was one school of thinking that was more particular. An article in the *Germantown Telegraph* for September 24, 1851, had this to say about pudding bags:

Your pudding or dumpling cloths should be squares of coarse, thick linen, hemmed, and with tape strings sewed to them. After using, they should be washed, dried, and ironed, and kept in one of the kitchen drawers, that they may be always ready when wanted.

68. Plum Pudding
(Pflaumen-Pudding)

Take 3 quarts of flour, a little salt, 12 eggs, 2 pounds of raisins, 1 pound of finely chopped suet, and 1 quart of milk. Mix all of this into a batter, put it in a bag dusted with flour, and boil 3 hours. Make a sweet sauce for it.

By the mid-nineteenth century, plum pudding was one of the commonest Christmas foods made and sold in Pennsylvania. It took its place beside the multitudes of other more traditional Pennsylvania-German Christmas specialties, such as mincemeat pie, *Baumkuche* (a rich layer cake), gingerbread, and sandtarts (a form of sugar cookie). Judging from period advertisements, the vast majority of plum puddings were made in confectioners' shops and sold over the counter, or imported in tins from England and sold at grocers and general stores. Those who could not afford the fancy commercial puddings had to make their own. Like the recipe here, the homemade species was often plain in the extreme, with the sugar omitted.

Those who fancied plum pudding (some Pennsylvania Germans did not) liked it because it was convenient to make several puddings at once. Plum pudding would keep almost a year if properly stored. They were perfect for emergencies because they could be reboiled in an hour, while dinner was being thrown together for unexpected guests.

When eaten as a dessert, it was customary to serve American plum pudding with the sweet sauce mentioned in the recipe rather than in flaming brandy as is still the custom in England. Sweet sauce was made by melting currant jelly in wine—red jelly in red wine, white jelly in white wine. Each guest at the dinner table was given a glass dish containing sauce, which would be spooned over the pudding according to taste.

Sweet sauces could also contain flour as a thickener, butter, powdered sugar, and nutmeg. Some people served the sauce with rum, or without any wine at all, in which case it became a hard sauce or glaze.

69. Apple Pudding
(Apfel-Pudding)

Peel and cook 3 pints of apples, mash them, add 4 [well-beaten] eggs, ¼ pound of butter, sugar, and some nutmeg or grated lemon rind. Wrap this in puff pastry and bake.

———————————◆ ◆ ◆———————————

By 1848 standards, this is an old-fashioned species of apple pudding, but its classification is actually somewhat borderline. This very same recipe appears in other cookbooks under the name of apple custard, which is misleading because there are not enough eggs in the recipe to create a true custard. In any case, this pudding belongs more solidly to the eighteenth century than to the nineteenth, and is further evidence of the conservative character of *Die geschickte Hausfrau*.

But old fashioned or not, this pudding was evidently still quite popular toward the end of the nineteenth century, for the recipe here was reprinted verbatim in the 1882 edition of *Der neue amerikanische Landwirthschafts-Calender* (The New American Agricultural Almanac: Reading, Pa.).

70. Transparent Pudding
(Durchsichtiger Pudding)

Beat 8 eggs to a froth. With a little grated nutmeg, ½ pound of butter, and ½ pound of powdered sugar, pour the eggs into a double boiler and stir until the mixture thickens. Then let it cool. Line a [pie] plate with thin pastry dough, add the filling, and bake in a moderately warm oven.

———————————◆ ◆ ◆———————————

The genealogy of this recipe is somewhat hazy and its appearance in *Die geschickte Hausfrau* somewhat roundabout. The German version, as it appeared in *Die geschickte Hausfrau*, was adapted from Anna Dorn's *Neuestes Universal- oder grosses Wiener-Kochbuch* (The Newest Universal, or Great Viennese Cook Book: Vienna, 1827).[102] But the same basic recipe also appeared in Mary Randolph's *Virginia Housewife* (1824) and Eliza Leslie's *Lady's New Receipt-Book* (Philadelphia, 1850). The ultimate source, even in the case of the Dorn version, seems to be Hannah Glasse's *New Art of Cookery*. One thing *is* certain: Transparent pudding was an English invention.

In terms of popularity, transparent pudding was a novelty food that appealed mostly to English and Anglo-American cooks of the upper classes. Anna Dorn's interest in it may have been motivated by its exoticness for Austrian cooks. Since the pudding was generally eaten cold in Pennsylvania (Mrs. Randolph served it hot in Virginia), it was customary to make it during the summer as a substitute for the rich dessert creams that were so popular during the early nineteenth century. Contrary to its name, transparent pudding is not transparent. It is diaphanous.

71. Potato Pudding
(Kartoffel-Pudding)

Whisk ¼ pound of fresh butter and gradually beat 10 egg yolks into it. When the eggs are completely mixed with the butter, stir in boiled, finely grated potatoes, some bread crumbs, powdered sugar, the grated rind of a lemon, and salt; and finally, bind this [together] with egg whites beaten to a froth. Since this pudding falls apart easily, it must be stirred properly so that it does not become runny. Bake 1 hour and serve with a butter sauce.

It has been taken for granted that the potato was important in Pennsylvania-German folk cookery, yet it is evident that the Dutch, like many of the other settlers who came to Pennsylvania before the Revolutionary War, did not look upon the potato as an important table vegetable. The Irish may have been the only exception, but in general, a European attitude prevailed.

Even though potatoes were grown in Flanders, Holland, eastern France, and parts of Switzerland during the late seventeenth century, their role in human diet was minimal, except, perhaps, at the lowest levels of society, for which period documentation is skimpy.[103] In late seventeenth-century Europe, as a rule, potatoes were eaten by humans

as a substitute for grain foods when grain was not available. Eating potatoes was equated with lowering one's standard of living, because in a
real sense they were a substitute for bread. This attitude was even
prevalent among the English in colonial Pennsylvania, who doted on
their manchet breads and treated potatoes with much less respect
than turnips or parsnips, or even sweet potatoes, which had found acceptance long before the so-called Irish potato came into fashion.

White potatoes did not enter the general European diet until
about 1770-71, during a period of extreme famine that forced the peas-
ants to turn to potatoes out of desperation.[104] What followed was what
the Swiss food historian Albert Hauser has called a "Potato Revolution," with potatoes quickly entering traditional diet as a bread or
grain substitute.[105] A similar "revolution" occurred here, but for different reasons and with different results.

Thomas P. Cope, a Quaker born in Lancaster County, noted in his
diary of 1808 that potatoes had become as common as bread in New
Jersey *only in the past few years*, and that there were farmers who
could still recall the days when at most two or three bushels of potatoes were thought to be sufficient for a family's use.[106] Cope's observation could also be applied to the Pennsylvania Germans.

Widespread assimilation of white potatoes among the Pennsylvania Dutch appears to have taken place in the period between 1780
and 1800, when the Hessian fly nearly forced many wheat farmers into
bankruptcy. Traditionally, the Pennsylvania Germans raised wheat for
cash and rye for home consumption. The Hessian fly caused many
farmers to turn to rye cultivation exclusively.[107] They sold their excess
crop not to Philadelphia brokers, but to local distilleries. This was followed by an upsurge in whiskey drinking, but there was no shortage of
bread because the Hessian fly did not damage rye. The potato did not
replace traditional Pennsylvania-German breads, but it did fill a gap left
by the wheat shortage, particularly in poorer households. For in practice, potatoes were brought into the cookery of the Pennsylvania Germans to replace certain wheat-based foods, such as noodles and dumplings. In more affluent households, this was not the case. The potato
simply found its place among the vegetable side dishes, partially replacing parsnips, but never fully replacing turnips until after the Civil
War. In short, potatoes were assimilated on a *secondary level* of Pennsylvania-German diet. Nowhere is this better illustrated than in the
recipe for potato pudding in *Die geschickte Hausfrau*.

One of the most significant features of this recipe is its flavor. The
ingredients have been assembled in a manner that creates the taste im-
pression of parsnips, which suggests something about the age of the
recipe. It probably dates from mid-eighteenth century, when potatoes
began to replace certain vegetable dishes on the Pennsylvania-German
table. In this case, parsnip pudding is now prepared with potatoes. Because of the taste coloration, the break with parsnip cookery has not

been complete. It is still transitional—the potato has not been allowed to stand on its own. This has fascinating implications when we consider that this old-fashioned recipe stayed in print with *Die geschickte Hausfrau* until 1883.

By the 1850s, however, potatoes served three times a day became very common in German Pennsylvania, so much so that one potato-weary workhand is said to have muttered this tableside prayer:

> *Marjets Grumbiere in aller Frieb,*
> *Middaags Grumbiere in geeli Brieb,*
> *Owets Grumbiere un alle Zeit,*
> *Grumbiere bis in Ewichkeit!*

> Potatoes served at breakfast,
> At dinner served again;
> Potatoes served at supper,
> Forever and Amen!

72. Calf's-Foot Jelly
(*Kalbfuss Gallerte*)

Wash 4 large calf's feet and boil them with 8 quarts [of water] until reduced to half, then strain and cool. Next, skim off the fat, pour the clear, jelled stock, without the sediment, into a kettle [over the fire], and when it has dissolved again, add 6 egg whites beaten to a froth, the juice of 6 lemons, 1 pint of white wine, and powdered white sugar to taste. Put the rinds of the lemons in a bag, and when everything is thoroughly cooked, strain the jelly through this bag, then cool it in a bowl.

In the culinary department, calf's-foot jelly was as basic to Pennsylvania-Dutch cookery of the nineteenth century as granulated gelatin is to cookery today. The basic jelly—without the egg whites, wine, lemon, and sugar—was an important ingredient in meat glaze (stock and jelly reduced to a thick consistency) and could be used to strengthen the jelling of other aspics. It was also added to thicken puddings, meat pies, and soups. When served hot, flavored with lemon juice and wine, it was itself a perfect starter soup for large dinners. When sweetened with sugar and served cold, as in the recipe here, it could be treated as a light pudding or even as a dessert. By itself, it was always considered light eating and an appropriate food for children.

Cakes and Pies

In his *Youthful Wanderer* (Orefield, Pa., 1876), George Heffner

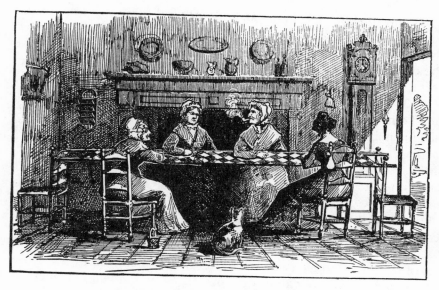

Quilting during the three o'clock break

lamented that the Dutch were at times much too eager to discard their distinctive cookery, particularly in the baking department:

> A score of new kinds of pies and cakes have become fashionable in our day, and it is the daughters that have the greatest opportunity to learn this baking of pastries quickest. The consequence is that the mother soon turns out to be only a *second rate cook!*[108]

Heffner made his observation at a time when Pennsylvania-German cookery was undergoing a radical change, and nowhere did it change more fundamentally than in baking. On this point, Heffner was not only nostalgic, he was right.

The reasons for this shift in taste are already apparent in the recipes in this cookbook. Aside from the pies, most can be classified as "tea cakes," what the Pennsylvania Germans sometimes called *Mietkuche* ("mead" cakes), since they were more often eaten with wine or mead than with tea. The cake-and-mead shop, discussed more fully in chapter 9, and the ubiquitous *Dreiuhrschtick* (three-o'clock break) greatly popularized this species of baked goods.

In general, however, cakes were expensive to make, so they appeared only on special occasions, such as weddings, funerals, and militia musters, or on important religious holidays. The truly elaborate cakes that sometimes appear in early accounts—such as the thinly layered hazelnut cakes of Reading—were rarely made at home. They were the work of professional bakers.

A more typical sort of dessert would be pie or fruit compote, the latter almost universally popular. Both pies and compotes were usually served as side dishes with the roast in a standard two-course meal, there being no formal dessert course. When formality demanded, as in the case of funeral banquets, the table was cleared and an array of dessert foods brought on, topped off invariably with wine and cheese.

By the mid-nineteenth century, it was not unusual for some funeral dinners to exceed a thousand guests, particularly if the deceased had been a well-to-do farmer or a figure in the community. The public at large was invited—including total strangers—so the family would literally cook for days in advance. There was extraordinary status attached to the number of people who attended the funeral dinner, and many families vied with one another in the expense and elaborateness of the meal, to the extent that a good part of an inheritance might be consumed at the funeral feast.

Aside from the huge display of food at funeral banquets, the buffet of the so-called *Deitscher Ball*, or "Dutch" Ball, was probably one of the most elaborate culinary events staged by the Pennsylvania Germans. Once commonplace in large Pennsylvania-German towns, and even in a great many small ones, the Dutch Ball was the equivalent of a fancy dance cotillion. The dancing and the chance for romance were always great drawing points, but so was the food, for the ball provided an opportunity to eat many things not otherwise found at home. If we are to believe period advertisements, the menus usually featured imported German wines and the most expensive dessert foods available. These were supplied by a local German *Conditor* (confectioner) or even a *Pastetenbäcker*, a specialist in pies. Although now mostly nonexistent, the Dutch Ball was once a major social institution; and in Philadelphia, at least, it served as a model for the fluffy debutante parties of the late nineteenth century.

To a certain degree, the art of baking in rural Pennsylvania was limited by the technical difficulties inherent in the traditional Pennsylvania-German oven. Unlike Anglo-Americans, who baked either in a wall oven in the fireplace or, more commonly, directly on the hearth, the Pennsylvania Germans baked almost exclusively out-of-doors.[109] For this reason, there was considerable similarity between the baking traditions of the Pennsylvania Dutch, the French of Louisiana and Quebec, and the Spanish of the southwest. While it was possible to bake cakes in outdoor ovens, these cakes were not much like cakes of today either in texture or consistency. For the most part, they were made with sweetened bread doughs or heavy, almost puddinglike, mixtures that resemble modern fruit cakes. Although the flour was not so highly refined as it is today, the most important difference was oven temperature, which could not be controlled with any exactness. Thus, the brick oven was more suitable for heavy, peasant breads, puddings, hard gingerbreads, and pies. But within this limited range, it could produce baked goods of extremely high quality, which can only be reproduced

Benefits-Ball
für
Mufikmeifter Reuss,

Es wird einem werthen deutschen Publikum bekant gemacht, daß die Washington Jäger Bande zu Gunsten ihres Capellmeifters Hrn. Reuß, einen Ball veranftaltet haben ; nemlich auf Montag Abend den 23ft. Januar, am Haufe des Hrn. Hill. Der Ball wird eröffnet Punkt fieben Uhr mit der ganzen Mtlitärmufik, fo wie dann in Zwifchenzeiten die Bande ganz neue Stücke vortragen wird welche zur Zufriedenheit der Anwefenden ausfallen werden. Ueberhaupt es wird von Seiten der Mufiker alles gethan werden um den Ball fo fplendit als möglich zu machen. Es wird daher von Seiten des deutfchen Publikums ein zahlreicher Befuch erwartet.

Eintritt 50 Cents.

Wafchingtou Jäger Bande.
Pottsville, Jan. 14.

in modern ovens by using thick slabs of stone or earthenware on which to bake.

Since outdoor bake ovens were large, Pennsylvania-German women could bake enough bread or pies for an entire week. It was common during harvest, for example, to bake forty or fifty pies at a time. In his "Amish Mennonites of Union County," John Umble quotes an 1875 Amish diary that mentions baking thirteen loaves of bread and forty-four pies in preparation for a dinner.[110] Such large bakings were not possible in cast-iron stoves. One of the many complaints Pennsylvania-German women had against cast-iron stoves was that they were too small, so housewives were forced to bake two and three times a week, which made more work, of course.

Since bake ovens were usually fired only once a week, a progression of bakings took place to make use of the heat produced during each firing. When the oven was at its hottest, it was used for baking breads. Then came the cakes, pies, and cookies. Once the temperature dropped to what we would consider a moderate heat, the oven was ready to receive puddings and custards. Lastly, there was usually sufficient heat left to dry fruit, corn, or herbs slowly on wooden trays.

In her *"Pennsylvania Dutch," and Other Essays* (1882), Phebe Earle Gibbons remarked that "the Dutch housewife is very fond of baking in the brick oven, but the scarcity of wood must gradually accustom us to the great cooking-stove."[111] Friend Gibbons put her finger on the problem more squarely than anyone else, for by the mid-nineteenth century, southeastern Pennsylvania had become denuded of its wood-lots to such an extent that coal replaced wood as the cheapest source of fuel. Since coal did not work in the traditional outdoor bake oven, the Pennsylvania Germans were forced by necessity to adopt the new stove technology.

With the passing of the outdoor bake oven came the hordes of new cakes and pastries that George Heffner complained of. Yet the change was gradual, for even in *Die geschickte Hausfrau*, many of the recipes represent a transitional phase between the heavy bake-oven cookery of the Siegfrieds' *41 bewährte Recepte* of 1834, with its gin-gerbreads, butter cakes, pound cakes, and honey cakes, and the lighter Victorian pastries that became so popular after the Civil War.

Even by 1848, many nontraditional recipes had been added to the basic Pennsylvania-German menu, and yet, there was still a re-markable difference between the baking recipes favored by the Penn-sylvania Germans and those commonly found in period cookbooks. To begin with, there was a difference in concept.

In German, there are many traditional terms for "cake." Some are much older than others, but *Torte*, from Latin *torta*, is now generally applied to fine layer cakes or to cakes baked in molds. It is a word that passed from the cloister bakery into middle-class German cookery, and one that replaced many older folk terms. With few exceptions, *Torte* appeared in Pennsylvania-German literature only in material reprinted or copied from Old World cookbooks. By adhering to a more ancient folk terminology, the Pennsylvania Germans used the word *Kuche* al-most exclusively in connection with anything baked that was not a form of bread. A *Raamkuche*, then, was a cream pie; a *Pundkuche* was a pound cake; and *Lebkuche* was gingerbread—even a gingerbread cookie, since there was often no linguistic distinction between large cakes and small.

Without diverging too far afield into Pennsylvania-German food terms and baking concepts, let us note only that the earliest Pennsyl-vania-German "pies" were considered a form of *Kuche. Gwetsche-kuche* (plum pie), for example, was viewed as a type of flat cake. Since pies as we know them today developed out of ancient flat cakes, this folk concept was technically correct. Consistent with this, the earliest Pennsylvania-German "pies" were usually square or round pieces of raised dough covered with a layer of fruit, spiced milk, preserves, sour cream, rice pudding, molasses, or even sweetened vegetables, such as beets. They were relatives of the Alsatian quiche and the Italian pizza. The first recipe in this section—for raised dough—has been added to show how these early crusts were made.

In Germany, the "pie" developed into a vast array of shapes and sizes, which gave rise to an equally vast terminology to describe them. Their history is now a complex science on which such German scholars as Oskar Rhiner and Annemarie Wurmbach have expended considerable time and energy. Their valuable studies are included in the list of references at the end of this book.

Being a mixed community with culinary elements drawn from several regional cultures of German-speaking Europe, the Pennsylvania Dutch once prepared a wide variety of Old World "pies," with Hessian, Palatine, Silesian, Swiss, Swabian, and Westphalian forms existing side by side. Gradually, the lines of delineation between various regional dishes blurred as the Pennsylvania Germans adapted their cookery to the New World, and especially after they began to assimilate Anglo-American cakes and pies.

Gustav Sigismund Peters must have recognized that by 1847 there was a growing confusion in Pennsylvania Dutch over what to call a pie and a pielike thing. For himself, he resolved the confusion by using the word *Pei*, which was nothing more than phonetic German. It looked somewhat odd (and still does), but as a catchall term, it worked. In fact, whenever Peters and his subsequent editors were in doubt, they simply Germanized English words, sometimes with peculiar and inadvertent results. Cornmeal muffins, for example, became *Kornmehl Muffins*, which was quite misleading, since *Korn* in Pennsylvania Dutch meant rye rather than corn or maize. But to clarify further what they meant, Peters's editors also supplied the English equivalent of each dish parenthetically after the German on the assumption that most Pennsylvania Germans could also read English. Every edition of *Die geschickte Hausfrau* was peppered with these curious reader's aids.

Granted these little linguistic irritations, granted the vague directions or recipes incorrectly translated from other sources, and granted the misprints and added inconveniences of few accurate means for measuring out ingredients or for controlling oven temperature (oven thermometers did not appear on the commercial market until the 1880s), how remarkable it seems today that Pennsylvania-German cooks were able to manage—and manage brilliantly—in spite of the deficiencies.

Even if they never turned out court pastries or brandied bonbons, Pennsylvania-Dutch housewives certainly had a faculty for making the most of their ingredients, a faculty that George Heffner sadly underestimated when he called them "second-rate."

Memories of the old kitchen hearth

Of the baking recipes in the original *Geschickte Hausfrau*, 74, 75, 76, 77, and 92 were translated into German from *The Kitchen Companion*, which in turn lifted recipes 74–77 from Thomas Cooper's appendix to Willich's *Domestic Encyclopedia* (1821). Most of Cooper's recipes were adapted from Maria Eliza Rundell's *New System of Domestic Cookery*.

A large number of crusts were used by the Pennsylvania Germans during the eighteenth and nineteenth centuries, much more of a variety than today. The most typical were doughs made with minced butter (which required chopping with knives), butter doughs made with cold water, puff pastries, and raised crusts (recipe 73). In order to save butter, which could be sold, many farm women adopted the "soft" crust (*Mürbteig*) made with lard, particularly when large bakings were called for. Even so, lard pastry never fully replaced the traditional Pennsylvania-German doughs until the turn of this century, when the assimilation of the English pie became complete.

Hannah Widdifield (1768–1854), a Quaker confectioner in Philadelphia, used a basic raised-dough recipe that, for all purposes, was the same as that used by the Pennsylvania Dutch in the eighteenth and nineteenth centuries. She liked this particular crust because it was "very nice for those who cannot eat rich paste," a good enough reason for reviving it in this calorie-conscious age. Her daughters later included the recipe in *Widdifield's New Cook Book* (Philadelphia, 1855). I reproduce it here because it would be helpful to know how this traditional crust was made.[112] It can be used in all of the pie recipes in *Die geschickte Hausfrau*.

73. Raised Crust for Pies

1 pound of flour
3 ounces of butter
1 tablespoon liquid yeast
Enough milk to form a dough

Rub the butter into the flour. Add the milk and yeast, and set it aside to rise. When light, roll it thin, and line your plates.

———————————— ❖ ❖ ————————————

There is a recipe for making liquid yeast at the end of this chapter.

74. Mince Pie
(Mince-Pei)

To [each] 2 pounds of chopped beef, free of skin and tendons, add 4 pounds of finely chopped suet, 6 pounds of well-cleaned and well-dried currants, 3 pounds of finely chopped apples, the [grated] rinds and juice of 2 lemons, 1 pint of sweet wine or cider, 1 [grated] nutmeg, ¼ ounce of powdered mace, and ¼ ounce of powdered allspice. Mix all of this together thoroughly, pack it into a deep crock, cover it tightly, and set it in a cool, dry place. Half of the above mixture is sufficient for a medium-size family.

———————————— ❖ ❖ ————————————

Technically, mincemeat pie belongs with chicken potpie and similar "savory" pies, rather than with dessert sweets. It is a remnant of a medieval tradition of spiced meat dishes that has survived because of its association with Christmas. This is why the Pennsylvania Dutch call it *Grischdaagboi*, literally "Christmas" pie, even though it was eaten throughout the winter.

Mincemeat pie, as we know it today, did appear in eighteenth-century German cookbooks, but generally under awkward names that immediately expose the recipes as borrowings from abroad, namely, from England. To the average German, it was foreign exotica. So it was not until they settled in Pennsylvania that the Pennsylvania Dutch came to know mincemeat pie. But they came to know it quickly, for there is good reason to suspect that it was one of the first Anglo-American pies assimilated into their diet.

The reason was quite simple. As the Quaker Elizabeth Ellicott Lea explained in her *Domestic Cookery* (Baltimore, 1853): "Where persons have a large family, and workmen on a farm, these pies are very useful."[113] By useful, she meant that the pies could be baked in large numbers, and, most importantly, during cold weather, they could be kept for as long as two months, provided the crusts did not sour. The mincemeat itself could be made ahead and kept even longer. Furthermore, cooks could stir in at the last minute meat leftovers, apple schnitz, dried cherries, grapes preserved in molasses, dried elderberries (when raisins were short), and other odds and ends from the pantry. Adaptation was the secret of mince pie's popularity—there was even a meatless variation made with green tomatoes. In fact, there was so much substitution and variation that one wonders how many Pennsylvania-German cooks would have followed this recipe verbatim.

75. Apple Pie
(Aepfel-Pei)

After the apples are washed clean, pare them and take out the cores. Boil the peels with a little water until the broth strengthens, then pour it through a cloth. Add some sugar and ground cinnamon, and bring it to a boil again. Meanwhile, line a pie plate with pastry dough, add the apples, and sprinkle each layer of apples with sugar and chopped lemon peel. Pour the above stock (or cider) over it. Cover the whole pie with pastry dough and bake. If the pie is to be eaten hot, serve it with butter after it is sliced.

Made as directed, this is a classic English apple pie. Without the upper crust, it becomes an apple tart, and if baked in a shallow pie dish, it would resemble a South German *Apfelkuchen*, or *Ebbelkuche* as it is called in Pennsylvania Dutch.

Ebbelkuche

Apparently, the Pennsylvania Germans knew about apple pies of the English sort long before they settled in America. Covered pies or *Pasteten* were popular in Germany during the Baroque period, and apple pies in particular show up in many of the cookbooks of that era. For example, it was called *gedeckter Apfelkuchen* in Conrag Hagger's *Neues saltzburgisches Koch-Buch* (New Salzburg Cook Book: Augsburg, 1719).[114] A hundred years later, it appeared as an utterly proper *Aepfel-Pastete* in Bratenwender's *Der kölnische Leckerfress* (The Cologne "Goody-Gobbler": Cologne, 1819).[115] However, most German versions of an apple pie also included sliced almonds and white wine.

76. Apple Puffs
(Aepfel-Puffs)

Pare the apples and either stew them in a stone crock on a hot hearth, or bake them. When thoroughly cooled, mix sugar and grated lemon peel with the apple pulp, and add a little of the liquid [left from cooking]. Put the apple mixture in thin pastries and bake them quickly. A quarter of an hour is sufficient [time] for baking.

This was a popular folk dish among the Pennsylvania Germans. Since the apple puffs in this recipe are in the same family as the baked apple dumplings mentioned in chapter 6, they were likewise served with cream and sugar and might constitute the equivalent of dessert after dinner.

The original recipe, as it appeared in *The Domestic Encyclopedia*, suggested that orange or quince marmalade could be added to the apples to improve their flavor. Also suggested as flavorings were cinnamon and orange flower water—an eighteenth-century touch.

77. Sweet Patties
(*Süsse Pasteten*)

Mince the meat of a boiled calf's foot (the stock may be saved for jelly), 2 apples, 1 ounce of candied orange and lemon peel, and a little rind and juice of a fresh lemon. With this, mix ½ a grated nutmeg, the yolk of 1 egg, 1 spoonful of brandy, and 4 ounces of currants, washed and dried. Bake in small patty pans.

The original German calls these sweet *Pasteten*, but nowhere does the recipe instruct us to cover the patty pans with dough. Nevertheless, this seems to be a recipe for mincemeat tartlets, and, as such, would be called *Grischdaagkichli* in Pennsylvania Dutch.

A *Kichli* is any sort of small pie or tart. A *Himbeerekichli* in Pennsylvania Dutch is the same thing as a French *tartelette aux framboises*. Tartlets of all kinds were generally eaten during the coffee breaks at ten in the morning or at three in the afternoon. They were also carried to church and fed to squirming children, sent home with guests who had far to go, or eaten with supper in the evening. Some *Kichli* were even baked in the shape of hearts, others as half-moons.

78. Dried-Apple Pie
(*Apfelschnitz Pei*)

Wash the apple schnitz in cold water,* put them in a pot and pour water over them so that the water stands 3 inches above the apples. Let

---

*Four cups of schnitz are intended here. Season with nutmeg.

this stand overnight, then set it over a moderate fire and let it simmer. Boil a lemon in water until you can stick a broom straw through the rind. Chop it fine and add it to the apples along with its liquid. Add ½ pound of brown sugar to each quart of apples, let them cook until soft, and then cool in bowls.

Butter a pie dish, line it with pie dough, and pour in the cooked apples until ½-inch deep. Roll out a thin crust in which 4 narrow vents are made, and lay this over the apples. Then bake the pie ¾ hour.

For the uninitiated, apple "schnitz" are slices of dried apple. They are so common in Pennsylvania that they are still sold commercially under their Pennsylvania Dutch name. Incidentally, the singular of *Schnitz* is *Schnutz*, a word with many comic meanings in Pennsylvania Dutch.

Schnitz are delicious in pie. In concept, the marriage of apple schnitz and dough is an ancient one. If we consider that apple schnitz have been found among the remains of Stone Age lake dwellings in Switzerland, we may begin to comprehend the role schnitz have played in the diet of Europeans down through the centuries. This culinary tradition seems quite unbroken from ancient times to the present, and nowhere has it developed more profusely than among the South Germans and their Pennsylvania descendants.

Apple schnitz pie decorated with crystallized apple schnitz and apricots

Apple schnitz form the basis of a multitude of Pennsylvania-German folk dishes, among them apple schnitz cake and *Schnitz un Gnepp*. It was through dishes like these that the Pennsylvania Dutch were able to increase the popularity of dried apples in this country, even though, as an article of food, schnitz were also known in traditional English cookery.

Amelia Simmons included what would have been a traditionally English recipe for "dried apple pie" in her *American Cookery* (Hartford, 1796), except that she gave it a New England touch by adding a handful of cranberries—not at all a bad suggestion.[116] Instead of cranberries, the Pennsylvania Dutch might include a handful of dried cherries (previously soaked), with equally blissful results.

79. Dried Cherry Pie
(Getrockneter Kirschen-Pei)

Wash 1 quart of [dried] cherries in cold water. Put them in a kettle with water and let them simmer over a moderate fire for ½ hour. Then add 1 pound of brown sugar and simmer it again for ½ hour. After your pie dishes are lined with dough, add a ½-inch layer of cherries and liquid. Lay a top crust over this and let it bake until the dough loosens from the dish, which should occur in about ¾ of an hour.

Sweet cherries, sour cherries, black cherries, red cherries, and most especially wild cherries—the Pennsylvania Dutch love them all. Not to be caught short of cherries over the winter, they dried them just like apple schnitz, hence the Pennsylvania-Dutch name *Kaerscheschnitz*.

Cherry trees were everywhere plentiful in Pennsylvania, and the wild varieties were encouraged to grow along country lanes. While traveling through the Pennsylvania-German settlements just below Pennsylvania's border with Maryland, Count Niemcewicz made this observation in 1798:

Not only are the houses surrounded by cherry trees but the roads are lined with cherry trees, some as big as the tallest oak trees. They are wild black cherries rather than ordinary cherries; I have not seen those we call morello anywhere. Whatever kind they may be, they provide both the traveller and the local inhabitants with a good taste and with pleasant refreshment. For those riding by, it is enough to reach out in order to get a handful. Many birds, and almost as many boys and girls perch on the branches right up to the very top without picking the tree clean of this abundant and prolific fruit.[117]

Until the 1820s, when commercial varieties of cherries became more readily available to the Pennsylvania Germans, the most commonly eaten fruits were the wild cherries mentioned by Count Niem-

cewicz. Even though they were small, these cherries were well flavored, and with a little ingenuity, they could be transformed into a
delicious meal. One old and very popular Pennsylvania-German recipe
for cherry pie, made with dried wild cherries stewed in maple syrup,
was a direct adaptation of a local American Indian dish.

Cherry pitter

80. Sour Cherry Pie
(Pei von sauren Kirschen)

Wash the cherries in cold water, line your [pie] dish with pastry dough,
and add the cherries. Pour enough cold water over them to partially
cover them, and sprinkle with flour. Add a large cupful of pure brown
sugar * to each quart of cherries. Grate a little nutmeg over the pie, and
cover it with a light crust. Bake the pie in a moderate oven until the
crust loosens from the dish.

Several recipes in *Die geschickte Hausfrau* note that when the
pie crust loosens from the dish, it has finished baking. Although this is
an easy way to tell when the pie is done, it works best when one is
baking in an old-fashioned Pennsylvania-German pie plate of earthenware. These plates were glazed inside and were somewhat deeper
than modern tin plates, running anywhere from 1¾ inches to 2½
inches deep. Many Pennsylvania-German cooks preferred to use these
older and more traditional pie plates long after the Civil War, and with
the revival of interest in Pennsylvania-Dutch folk culture, several local
potters have begun making them again.

81. Peach Pie
(Pfirsischen-Pei)

Peaches should be ripe but not soft. Pare them, cut them in thin slices,
and prepare in the same manner as for apple pie.

The Pennsylvania Germans call peaches *Pasching* and a peach
pie *Paschingkuche*. There are even peach schnitz (*Paschingschnitz*),
which are delicious, when you can find them. In the 1850s, they were
common. Grim and Reninger, Pennsylvania-Dutch grocers in Allentown, for instance, advertised peach schnitz regularly in *Der Lecha
Patriot*.

---

*Something akin to Demerara sugar may be intended here. Light brown sugar
will work satisfactorily.

In *Peach Industry in Pennsylvania* (1897), George Butz noted that by the 1890s there were three major peach belts in the state, every one of them in the Pennsylvania-German region.[118] But long before the 1890s, and long before the first Germans settled in Pennsylvania, peaches were growing both wild and in cultivated orchards in most parts of the colony. The Indians, being fond of peaches, obtained plants from the early Dutch and Swedish settlers along the Delaware. Peaches had become so plentiful by the early eighteenth century that they were often fed to the pigs or converted into peach brandy. Peach brandy figured prominently in Pennsylvania-German cookery and was often used to flavor the whipped cream that invariably came to the table with peach pie.

82. Cranberry Pie
(Cränbeeren-Pei)

Take 1 quart of cranberries, pour 1 pint of water over them, and set them on a moderate fire. Add 1 pound of pure brown sugar,* and let this simmer until the cranberries are completely soft, then press them with a spoon and let them cool in a bowl. Put them into pies or tarts and bake.

Cranberries are called *Grembeere* or *Krambeere* in Pennsylvania Dutch. Cranberry pie was eaten in Pennsylvania mostly during December, usually around Christmas or New Year's Day. Historically, cranberries were not plentiful in the wild and were not available on a commercial basis in the commonwealth until after the Civil War. For the most part, it was the *Vaccinium Oxycocus*, or "small" cranberry, that could be found in Pennsylvania's bogs, but never in great quantities. New Jersey, on the other hand, provided a plentiful source of berries. The so-called "hog" cranberry—not a proper cranberry but growing wild in great numbers on the Jersey Pine Barrens nonetheless—was easy to pick and ship in barrels to urban markets.

Insofar as the Pennsylvania Germans were concerned, cranberry pie was a culinary waif that had lost its way from New England. It would have been out of place in *Die geschickte Hausfrau* were it not for the fact that there was a short-lived cranberry craze in Pennsylva-

*Use dark brown sugar. This recipe is excellent, but grated orange rind will make it even better.

nia during the late 1840s and early 1850s. Lutz and Scheffer were in the thick of it.

They not only published enthusiastic editorials on cranberry culture in *Der amerikanische Bauer*, but also included large and glowing advertisements for the cranberry nursery of T. Trobridge of New Haven, Connecticut. Trobridge claimed that cranberries could be grown anywhere, but he had a special angle aimed at the Pennsylvania Germans. Since Dutch farmers irrigated their meadows, they created patches of ground too boggy for practical use. According to Trobridge, these man-made bogs were ideal for cranberry culture. There was gold in that muck if farmers would only plant their cranberries at 50¢ per 100. Since Trobridge estimated that it would take 10,000 of his plants to cover an acre of bog, anyone with a rudimentary knowledge of mathematics could figure out who was really dredging up the gold.

In his book on cranberry culture (1870), Joseph White took nurserymen like Trobridge to task for what he felt was intentionally deceptive advertising. White had the benefit of hindsight, which was not available to the unwary farmers of the 1840s. Lutz and Scheffer were doubtless overly optimistic when they allowed cranberry pie to find a place in *Die geschickte Hausfrau*. Certainly, the surging harvests of cranberries never materialized, for if the Pennsylvania Germans fell victim to the cranberry craze, their fever did not run high or for very long. Because the outlay was expensive and cranberries had only a limited season, enthusiasm soon dried up. After all, there were scores of other berries growing wild in the state, and all were free for the picking. For the Pennsylvania Dutch, this New England dish remained a culinary oddity.

83. Rhubarb Pie
(Rhubarb-Pei)

Cut off the stems at the base of the leaves. Pull off the outer skin and cut the stems into pieces ½-inch long. Line a dish with rolled dough and add a layer of rhubarb 1-inch deep. To each quart of chopped rhubarb, add 1 large teacup full of sugar. Sprinkle this sugar over the rhubarb with a little salt and ½ a grated nutmeg. Cover this with a nice crust, which must have a slit in the middle, then bake until the pie loosens from the dish.

Rhubarb pies made in this manner are by far tastier than those that are filled with cooked rhubarb.

Before the 1830s, rhubarb pie was not as commonly eaten in this country as many now assume, for until the early 1800s, rhubarb was grown mostly for the medical virtues of its root. Even though the rhubarb used in medicine and the rhubarb used in cooking were different, many cooks were not at all convinced that the plant was safe to eat in the amount commonly found in pie. Doctors, however, particularly those of the homeopathic school, championed stewed rhubarb as a home remedy. With that seal of approval, rhubarb eventually caught on.

Thus, rhubarb pie became spring's blessing. Like sorrel pie, dandelion salad, and other early spring favorites of the Pennsylvania Germans, rhubarb pie became one of those dishes whose appearance was enthusiastically welcomed because it corrected a diet deficiency caused by a lack of fresh green vegetables during the winter.

Some Americans referred to rhubarb as "Persian Apple," a name alluding to its supposedly exotic place of origin (actually Central Asia) and to its treatment when cooked in pie. But the Pennsylvania Dutch coined their own name: *Boigraut*, or "pie plant." Today, many people still use this term, even in English.

Older rhubarbs had somewhat tougher skins than modern varieties, which seems to have necessitated the almost universal custom of peeling the outer red skin; hence the reason for the directions in the recipe above. It was also true that there were cooks who thought the skins, like the leaves, were poisonous. Others, particularly in the early nineteenth century, treated rhubarb pie as a kind of mock apple pie, and the red color in the skins simply detracted from this illusion.

84. Huckleberry Pie
(Heidelbeeren-Pei)

Put 1 quart of huckleberries in a washbasin, take out all those that float [and throw them away]. Then take out the [remaining] berries, removing the stems and culling the unripe ones. Line a buttered baking dish with dough and make a layer of berries ½-inch deep. Add 1 teacup full of brown sugar to each quart of berries, and pour ½ teacup of water over this. Sprinkle the berries with 1 teaspoon of flour, 1 salt spoon of salt, and ½ a grated nutmeg. Cover this filling with pie crust, make some incisions in the top, pinch both crusts together around the edge, and bake in the oven for ¾ hour.

Huckleberries, or whortleberries, belong to that large tribe of wild berries most people now commonly lump together as blueberries. Actually, blueberries are only one type of huckleberry. The Pennsylvania Dutch called all of them *Hockelbeere*. The "Pennsylvania Huckleberry" (*Vaccinium pennsylvanicum*), found on the ridges of the Blue Mountains, was considered the choicest of all the wild varieties because of its sweetness.

The presence of so much natural sugar allowed the Pennsylvania Dutch to convert them into an unusual delicacy called huckleberry raisins. A few trays of fresh berries were laid up in the *Rauchkammer* to dry and take on a smoky flavor. A handful of these berries thus prepared might be added to sausage, dumplings, or stuffings—the three major uses—or boiled and added to cornmeal mush for breakfast.

85. Cream Pie
(Rahm-Kuchen)

Simmer a quart of sweet cream, beat 4 or 5 eggs lightly, and stir them into the cream. Add 1 salt spoon of salt, 1 teaspoon of lemon essence, ½ a grated nutmeg, and 2 teaspoons of sugar. Take shallow pie dishes with slanting sides, rub them with melted butter, line them with very thin dough, and set them in the oven for 10 minutes. Then pour the above cream mixture into the dishes and let them bake for ½ hour.

This Pennsylvania-German recipe is much plainer than most I have seen but makes an excellent *custard*. Plainer yet, however, is the cream pie of Elizabeth Denlinger Leaman (1824–1902), a Mennonite from Lancaster County, whose recipe was written down in 1867 in her daughter's manuscript cookbook. Since daughter Barbara was selling these pies at the Lancaster farmers' market, perhaps it would be instructive to see how her cream pies were assembled: "4 eggs, 1 cup sugar, 1 cup sour cream, 1 cup sweet milk."[119] Coming as it did from oral tradition, this recipe may date from the early eighteenth century.

Honey can be substituted very easily for the sugar—one of the characteristics of eighteenth-century Pennsylvania-German recipes.

86. Custard Pie
(Custard-Pei)

Beat 4 eggs with 4 spoonfuls of flour until they are light. Then gradually stir in 1 quart of milk, as well as 1 salt spoon of salt, ½ of a grated nutmeg, and 2 spoonfuls of sugar. Lightly butter a square tin pan, pour the above mixture in, and let it bake for ½ an hour. This is an excellent custard.

Custard kettle

This recipe is structurally different from the last one in that milk has been fortified with flour—at the expense of using cream. The old Pennsylvania-German term for custard was *Oierraam* ("egg-cream"), so by this etymological definition, there *must* be cream and eggs or it is not custard.

87. Rice Pie
(Reis-Pei)

Wash 1 full wineglass of rice and boil it in 1 quart of milk until soft. Take it from the fire and gradually stir in 3 lightly beaten eggs. Then add 1 small teacup of sugar, 1 small grated nutmeg, ½ teaspoon of salt, and 1 small teaspoon of lemon essence. Line shallow pie dishes with dough, fill them nearly full with the above mixture, and bake ½ hour.

This is rice pudding baked in a pie shell, which is why it is also called "pudding" pie. Rice pudding pie was well known in Germany. Friederike Löffler published a recipe somewhat similar to this one, but much richer in eggs and much lighter in texture.[120] This recipe, however, is English. It is quite possible that Josiah Marshall, author of a handbook for emigrants, put his finger on its direct source when he wrote in 1845 that "this form of pastry (or its name, at least) is, we believe, peculiar to the county of Kent [England], where it is made in abundance, and eaten by all classes of people during Lent."[121]

88. Pumpkin Pie
(Kürbiss-Pei)

Cut 1 nice pumpkin in half, remove the seeds and the pulp, pare the skin, cut the pumpkin halves into small pieces, and put them in a kettle with 1 small tea saucer of water. Cover the pot and set it over a moderate fire until the pumpkin is soft enough to mash gently. Then, with a spoon, press the pumpkin through a colander or sieve into a bowl. Add enough milk to make a thin paste. Add to each quart of pumpkin 4 well-beaten eggs, 1 teaspoon of sugar, 1 salt spoon of salt, 1 finely grated nutmeg, 1 teaspoon of lemon essence, and some ground ginger.

Line shallow pie plates with dough and fill them with the pumpkin mixture. Lay a little strip of dough around the edge of each dish and bake in an oven for ¾ hour.

Pumpkin pie was certainly not among the favorites of the Pennsylvania Germans during the nineteenth century, mainly, I suppose, because the Dutch did not associate it with any particular holiday, especially not with Thanksgiving or with Christmas. On the other hand, some Pennsylvania Dutch did make pies with pumpkin, but the traditional Pennsylvania-German *Karrebseboi*, or more correctly *Karrebsekuche*, was somewhat different from the recipe here, which is most probably of New England origin. To begin with, the Pennsylvania Germans used an entirely different kind of pumpkin for cookery.

The historical culinary pumpkin of southeastern Pennsylvania was the crookneck pumpkin, variously called the winter crookneck squash, the gooseneck pumpkin, and, in Pennsylvania Dutch, the *Halskarrebs*, or "neck" pumpkin. It was this pumpkin that was traditionally used for cooking because of its fine texture and good keeping qualities. The large, round, orange pumpkins sold today at Halloween, were called "cow pumpkins" or field pumpkins and were used only as fodder for livestock. The local Indians, however, did utilize them as food. They cut them into long curled strips, hung them from poles to dry in the sun, and then stored them for winter use in stews.

This method of preservation gained a certain vogue for foddering cattle in Pennsylvania during the 1840s, but it did nothing to promote cow pumpkins for human consumption. To serve cow pumpkins to people in any form would have been quite an insult to the Pennsylvania Dutch.[122]

Traditional Pennsylvania-German pumpkin pies made with *Halskarrebse* were hardly like modern pumpkin pies anyway. They were actually pumpkin flans or tarts, as Peter Kalm confirmed during his visit to Pennsylvania in the eighteenth century.[123]

Slices of gooseneck pumpkin about the size and shape of orange sections were simmered in cider or water until soft; then they were arranged in a spiral pattern or simply stuck into the tart pastry. A mixture of sour cream and eggs flavored with molasses, whiskey, or rum was then poured over the pumpkin, and the tart was baked like a shallow quiche.

Only in the late nineteenth century did the Anglo-American version of pumpkin pie gain widespread acceptance among the Pennsylvania Germans, and since it is now associated with Thanksgiving, it has replaced the traditional Pennsylvania-German form altogether. Alas!

89. Johnny Cakes
(Johnny-Kuchen)

Place 1 quart of freshly ground cornmeal in a bowl together with 1 large teaspoon of salt. Stir water into this until it is completely moist, and using the hands, form it into cakes ½-inch thick, which you then fry slowly in a greased pan. When one side is done, flip it over to the other. The cakes should be split in the middle, buttered, served hot, and eaten with roast pork.

I suppose the pork would recommend this to Pennsylvania-German taste. In any case, the Pennsylvania Germans were much more likely to make buckwheat cakes than corn cakes and had a species of wheat cake called *Eisnerkuche* (made between two plates) that they preferred above all else. There were also flat cakes made with bread dough called *Blatz*.

If we recall that in 1847 Eliza Leslie published a cookbook on cornmeal cookery, and that nationally, there was extensive publicity about cornmeal foods as a result of the failure of the potato crop in Ireland, we may see the rationale for including two cornmeal recipes in *Die geschickte Hausfrau*.

The lack of a specific word for johnny cake in Pennsylvania High German and Pennsylvania-German dialect should be evidence in itself that this item of food was a latecomer borrowed (if borrowed at all) from English-speaking Americans. During the eighteenth century, Pennsylvanians in general—English and German—considered johnny cakes a peculiarity of Maryland, as illustrated in the following anecdote.

During the Revolutionary War, Philadelphian Alexander Graydon was held captive by the British on Long Island. In his memoirs of the event, he related that his mother came north to see him, and while living nearby to work for his release, she learned from one of the other

American captives how to make johnny cakes "in the true Maryland fashion."[124] This novel exercise consumed the better part of an afternoon, because Mrs. Graydon, a native Pennsylvanian who had run a boardinghouse in Philadelphia before the revolution and who knew very well how to cook, did not know how to make johnny cakes.

Her ignorance was not exceptional. In southeastern Pennsylvania, cornmeal was viewed as a poor man's wheat; it was not widely accepted as a wheat substitute in breads or cakes, and in Pennsylvania-German cookery, it simply did not work in traditional noodle pastes, dumplings, raised crusts, or roux.

In Pennsylvania, johnny cakes were more typical of the cookery found in the western sections of the state, which were settled by southerners and Ulster Scots. In that area, where farming was often at a subsistence level, corn was the predominant food grain rather than wheat. Because of this, outdoor bake ovens, which are not well suited to cornmeal bakery, were an exception rather than the rule, even among the Pennsylvania Germans who settled in that region. Many people were forced to prepare their bread directly on the hearth, the traditional pattern among the poor in Britain.

A similar relationship between white bread and outdoor bake ovens, and corn bread and subsistence farming was observed among the Creoles of Louisiana by Professor Fred Kniffen of Louisiana State University.[125] His work on this subject has reinforced the many similarities between Pennsylvania-German and French-Creole baking traditions.

90. Cornmeal Muffins
(Kornmehl-Muffins)

Pour boiling water over a quart of unroasted cornmeal, stirring it all the while until it becomes a thick paste, which you [then] let cool. Before it has completely cooled, add 1 small tea saucer of [melted] butter, 1 teaspoon of salt, 1 teaspoon of yeast, and 2 well-beaten eggs. Set this in a warm place for 2 hours, then stir it until smooth and even, and fry in small cakes in a hot frying pan. When one side is golden brown, flip them over to the other. Then lay them each on a hot plate and serve.

Generally speaking, cornmeal muffins were probably not so popular among the Pennsylvania Dutch as rusks. Rusks of wheat flour were used as *Dunkes*, that is, for dipping in coffee or for crumbling into coffee to make a thick "cup soup" called *Kaffisupp* or *Kaffibrockle*, a popular breakfast dish. The taste and texture of cornmeal muffins or cornmeal rusks were not well suited for *Dunkes*.

In areas where the land was poor, cornmeal naturally played a much more significant role in Pennsylvania-German cookery than, for instance, in Lancaster or York counties, which at one time formed the heart of Pennsylvania's colonial breadbasket. But this cornmeal was considerably different from that used in the South, because the Pennsylvania Germans almost always roasted their corn before grinding it for meal. This explains the reason for specifying unroasted meal in the recipe above.

Roasted cornmeal has a distinctively nutty flavor, and since it is tan rather than yellow and powdery in texture, it is almost undetectable as an adulterant in rye bread. When scalded, it can be used in white bread. Either way, it allowed frugal Dutch housewives to stretch more loaves from their flour and thus turn a little higher profit at market.

91. Waffles
(Waffeln)

Into thoroughly sifted flour,* stir 3 teacups of fine powdered sugar, 1 cup of butter, 3 well-beaten eggs, and ½ teaspoon of saleratus [potassium bicarbonate] dissolved in a small teacup of milk, until it works into a thin batter. Then add ground mace and salt. The batter must be thin enough so that it can be poured into a waffle iron. Once the iron is hot, grease it with bacon, or butter it, add 1 or 2 spoonfuls of batter, bake the waffles until brown, and sprinkle them with sugar and cinnamon. After they are done, do not set them immediately on top of one another, rather, set them on a plate by the fire where they can become crisp.

Waffel is a cognate of the English word "wafer," and in a sense, both are made in a similar way. As an item of food, waffles were known in Germany even in the Middle Ages, and according to Ernst Thiele's *Waffeleisen und Waffelgebäcke* (Cologne, 1959), they were originally eaten only during times of festivity (Christmas, for example) or fasting, such as Lent. They were not everyday foods. The earliest waffles were nothing more than slices of buttered bread pressed between hot iron molds. The name derives from the pattern (*Waben*), not from the ingredients.

Batter pail

A seventeenth-century manuscript cookbook compiled by Anna

---

*Technically, the procedure in this recipe is backwards. After mixing the other ingredients, one should add only enough sifted flour to make a thin batter.

ter Braeck, now in the East Friesian State Museum at Emden (Federal Republic of Germany), contains a recipe for waffles that appears to be a prototype for the basic "Dutch" recipe that reached the shores of England in the late 1600s. What separates the Pennsylvania-German recipe above from earlier recipes is the use of saleratus (baking soda), which eliminates overnight fermentation of the batter, the addition of yeast, and other traditional leavening techniques.

After waffles became crisp by the fire as directed in the recipe above, they were served like cookies, dusted with powdered sugar and cassia, or as a dessert, with alternating layers of waffles and whipped cream flavored with such things as rum, sugar, and fruit—particularly cherries. Pennsylvania-Dutch waffles could also be used for simple meals, dispensing with the sugar and spices, and served like toast with chicken or meat and a thick gravy, thus elevating them to the level of a main course or substitute roast. Chicken and waffles was a combination that was particularly popular among the Dutch of central Pennsylvania.

In the 1850s, while *Die geschickte Hausfrau* was at the height of its popularity, there was a local craze for sweet potato waffles, a revival, actually, of a novelty food once popular in early eighteenth-century Pennsylvania. For the adventurous lovers of orange-colored waffles, the following is a translation of the recipe as published by Carl Friederich Egelmann in his *Der neue amerikanische Landwirtschafts-Calender* (New American Agricultural Almanac: Reading, Pa., 1853).[126]

Sweet Potato Waffles

Take 2 tablespoonsful of [cooked] pureed sweet potato, 1 tablespoon of butter, 1 tablespoon of sugar, a pint of milk, and 4 tablespoons of flour. Mix these ingredients together thoroughly and bake the batter like any other waffle.

American food historians generally give the Holland Dutch in New York much of the credit for introducing waffles to Americans. But the Pennsylvania Germans brought a penchant for waffles that probably had a great deal more influence if for no other reason than that the Germans came here in such large numbers. Their demand for waffles in eighteenth-century Pennsylvania can be gauged in part by the frequency of newspaper advertisements for waffle irons. Friedrich Wilhelm Starmann, a German merchant in Philadelphia, often advertised German goods in local newspapers. For example, in the August 31, 1791, issue of the *Neue unpartheyische Lancaster Zeitung*, he advertised a shipment of German coffee mills and waffle irons, not to mention Flemish bed linens, flowered and single-color wash cloths, fine white Dutch table linens, and, for the children, little boxes of sugar candy.

92. Jumbles
(*Jumbeln*)

[Sift] 3 pounds of flour [into a bowl]. [Mix] 1½ pounds of butter, 1 pound of sugar, 6 well-beaten eggs, ½ a grated nutmeg, and 1 teaspoon of lemon essence, or 1 teaspoon of powdered cinnamon. Work this together thoroughly, then roll out the dough about ¾-inch thick. Sprinkle sugar over it, cut into round cakes, making a hole in the center of each, then lay them on light [baking] tins and bake 10 minutes in a [quick] oven.

Being cookies, jumbles would fall under the Pennsylvania-Dutch classification of *Kichelcher*, meaning "little cakes." These particular little cakes were sometimes called *Tschumpels* in dialect because that is just how the Pennsylvania Dutch pronounced it. Otherwise, they were called *Krenslin*, meaning "little wreaths." For the Pennsylvania Germans, this last term was the most traditional one because *Krenslin* was what jumbles were also called in the Palatinate and other parts of Germany from which the Pennsylvania Dutch originated.

In English, a jumble is a mixture, but this meaning has no connection with the origin of the name of the cookie, which evidently traces to Latin *gemel*, meaning "twin." The original jumbles, it seems, were knotted into double rings somewhat like pretzels. They were known in various parts of Western Europe under different and somewhat amusing names: *ciambelline* in Italy, *gimblettes* in France, *Bretzeln* in parts of Austria, and so forth. In seventeenth-century England, *Iambales* (a corruption of the French) were generally any sort of sugared paste wreathed into knots. Some recipes even boiled the cookies before baking them—another connection with pretzels. However, it is fairly clear from other nineteenth-century recipes that the basic ingredients in most early American jumbles were much like those in the recipe here. And while jumbles could be any shape desired, a great many Victorian cooks preferred to cut them in rounds with a small hole in the center, like flat doughnuts—a lingering memory of the original ring form. More conservative cooks rolled their dough out into long strips, cut it into eight-inch lengths, and then curled it into rings. This was definitely the older and most traditional method of preparation.

Jumbles were standard fare in early Pennsylvania. They were sold year around by street vendors and could be purchased at any inn or tavern. A plate of jumbles and a bottle of Madeira was considered a flattering welcome for guests whose visit was deemed worthier than a bowl of tea or hot chocolate.

93. Soft Gingerbread
(Weiche Lebkuchen)

Take ½ pint of sour milk or buttermilk, ½ pint of molasses, 1 teacup of butter or salted lard, 1 large teaspoon of saleratus dissolved in a little hot water, 2 well-beaten eggs, ½ a nutmeg, 1 teaspoon of powdered cinnamon and 1 heaping tablespoon of finely ground ginger. Add [some] sifted flour and work all of it together into a batter that can be stirred with a spoon easily. Beat the batter a little while, then pour it into square, buttered baking pans [so that the batter stands] 1-inch deep. Bake ½ hour.

This was called "soft" gingerbread because it was a gingerbread loaf rather than a hard cookie. But it was also called just "sweet cake" by the Pennsylvania Germans and was considered a special treat for children. In its plainest form, it was baked in long or square pans and cut into squares for the table. As a cake, it was served hot with butter, as is evident in the old Pennsylvania saying: "May your virtues ever spread, like butter on hot gingerbread."

Although the original meaning of *Leb* is lost, some etymologists suppose that it derives from *Laib*, a molded bread,[127] plus *Kuchen*, a flat cake. Whatever its origin, perhaps the most accurate way to translate *Lebkuchen* is to call it a "spice" cake, since ginger is certainly not always the major ingredient. In an attempt to be somewhat clearer than this, some old Pennsylvania-German recipes called it *Ingwerbrod*, a literal translation of the English. A recipe for soft *Ingwerbrod* appeared in Jakob Landis's *Lese und Prüfe* (Harrisburg, 1882), one of the last Pennsylvania-Dutch recipe books to be published in German.[128]

In some Pennsylvania-German quarters, there seems to be confusion over the difference between *Lebkuchen* and *Honigkuchen*. Honey cake is a type of *Lebkuchen*, a much older cookie than those Anglo-American hard gingerbreads (using sugar or molasses) sold today as "Pennsylvania Dutch." For purposes of comparison, the following recipes will illustrate the difference.

The first is a translation of an authentic recipe for Pennsylvania-German honey cake as published in Samuel and Solomon Siegfried's *41 bewährte Recepte* (41 Proven Recipes: Millgrove, Pa., 1834).[129]

To Bake Honey Cakes

For which, take 6 pounds of flour, 2 pounds of honey, 1 pound of sugar, 2 ounces of cinnamon, 1 ounce of ginger, and some candied orange peel. [Beat] 6 eggs and 2 teaspoonfuls of pearlash dissolved in milk. Mix all the ingredients together, knead thoroughly, add additional milk if necessary. Bake for 20 minutes.

The next recipe is for Anglo-American hard gingerbread as published in *The Family's Guide*, an upstate New York cookbook printed by Lutz and Scheffer (under Gustav Peters's name) in 1848.[130]

Hard Gingerbread

Take 3 pounds of molasses, 4 beaten eggs, 1 pound of brown sugar, 2 ounces of finely powdered ginger; of cloves, mace, and nutmeg, ¼ of an ounce each; of fine coriander seed and caraway seeds (if you have them) 1 ounce each; and 4 pounds of melted butter. Mix the whole together, and add as much flour as will knead it into a stiff paste. Roll it out. Cut into any form you please, and put into a hot oven.

Incidentally, this makes a huge batch of cookies, easily sixteen to eighteen dozen.

Gingerbread cookie cutters

94. Composition Cake
(Composition-Kuchen)

Take 1 pound of sugar, ½ pound of creamed butter, 4 well-beaten eggs, 1 cup of milk, ½ teaspoon of saleratus dissolved in some warm water, ½ a finely grated nutmeg, and 1 teaspoon of lemon essence. Add enough sifted flour to make a thick batter.

Beat this thoroughly until the batter is light and frothy, then add 1 pound of chopped, seeded raisins and 1 pound of washed and dried currants. Line tin baking pans with buttered paper, pour a 1-inch thick layer of the above mixture into the pans, and let them bake in a moderate oven for ½ hour. This batter makes 2 cakes 8 inches wide and 12 inches long.

———————◆◆———————

This tea cake resembles light fruit cake because of its large quantity of raisins and currants. In point of presentation, the next recipe is a variation of the one above, although in terms of age, almond cake is by far the older of the two.

95. Almond Cake
(Mandel-Kuchen)

Make a batter as given in the foregoing recipe. [Then] shell ¼ pound of almonds, chop them fine and instead of raisins and currants, stir them into the batter. Then proceed as with composition cake.

———————◆◆———————

Both this and the preceding recipe may ultimately trace their origin to Italy, since they are similar to certain old renaissance *Weinkuchen*, or sweet wine cakes, that Italian cooks popularized among the upper classes in Germany. This may explain why both composition cake and almond cake were served with wine in Pennsylvania, particularly at funerals, but also at inns and cake-and-mead shops. Lacking almonds, however, some creative Pennsylvania-Dutch cooks substituted hickory nuts, hazelnuts, or walnuts. With or without almonds, "almond" cake was generally cut and served in small diamond-shaped slices.

96. Yellow Lady Cake
(Gelber Damen-Kuchen)

Take 1 pound of fine white sugar, ½ pound of creamed butter, the yolks of 8 eggs beaten until thick and smooth, 1 cup of sweet milk, 1 small teaspoon of lemon essence, and enough sifted wheat flour to make a thick batter. Beat [all of] this [together] until it is light and creamy. Then crush ¼ pound of almonds and mix them into the batter thoroughly. Pour this 1-inch deep in tin pans lined with white, buttered paper and bake ½ hour in a hot oven, or 40 minutes in a moderate oven. This is a first-rate cake.

This is yet another species of wine cake that became popular in Pennsylvania during the nineteenth century. After the cake came out of the oven, it was usually sliced into thin strips or "fingers." Although lady cake was not a traditional Pennsylvania-German dish, it was popularized by many late nineteenth-century church cookbooks, such as *Help for the Marthas*, a German Reformed cookbook published in Reading in the 1890s.[131]

97. Pound Cake
(Pfund-Kuchen)

For 1 pound cake, take 1½ pounds of [sifted] flour, 1 pound of fine white sugar, 10 eggs, 1 gill of brandy, ½ a grated nutmeg, and 1 teaspoon of vanilla or lemon essence. Then cream the butter with the sugar. Beat the eggs to a froth, mix the ingredients all together and beat until light and creamy. Line a baking tin with buttered paper. Pour a layer of batter 1½-inches deep, and bake 1 hour in a moderate oven. When done, turn the tin over slowly and take out the cake. Set the cake on the bottom side of the tin to cool. Before the cake is sliced, remove the paper.

A classic pound cake should have equal weights of eggs, flour, butter, and sugar. This recipe fails to specify the amount of butter, but it should be about 1½ pounds.

As in other parts of Europe, *Pfundkuchen* was well known in Germany, even in the eighteenth century. Some popular recipes saw a wide circulation that crisscrossed national boundaries. Anna Dorn published a recipe similar to this one in her 1827 Austrian cookbook, but flavored her cake with wine, cloves, cinnamon, nutmeg, and caraway—a spicy touch found in many German renditions. Other versions of the recipe, as published in *Die geschickte Hausfrau*, appeared later in *Cookery as It Should Be* (Philadelphia, 1853), and again in

John Marquart's *600 Miscellaneous Valuable Receipts* (Lebanon, Pa., 1860). Since it is also similar to the recipe for "Pound, or Bride Cake" in *The Kitchen Companion*, this recipe was evidently well known long before its appearance in *Die geschickte Hausfrau* and may very well trace to Mrs. Rundell's *Domestic Cookery*, a book that was heavily plagiarized by American almanac printers.

98. Sponge Cake
(Schwamm-Kuchen)

One pound of powdered sugar, ½ pound of sifted flour, 8 eggs, 1 teaspoon of salt, 1 teaspoon of rose brandy or 1 teaspoon of lemon essence. Beat the egg yolks, the flour, and the sugar together until smooth and light. Beat the egg whites to a froth. Mix all of this together well, and add a little saleratus. Butter a square tin pan, line it with paper, pour a layer of the above batter 1-inch deep, and bake in a moderate oven.

Sponge cake, in its most simplified form, never lost popularity in Germany or in Pennsylvania. In German cookbooks it is now the ubiquitous yet richly flavored *Sandtorte* baked in a springform mold. In Pennsylvania, however, the tendency was to make the cake as plain and as light as possible, serving it only with a light dusting of powdered sugar and, preferably, fresh fruit, such as strawberries or raspberries. It is in this form that sponge cake invariably appears at county fairs, church suppers, picnics, grange banquets, and funeral dinners. The Dutch fondly call it *Schwammkuche*, or even *Schpunchkuche*, as it appeared in George Girardey's *Handbuch über Kochkunst*.

It is interesting to note that the recipe in *Die geschickte Hausfrau* is derived from a sponge cake recipe that belonged to Mary Pennington, wife of Benjamin Smith Barton, the great Philadelphia botanist. Mrs. Barton's recipe appeared in Frances Harriet McDougall's *Housekeeper's Book* in 1837.[132]

99. French Tea Cake
(Französischer Thee-Kuchen)

Beat 10 eggs to a froth. Dissolve ½ teaspoon of saleratus in some warm water and let it cool. Add this to the eggs and beat them again for 10 minutes. Then add 4 ounces of powdered sugar and 4 ounces of flour, and whisk the ingredients together well. Pour the batter in a layer 1-inch deep in a buttered pan lined with paper and bake in a hot oven.

Even though the Pennsylvania Dutch preferred rusks and coffee instead of tea at 3:00 P.M., cooks in more formal homes did make tea cakes, which were cut in strips while warm, buttered, and served hot. Otherwise, *Theekuche* were more often found among the dainties served at the Dutch Ball.

100. Wedding Cake
(Hochzeit-Kuchen)

One pound of flour, 9 eggs, the yolks and whites of which must be beaten separately, 1 pound of creamed butter, 1 pound of brown sugar, 1 tea saucer of molasses, 1 ounce of grated nutmeg, 1 teaspoon of powdered cinnamon, 1 teaspoon of powdered spices, and 1 gill of brandy. Mix these ingredients together well. Wash and dry 3 pounds of currants, halve 3 pounds of large raisins and seed them. Sprinkle ½ pound of flour over the currants and raisins, mix them together well, and stir them into the batter with a pound of finely chopped candied lemon rind. Line tin pans with buttered paper, pour a layer of the above batter 1½ to 2-inches deep, and bake in a moderate oven 1½ to 2 hours.

Bride cake pan

This appears to be a New England recipe, for it is often called "Black Cake" or "New England Wedding Cake" in other period cookbooks, not the sort of wedding cakes made by the Pennsylvania Dutch anyway.

After baking, the cake was allowed to cool in the oven, then was iced when cold. Some recipes required five hours for baking, either in two small pans and then stacked like a layer cake, or in one large pan and served like the modern box cake. This cake could also be baked in an iron cake mold.

101. Rich Bride's Cake
(Vorzüglicher Braut-Kuchen)

Take 4 pounds of sifted flour, 4 pounds of sweet, fresh butter that has been worked to a cream, and 2 pounds of powdered white sugar. To each pound of flour, add 6 eggs, 1 ounce of ground nutmeg, and 1 teaspoon of lemon essence. Wash 4 pounds of currants well, lay them on a double-folded cloth, and let them dry. Seed 4 pounds of large raisins, cut 2 pounds of candied lemon peel into thin strips, and chop 1 pound of shelled almonds. Beat the egg yolks with the sugar into a smooth batter. Mix the flour and butter together, and add it to the batter, along with the spices, ½ pint of brandy, and the egg whites beaten to a froth. Stir this together well and sprinkle ½ pound of flour over the raisins. Mix well and form it all into a cake.

Grease large tin pans, line them with white paper, pour the above batter in a layer 2 inches deep, and bake 2 hours in a moderate oven. The raisins and currants should be prepared a day before the cake is made.

I suspect that this recipe wore two veils because in spite of its name, it is not much different from the once-famous "Dutch Cake" baked throughout Pennsylvania at Christmas. The only real difference seems to have been that Dutch cake contained more brandy. During the rest of the year, it belonged to brides and lotteries, and, appropriately, one took a chance on both.

At Christmas, Pennsylvania-German newspapers overflowed with alluring advertisements for Dutch cake. Many bakers offered them as prizes in Christmas bake-offs between pastry shops. And what they did not sell that December was often donated as part of the loot in the charitable spring lotteries that were once so popular for raising money to pay for bridges, roads, schools, and even churches in German Pennsylvania.

Some Dutch cakes were true window showpieces, often the size of wagon wheels (a common claim!), and one determined soul baked a Dutch cake that weighed in at something more than 1,000 pounds. The oven had to be built around the cake. However, most Dutch cakes were not so large, for the *Philadelphia Ledger* of December 26, 1846, advertised them this way: "Superior Dutch Cakes, equal to Fruit Cake, may be had fresh every day in 6, 12, 25, and 50 cent loaves." Of course, little Dutch cakes were loved most of all by children.

102. Plum Cake
(Pflaumen-Kuchen)

To make the cake, take 2 cups of butter, 2 cups of molasses, 1 cup of sweet milk, 2 well-beaten eggs, 1 teaspoon of powdered saleratus, 1 teaspoon of grated nutmeg, 1 teaspoon of ground allspice, 1 teaspoon of cinnamon, and 1 gill of brandy. Add some flour to make the batter thick enough that it can be stirred with a spoon easily. Whisk this until it becomes light, then add 2 pounds of raisins and 2 pounds of washed currants, and ½ pound of chopped, candied lemon rind, then bake in a hot oven. This is a good, elegant cake that is easy to make and is not expensive.

This last remark explains the popularity of the recipe a century ago. Plum cake was once a Christmas specialty in Bucks County, where it was eaten as frequently as fruit cake and Dutch cake.

103. Kisses
(Küsse)

Beat the whites of 4 eggs to a froth and stir in ½ pound of powdered sugar. Season with vanilla or lemon essence and continue to beat it until it is stiff. Then form [scoops] of batter in the shape and size of half an egg, [and set them] an inch apart from one another on cooking parchment. If the batter loses its shape or runs, it has not been beaten enough. Put the parchment on a hardwood board and set it in a hot oven. As soon as the kisses begin to turn yellow, take them out, lay the parchment on a table, and let them cool 3 or 4 minutes. Then insert a knife blade under them, holding the knife in the left hand, and separate each kiss from the paper. Join their flat sides together and set them carefully on a plate.

The recipe here is similar to one published in Laura G. Abell's *The Skillful Housewife's Book* (New York, 1846).[133] Kisses were simple enough to make when there were ample egg whites left over from other bakings. Proper kisses should be feather light, and for this reason, the Pennsylvania Germans often hung them as decorations on Christmas trees.

104. Icing for Cakes
(Eis auf Kuchen)

Beat the whites of 2 small eggs to a froth, add ¼ pound of powdered white sugar and some vanilla or lemon essence. Beat this until it is white and light. The more it is beaten, the thicker it will become. Then spread it over the cake with a little piece of cardboard and let it dry and harden in a warm place.

Eis is not the old word the Pennsylvania Germans used for icing. That seems to be Gustav Peters's peculiar invention, because *Eis auf*

Kuchen in his day meant ice cream on cake, what we would call cake à la mode today. The correct term was *Guss*, a standard culinary term that was once common usage in nineteenth-century Pennsylvania-German almanacs and newspapers. Flannel cakes were called *Guss-kuche*, because *Guss* comes from the German verb *giessen*, "to pour."

This *Guss* is an old-fashioned royal icing that becomes stiff rather quickly, which is why it is ideal for decorating gingerbread cookies or anything else requiring the use of a pastry bag. However, as an icing for large cakes, it is almost too brittle, except, perhaps, where a hard decorative icing is desired. To beat it properly, use a broad-bladed whisking knife.

105. Molasses Taffy
(Molasses-Zucker)

Pour 1 pint of ordinary molasses into a pan over a moderate fire. Let this boil, stirring constantly so that it does not bubble over. After it has boiled ½ hour, cool a little of the molasses in a saucer. If this hardens and breaks easily, then it has boiled enough. Add a little lemon, sassafras, or vanilla [essence] and some coarsely chopped almonds, then pour it into shallow buttered tin pans [to cool].

Aside from the ingenious clear toys that the Pennsylvania-German children prized at Christmas, molasses taffy, or *Moschi*, was probably the most popular candy found in the home. It was made with caramelized sugar or boiled molasses and nuts. Some types of *Moschi* were hard, others not absolutely so due to the addition of baking soda. Soda produced bubbles in the taffy, thus making it softer. To make soft *Moschi*, it would be necessary to add ¼ teaspoon of baking soda to the recipe above before adding the flavoring and nuts.

The term *Moschi*—which now commonly appears in English as moshey—is evidently a dialect corruption of *moschkiwado*, a Pennsylvania-German term for muscovado sugar. Muscovado sugar (unrefined sugar) was commonly used for making the cheapest grade of *Moschi* before molasses became a more popular substitute. A fuller discussion of muscovado sugar appears on pp. 155–56.

Early recipes for *Moschi* are extremely rare, but doubtless the prototype for the Pennsylvania versions is the recipe for *Moschi* found in Marcus Loofft's *Nieder-Sächsisches Koch-Buch*. It is translated as follows:[134]

Loofft's Muscovado Almond Taffy

Take shelled almonds, as many as you like, and somewhat more than half as much grated sugar. Then you can either cut the almonds in very thin slivers, or chop them up small in the sugar. Put the sugar and nuts in a pan and stir over the fire until the mixture is a nice dark brown, verging on red. While it is hot, press this into small, fluted molds. Press the sugar down completely all around the edges until it is about the thickness of a finger, leaving no spaces. To make certain that the molds are completely free of residue, they should be well cleaned beforehand and laid for an hour in clean, cold water. Once the taffy is in the mold and begins to stiffen, take it out quickly before it hardens. This taffy can be put into any mold you choose, large or small, but the mold must be thoroughly wet first.

If muscovado sugar is stored for any length of time, it will harden into a lumpy mass; when fresh, it is coarse and sticky. This is probably one reason why Loofft was obliged to grate his sugar, and no simple task either. When caramelized with nuts, as in the recipe here, it takes on the consistency of hot macadam, which is why all the pushing and pressing is necessary. Boiled molasses retains the flavor of muscovado sugar, and because it flows easily when poured into molds, it presents similar results with less work. That is probably why molasses became more popular with busy Pennsylvania-German housewives. They also used fewer nuts.

Making *Moschi*

Historically, Pennsylvania-German *Moschi* was always made in round, fluted molds, so it is interesting to see in Loofft that this shape was also traditional in Germany. Considering that the first edition of Loofft's cookbook appeared in 1755, his recipe may be considered fairly standard for the entire eighteenth-century, for he was already well established as a chef when he wrote it.

106. To Make Yeast
(Hefe zu machen)

Boil 1 pound of good flour, ¼ pound of brown sugar, and a little salt in 2 gallons of water for 1 hour. Then let the liquid cool until it is luke-warm. Next, pour it into bottles, which must [then] be sealed tightly. A pint of this yeast will be sufficient for 18 pounds of bread.

Hops

Like most women in her day, my great-grandmother made her own yeast. The process involved other members of the family, for as a child, it was my grandmother's assignment to pick the hops that grew like grapevines up the side of the house by the kitchen. Those people who were not lucky enough to have their own hops had to rely on recipes such as the one here in *Die geschickte Hausfrau*. Otherwise,

cooks were obliged to buy what yeast they could obtain, and that was usually brewer's yeast, also made from hops.

Actually, when it came to baking, many Pennsylvania-German women preferred brewer's yeast to liquid yeast, or *Satz*, as it was called in dialect. According to Jacob Graeff's reminiscences of Reading during the 1820s:[135]

> No housekeeper thought she could make fine cakes without brewer's yeast, and just before Christmas a large, lively crowd gathered at the brewery several hours before day. As the quantity of yeast was limited and only 2 cents worth allowed one person, the strongest half of the crowd secured the prize and the other half went without.

The brewery in question was High's on Penn Street, which sold yeast once a week. Such brewer's yeast was much more active than most homemade mixtures, which meant the woman who used it could eliminate some steps in baking.

This, of course, was the situation before the development of commercial yeast tablets and powders. Until that time, yeast was generally liquid, whether made from hops or from sugar and flour. Because of this, the other liquid ingredients in baking recipes must be adjusted accordingly for modern adaptations. As a rule—and a very loose one—½ pint of liquid yeast usually equals one modern yeast cake. In light of this, the recipe in *Die geschickte Hausfrau* makes impressive claims.

8

"Siesses" and "Saueres"

Sauerkraut un Schpeck
dreibt alle Sarje weck.

Translation

Sauerkraut and pork
drive all cares away.

A FOLK SAYING

The sweets and the sours—*Siesses un Saueres*—is the most recently developed branch of Pennsylvania-German cookery, one that took its final form (and one we know today) a good fifty years *after* the appearance of *Die geschickte Hausfrau*. Gustav Peters's cookbook probably had little to do with this shift in taste, but if his recipes are any indication, a transition was already underway by the late 1840s, for the recipes represent a combination of two different approaches to sweets and sours.

By the early nineteenth century, at least two distinct "taste cultures" had developed in southeastern Pennsylvania, three, actually, if we treat Philadelphia by itself. Philadelphia possessed a sophisticated cuisine that was more international in tone and is more readily accessible today through period cookbooks than the other two. Thus, in practice, its cookery was somewhat separate from the countryside around it.

In the countryside, two taste cultures existed side by side. The first was that of the Quakers and other English-speaking farmers who came to Pennsylvania for the most part from western England and Wales. They brought with them a cookery based on dairy culture. Theirs was a "white gravy" cookery, which used butter and milk (thickened with flour), or cream, in a vast number of sauce or gravy combinations. The most common table meats consisted of salt pork, "flitch" (local dialect for unsmoked bacon), and dried beef. Each of these meats was usually prepared in some way with cream or milk, as in "frizzled beef" (dried-beef gravy) and "flitch-in-cream" (a variation of dried-beef gravy). As a contrasting flavor to this milk-based cookery, Anglo-Pennsylvanians generally preferred fruity sweets or preserves, so much so that in some households the use of pickles was unknown. In general terms, this system of taste was probably a continuation of certain aspects of Philadelphia cookery as it had existed in the late seventeenth and early eighteenth centuries.

In absolute contrast to this was the taste culture of the Pennsylvania Germans. Their cookery was pork and flour based, with particular emphasis on dough dishes (noodles, dumplings, etc.) as accompaniments to fatty meat. Their brown gravies were usually made of drippings or stock thickened with roux. This required the acid contrast of vinegar or fruit juice to combine with the fat to make it more palatable. Thus predisposed to acidity in their cookery, Pennsylvania-German cooks placed greater importance on tart pickles than on sweet

151

preserves. For this reason, pickles with tart fruits—especially cherries and crab apples, apple butter without sugar, raspberry-flavored vinegar, slightly green peaches, gooseberries, and currants—all found great favor among the Pennsylvania Dutch.

One of the first intrusions into these two taste systems appeared in the form of Asiatic pickles, such as chutney, chow-chow, and "mangoes" (recipe 121). These highly spiced sweet pickles were rapidly assimilated into British cookery because they were for the most part originally intended as condiments with mutton in their native cuisines, and mutton was the staple meat of Britain. Through British trade contacts and British cookbooks, these pickles found their way to America. But in Pennsylvania, where large-scale mutton eating was generally limited to Philadelphia, adjustments had to be made to make the pickles more suitable for pork.

By the outbreak of the Civil War, these traditional taste systems in rural Pennsylvania began to undergo modification, which was accelerated by the rapid industrialization of the state after 1865. As eating habits became more urbanized, pork consumption declined in favor of beef shipped in from the west. By degrees, the Pennsylvania Germans assumed the taste preferences of their Anglo-American neighbors. In short, they assimilated many Anglo-American sweet pickles and began adding more sugar to their sours.

The full range of sweet and sour pickles now associated with Pennsylvania-German cookery was not possible until refined white sugar became cheap and everywhere available, which did not happen until the acquisition of Puerto Rico and the Philippines after the Spanish-American War.

This increase in consumption of white sugar did not go unnoticed by the Pennsylvania Dutch. Period editorials wondered whether this change was really progress (a sign of new wealth) or just bad diet. *The Inglenook*, a publication of the Church of the Brethren (a Pennsylvania-German sect) remarked with a cautious note of wonder in its January 31, 1911, issue that by 1910 American sugar consumption had reached an all-time high of eighty-one and one-half pounds per person. These figures were based on U.S. government statistics that showed the average per capita consumption of sugar in 1880 was forty pounds. In thirty years, sugar consumption had doubled, with the largest jump occurring between 1900 and 1910. Thus, as a culinary development, the sweet and sour pickle was not so much a product of traditional Pennsylvania-German cookery as it was part of a larger American pattern. Most sweet and sour pickles now sold in the Pennsylvania-German area are typical of what was found throughout the United States at the turn of this century. The basic interplay of tastes in Pennsylvania-German cookery was the tart flavor of fruits contrasted against the salty or smoky flavor of meats, not the sweet-sour taste of refined sugar and vinegar.

The practice of placing so many sweets and sours on the table reached rural America by the turn of this century. In Appalachia, in poor families where good meat was not affordable, sweets and sours often took the place of meat or allowed cooks to reduce the meat portions, because the relative cost of sugar-based foods was cheaper. This also occurred in German Pennsylvania, as the consumption of fresh pork fell with the decline of home butchering.

Rural cooks did not develop the "sweet and sour table" with which we are now so often confronted. They took their cue from church or charitable cookbooks and "family style" restaurants that perfected a simplified version of the old French style of arranging symmetrically on the table all the food of a given course. In eighteenth-century America, the table for each course was completely covered with the main dish and its side dishes. The pickles in *Die geschickte Hausfrau*, such as melon mangoes (recipe 121), pickled walnuts (recipe 119), and red cabbage (recipe 124), were all typical side dishes for an upper-class eighteenth-century American dinner, that is, as conditure for the roast. The placement of "seven sweets and seven sours" on one table—or any other balanced number of side dishes—is strict *service à la française*. It is not of Pennsylvania-Dutch origin, whatever the number.

Any further similarity to *service à la française* stops here, for in Middle America, the term has lost its classic meaning. As for the pre–Civil War Pennsylvania-German table, it offered several kinds (or cuts) of meat rather than fourteen kinds of sweets and sours. In fact, in many households, sauerkraut took the place of other pickles altogether.

Pickles were not unknown, however; quite the contrary. But economics had a great deal to do with the type and number of pickles available in any given household. Certainly, sauerkraut was considered basic. Pickled cucumbers and string beans were probably next in order. Some of the earliest surviving Pennsylvania-German pickle recipes are specifically for theses two vegetables.

Johann Krauss included two recipes for preserving string beans and *Salzkummern* (salted cucumbers, like dill pickles) in his *Haus- und Kunstbuch* (1819).[136] Both of his recipes demonstrate very clearly that early Pennsylvania-German pickles were not intended to be sweet or mild, but that they shared a salty sharpness of flavor akin to sauerkraut. Many other pickling recipes appeared even earlier than this in Pennsylvania-German agricultural newspapers and almanacs, for pickling was traditionally the husband's sphere in the Pennsylvania-Dutch household.

Originally, in medieval German culture, pickling was mostly limited to the preservation of meat and fish, exclusively a man's task. A typical medieval German recipe for pickled fowl called for a brine of vinegar, salt, juniper berries, and caraway seed—strikingly similar to some later recipes for pickled cucumbers.[137] According to the German cultural historian Karl Rhamm, the technique for pickling sauerkraut, beets, cucumbers, and beans came to Germany from Slavic Europe.[138] These pickles were gradually added to the traditional list of culinary chores expected of men, and in many cases, such as the pickle for fowl, older recipes were applied to new ingredients.

While most traditional Pennsylvania-German pickles were designed to humor the meat, preserves were generally intended for some type of *Heemgebackenes* (homemade baked good), eaten with the meal, one might say, as a fruit substitute.

The principal "sweet" condiment (if it had sugar in it at all) was apple butter, called *Lattwaerrick* in Pennsylvania Dutch. *Lattwaerrick* is derived from German *Latwerge*, which in turn stems from Latin *electuarium*. *Lattwaerrick* is bound up with old medical connotations, for *electuarium* itself comes from Greek *eleigma*, an internal medicine. During the Middle Ages, and even into the seventeenth century, preserves containing sugar were considered medicines in Germany. Thus, they were the province of the apothecary shop.[139] On the folk level, this attitude lingered in rural Pennsylvania even into the early nineteenth century. Blackberry jam, for example, was a standard medicine for gall stones.

Most Pennsylvania Germans ate rye bread as daily fare (until the 1860s at any rate). Jams and jellies were not used so much as *Schmieres* (a spread) on bread as they were garnitures for cakes, pies, and cookies—items served only on unusual occasions. Butter and jam on a slice of white bread was a middle-class, Anglo-American symbol of status in the eighteenth century. Apple butter and cottage cheese on a slice of rye bread was the Pennsylvania-German equivalent. In working-class rural households, rich confections like raspberry jam might be spread across the top of a freshly baked pie (made with raised crust), or mixed with vinegar and served hot over pork. Where formality was in order, jams and jellies were served as side dishes among the desserts and were generally eaten as spreads on cake, not bread. One reason for the popularity of almond cake and sponge cake among the Pennsylvania Dutch was that they could be eaten with a sweet *Schmieres*.

In any case, Pennsylvania-German preserves, even in *Die geschickte Hausfrau*, would hardly pass for sweet by modern standards. The sugars used then were quite different from those known in the United States today. Perhaps it would be useful to review the various grades of wholesale sugar as they were designated in Pennsylvania during the nineteenth-century. The following list is taken from *Hope's Philadelphia Price-Current* for October 5, 1807.

Havana white
Havana brown (like Brasilian Demarara)

Muscovado 1st quality
Muscovado 2nd quality
Muscovado ordinary
West India clayed white
West India clayed brown
Calcutta white
Batavia white

Of these, ordinary muscovado was the cheapest, just about half the cost of Havana white, the most expensive sugar then available and the one sugar on this list most like the white granulated sugar of today. Cheap, black, sticky muscovado or brown Demarara-type sugars were the most common table sugars used by the Pennsylvania Germans. Like molasses, muscovado sugar was always in great demand, even in the eighteenth century, for it was one of the first sugars to be advertised in the Philadelphia *American Weekly Mercury* of 1719.[140]

Making loaf sugar

Regardless of grade, sugar was imported in large cones or loaves, called *Hutzucker* ("hat" sugar) by the Pennsylvania Dutch because the cones resembled tall pointed hats. In his *Island of Cuba*, Alexander von Humboldt described these cones and how muscovado sugar was manufactured:[141]

Of each loaf, or cone with the base uppermost, the upper part gives white sugar, the middle gives brown, and the lower, or point of the cone gives *cucurucho*; these three grades of Cuba sugar are purged, and but a small portion is manufactured as raw, or *moscabado* sugar. As the purging forms are of different size, the loaf varies in weight; it is usually about twenty-five pounds after being purged. The sugar masters desire that each loaf should give 5/9 of white, 3/9 of brown, and 1/9 of *cucurucho* sugar.

The word muscovado comes from Spanish *masacabado* or Portuguese *mascavado*, meaning "unrefined." Muscovado sugar is still available in Britain and in some import shops and health food stores in this country. One may make a close approximation, for immediate use only, by mixing one tablespoon of unsulfured molasses to each cup of dark brown sugar.

Once the loaves of sugar reached the United States, they were usually purged or refined again and converted into smaller loaves for retail, wrapped in blue paper to preserve the whiteness. In spite of this precaution about appearance, none of the retail loaf sugar was usable until it was again boiled in water to remove insects and other extraneous material. This irksome process involved egg whites, charcoal, and constant skimming. The syrup was then strained through a cloth bag until clear, returned to the fire, and boiled down. "This practice has long been pursued in my family, and I never allow the use of any sugar for culinary purposes, which has not been cleansed," remarked a letter to the editor of the *Germantown Telegraph* of June 25, 1851. To put it more bluntly, women who did not clean their sugar before using it were considered worse than poor cooks.

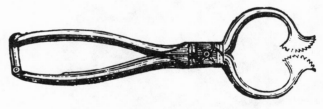

Sugar shears

As for actual preserving techniques before the 1850s, Pennsylvania-German cooks were still using traditional glazed redware crocks instead of canisters or jars for preserving their fruits and vegetables. These crocks were usually glazed on the inside only and sealed with a bladder, a sheet of paper, and a string. Jams and marmalades in particular were stored this way, while pickles and other acidic foods were kept in unglazed or salt-glazed stoneware because of the danger of chemical poisoning from leaded redware glazes. Most of the recipes in *Die geschickte Hausfrau* call for the use of glass jars, because by 1848 a number of fairly reliable commercial jars were available. Even so, Pennsylvania-German women at this time tended to look upon glass jars in the same light as many women today view overpriced French culinary gadgets: interesting, but unnecessary.

In this chapter, recipes 108, 109, 110, 111, 112, and 113 were reprinted in volume 3 of *Der amerikanische Bauer*, and recipes 117, 118, 119, and 120 may be traced to Mary Randolph's *Virginia House-Wife*.

107. To Put Up Quinces
(Quitten einzumachen)

Quince

Pare nice quinces, cut them lengthwise into several pieces, and boil them in water, though not until soft. Then strain them and put them in a pot, boil, and clarify. To each pound of quinces, [mix] 1 pound of sugar with ⅙ of a quart of the hot water in which the quinces were cooked. When this clarifies, pour it over the quinces and let them stand 2 days well covered. Next, pour off the syrup and set it over the fire. When it boils, add the quinces and let them cook ¼ hour. Then take the quinces out, and if the syrup is not yet thick enough, boil it down a little longer. After both syrup and quinces are sufficiently cool, put the fruit in jars and pour the syrup over them.

———————————◆◆———————————

Quinces were among the very earliest fruits brought to Pennsylvania by the Germans, and by the 1740s, Peter Kalm noted that they were common everywhere. Aside from canning quinces in syrup, one of the most popular Pennsylvania-German recipes was quince marmalade, known among the Dutch as *Quittehunnich*, or quince honey. It had to be made with white sugar, so it was a specialty dish, served only on festive occasions.

Of course, pouring the syrup cold over the quinces, as directed here, flies in the face of everything we now know about sterilizing canning jars. This doubtful practice was commonplace until the late nineteenth century.

108. To Put Up Peaches or Apricots
(Pfirsichen und Aprikosen einzumachen)

[Use] peaches or apricots that are only half ripe. Pare them, take out the pits, and split them into halves. To each pound of cooked fruit, dissolve 1 pound of sugar in some water. When this boils, add the fruit and let the syrup boil up several times. Then take the fruit out carefully with a skimmer and let the syrup cook down until somewhat thicker. When both the fruit and syrup are sufficiently cool, pack the fruit in jars and pour the syrup over them. If in time the syrup should become watery, pour it out and boil it again.

George Girardey published a recipe for preserving peaches and apricots very similar to this one.[142] But many other Pennsylvania-German recipes also suggest that the peaches may be brandied with sliced oranges. Among the Pennsylvania Germans, brandied peaches were commonly served with chocolate cake.

109. To Put Up Crab Apples
(Wilde Aepfel einzumachen)

Pare the apples and core them. Put them in boiling water with a stick of cinnamon and boil for some time. Then take out the apples and let them drain in a colander. Meanwhile, to each pound of apples, mix 1 pound of sugar with 1 cup of water, [and] set [this] over the fire. After this syrup has been skimmed and cooked down until thick, add the finely chopped rind of 2 lemons and their juice, as well as the apples, and let this boil until the apples are clear and fairly soft. Then, remove the fruit, reduce the syrup until it is thick, and when sufficiently cool, [pour it] into jars with the apples.

The *Holzabbel*, or crab apple, is still popular in some areas of Pennsylvania. It makes a deliciously tart preserve that can be served on white bread or as a condiment with pork, duck, or goose.

110. To Put Up Currants
(Johannisbeeren einzumachen)

To each pound of red, ripe, stemmed currants, dissolve 1 pound of sugar in some water. When this syrup thickens, add the currants and let them boil until they reduce. Then remove the currants, reduce the syrup further, pour it over the berries, and cover them tightly once they are thoroughly cool.

At one time, wild and domesticated currants were among the most widely consumed fruits in Pennsylvania. Several varieties are native to North America, but they are generally quite different from the currants known in Germany and brought to Pennsylvania for garden cultivation. Most Pennsylvania-Dutch kitchen gardens included red, black, or white currants. Of the three, the red were the commonest. The white currants demanded more attention, but being sweeter than the others, they were also most in demand for the table.

Girardey also preferred the white currants and published a recipe for making jelly from them, which he suggested keeping in small earthenware jars sealed with paper doused in brandy or Kirsch.[143] This jelly could then be used for cakes.

111. Currant Marmalade
(Marmalade von Johannisbeeren)

Press the currants and boil the juice until it thickens. Next, mix this with sugar of equal weight, and boil it in a brass kettle until a smooth syrup forms. Three fourths of a pound of sugar is sufficient for each pound of berry juice. Marmalade from raspberries, mulberries, and strawberries is prepared in this manner. In no case, however, should skimming be omitted.

————————◆◆————————

Currant marmalade, whether from black, white, or red currants, was used in a multitude of ways, but particularly in sauces for puddings and in pies. It was served as a condiment with venison, duck, or pork, and it was even applied as a topping on cheesecakes.

112. To Put Up Plums
(Pflaumen einzumachen)

Make a syrup with brown sugar [and water]. When the sugar has dissolved completely and is boiling hot, pour it over stemmed plums. Let them stand in this syrup for 2 days. Pour off the syrup and boil it again. Skim it, then pour it a second time over the plums, which must stand in it another 2 days. Then [remove the plums], heat up the syrup, pour it over the plums, and after 2 days, set it all over the fire in a brass kettle, and simmer it until the syrup thickens. To each pound of plums, use 1 pound of brown sugar.

————————◆◆————————

The most common use of this dish was to serve it hot as compote. Otherwise, it would have served as a filling for pies.

In the early eighteenth century, plums were evidently scarce outside the immediate environs of towns. Dried plums were imported

from Germany in large quantities, but domestically, they seem to have been a gentleman's fruit, grown mostly in protected urban gardens, yet even there, subject to odd blights and fallen fruit. That plums were not as plentiful as in Germany is evident from period accounts and from the many traditional plum dishes in which apples were substituted. For example, in the Rhineland, *Lattwaerrick* is actually plum butter, not apple butter as in Pennsylvania; and Palatine *Hutzelbrod* is often made in Pennsylvania with dried pears instead of real *Hutzel* (dried plums).[144] The plum shortage continued long enough for plums to fall into the category of a secondary fruit among the Pennsylvania Dutch, a position that did not change even when plum culture became more extensive after 1800. One of the most widely planted varieties in Pennsylvania was "General Hand," developed in 1852 and named for a Revolutionary War figure from Lancaster County.

113. To Put Up Pears
(Birnen einzumachen)

Pare small ripe pears that are still firm. After removing the stems, halve the pears and put them in cold water. Next, to each pound of pears, make a syrup with 1 pound of sugar and some water. Drain the pears, put them in the syrup, and simmer until they are soft. Then remove the pears and let the syrup cook down somewhat thicker. When the syrup has cooled, pour it over the pears in glass jars.

This recipe works excellently with the small Seckel pears that were so much a part of Pennsylvania-German cookery in the last century. The pears took their name from Lorentz Seckel, a Pennsylvania-German wine merchant who found a tree of them growing on his farm along the Delaware River. They are said to be a natural hybrid related to the German Rousselet pear. Whatever the case, Seckel pears and Bergamot pears were the oldest varieties of pears raised in Pennsylvania, dating at least from the 1740s, and their popularity did not wane among the Dutch even in the 1840s when so many newer varieties were available.

114. To Put Up Tomatoes
(Tomatoes einzumachen)

Pour boiling water over small red or yellow tomatoes about the size of plums, and remove the skins.* Make a syrup with sugar and some water, and when it is hot, add the tomatoes and let them simmer. Boil 2 lemons in water until their rinds are soft, then slice and mix them with the tomatoes in the syrup. Let this boil until the fruit is completely clear, then remove the tomatoes, let them cool, and boil the syrup until it becomes thick and rich. Let the syrup cool, then put the tomatoes in glass jars, and pour the clarified syrup over them.

During the 1840s and 1850s, red and yellow pear (or plum) tomatoes were much more in vogue for table use than the other types of available tomatoes. This was particularly true for the Pennsylvania Germans, because plum tomatoes could be treated as fruit in traditional recipes. The recipe here uses more or less the same approach as stewed tomatoes, and like stewed fruit, stewed tomatoes were originally served as compote, the most popular of all nineteenth-century desserts among the Pennsylvania Dutch.

That tomatoes were generally looked upon as fruit and not salading is also evident in the popularity of tomato figs. Tomato figs became popular during the 1840s, and in some rural households, they assumed a place in the diet traditionally held by plums, particularly dried plums. Since tomatoes were in season longer and were more plentiful, there was an underlying economic consideration that may not be immediately apparent today. Furthermore, tomato figs were something of a novelty, and they made an interesting snack food for children. Since

---

*Use about 1½ quarts of tomatoes. The syrup can be made in the proportion of 4 cups of sugar to ¾ cup of water.

manuscript cookbooks from this period usually have at least one recipe for tomato figs, I supply the following from the Byers family cookbook (ca. 1870–1915), from Upper Strasburg Township in Franklin County.[145]

Tomato Figs

To 4 lbs. of figs or small tomatoes, take 1½ lbs. of brown sugar, scald and skin the tomatoes. Place in your preserving kettle, sprinkle the sugar among and over them and let them stand until a juice is formed. Do not add water. Put on the stove and boil slowly until they look clear, then take them out in a large platter, flatten them slightly, dry in a clean sunny place, sprinkling on them occasionally while drying, a little of the syrup in which they were boiled. When dry, they may be packed in layers with powdered sugar between. If the figs are desired very sweet, more sugar may be added to that in which they are cooked.

It should be evident from the first line in this recipe that one of the common names for pear or plum-type tomatoes in central Pennsylvania was "fig tomatoes."

115. To Put Up Wine Grapes
(Weintrauben einzumachen)

When almost ripe, remove the grapes from their stems. To each pound of grapes, make a syrup of 1 pound of sugar and 1 small teacup of water. Bring this to a boil and pour it over the grapes. Let them stand 2 days [remove the grapes from the syrup], then bring the syrup to a boil.

Again, pour it over the grapes. After 2 days, simmer the grapes in the syrup until they are clear. Then [again] remove the grapes with a skimmer and let the syrup cook down. Cool the syrup, and finally, pour it over the fruit and store in glass jars.

———————————◆◆———————————

The key word in this recipe is *Weintrauben*: wine grapes, not the wild fox grapes or frost grapes that are common throughout Pennsylvania, but *wine* grapes. Between the 1790s and the 1860s, the Pennsylvania Germans had extensive private vineyards, some of which exceeded 500 acres in Berks County alone.[146] One of the most famous was the "Schweizerhalle" vineyard of Johann Auer (1788–1858) in Bethel Township.

It had been the goal of Pennsylvania-German vintners to produce a white *Rheinwein* much like the wines they had known in Germany. The Pennsylvania Germans almost succeeded until an economic depression, competition from Ohio and California, and the Temperance Movement rooted up all but the smallest plots. As the vine retreated from the field to the backdoor arbor, its shady trellis grew into a special kind of porch for the Pennsylvania Dutch, a summer meeting place for families, for lovers, and, of course, for children, whose job it was to pick the grapes so *Grossmammi* could can them.

What did the Dutch do with canned grapes? They put them in pies, either alone or as substitutes for the raisins in mincemeat.

116. To Put Up Cherries in Vinegar
(Kirschen in Essig einzumachen)

Boil 1 quart of good wine vinegar with 1 pound of sugar in a kettle. Skim well and let this cool. Then take large, sour cherries and cut off [the top] half of each cherry stem. Sprinkle the bottom of a canning jar with small pieces of cinnamon and cloves. Place a layer of cherries over this and proceed in alternating layers of cherries and spices until the jar is full. The top layer, however, must consist of spices. Finally, pour the reduced wine vinegar over the cherries, covering the jar with a bladder and thick paper. Store in a dry place.

This is a thoroughly traditional Pennsylvania-German recipe. An excellent eighteenth-century version, with the very same ingredients, appeared in the 1797 *Landwirtschafts Calender*, a Lancaster County almanac.[147]

117. To Put Up Cucumbers
(Gummern einzumachen)

Take cucumbers fully grown, but still young. Pare away the green skin and slice them tolerably thick. Make a layer of cucumber slices in a deep dish, sprinkle finely chopped onions and salt over them, and continue in this manner until the cucumbers are all in. Sprinkle salt on top and let this stand 6 hours. Pour the cucumbers into a colander so that the liquid can run off completely. Then put them in a crock, sprinkle a little cayenne pepper over each layer, and pour strong, cold vinegar over them. When the crock is full, add some olive oil and cover tightly. After 8 days, pour off the vinegar [and oil] and put on fresh.

"Oil Cucumbers" (the recipe here) and numerous other cucumber pickles are as much a part of the Pennsylvania-German cookery as *Schnitz* or gingerbread or pickled beets. Recipes for cucumber pickles, with or without olive oil, appear in many eighteenth-century Pennsylvania-German sources. But to state that one recipe was more common than another would be a rather grave error, because variety seems to have been the rule and individual taste the ruling fashion. Yet certainly most old Pennsylvania-Dutch cucumber pickles could be classified as salt pickles of one form or another. Typical of this old school was the briny recipe published by George Girardey in 1841 called *Eingemachte Kukummern mit Salz-Wasser*—pickled cucumbers in salt water—to which he added mace, nutmeg, and cloves for flavor.

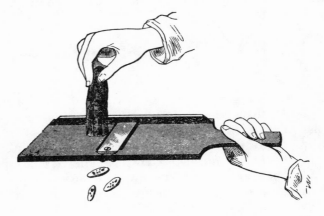

118. To Put Up Onions
(Eingemachte Zwiebeln)

Take small white onions and remove the tops with a sharp knife. Pour boiling water and salt over them and cover the pot carefully, letting them stand thus for 8 days. Every day, put fresh water and salt on them and stir so that none of the onions float on top. After 8 days, remove the skins and outer shells, and put the onions in plain cold vinegar with a little turmeric.

The Pennsylvania Germans usually ate pickled onions as condiments with roast veal or roast pork but often added them to sauces served with other meats as well.

119. To Put Up English Walnuts
(Englische Wallnüsse einzumachen)

Walnuts for pickling should be hulled only when the kernel is so soft that a pin can pierce it easily. Pour boiling water and salt over the nuts and let them stand well covered for 9 days, and every third day pour fresh salt water over them. Afterwards, [discard the brine and] set the nuts on dishes in the open air a few minutes, taking care to turn them over. Then put the nuts in a pot and sprinkle some whole pepper, cloves, a little garlic, mustard seed, and grated horseradish over them, and cover with strong cold vinegar.

This is actually walnut catsup, a "store sauce" once popular as a condiment with fish. It can be found in almost every period cookbook, both English and German, because the homemade facsimile was half as expensive as the commercial product, provided, of course, that one could find decent walnuts.

The walnuts used in this recipe had to be thoroughly green, and the pin test was an age-old trick for determining their proper ripeness. However, the reason for setting the walnuts in the open air (actually, in the direct sun) is not always explained. It was done to blacken the nuts, since this color was thought to improve the appearance of the pickle.

Another improvement was age: the older the better. Marion Harland wrote in her *Common Sense in the Household* (1884) that she had "eaten walnut pickle ten years old that was very fine."[148] We may suppose from this that some people served it a great deal older.

120. To Put Up Peppers
(Pfeffer einzumachen)

Take large, young, longish bell peppers, leaving the seeds in and the stems on, and cut a slit on one side between the large veins to draw the water in. Pour boiling salt water over the peppers, changing this every day for 3 weeks, and keep tightly covered. At the end of this time, if the peppers have turned a nice green, then pour cold vinegar and a little turmeric over them and put them away carefully. Be mindful not to cut through the large veins, as the heat of the peppers will be drawn out of the pods instantly [by the salt water].

Because of Philadelphia's trading contacts with the West Indies, both sweet and hot peppers were common in Pennsylvania by mid-eighteenth century. For a while, the hot ones were most in vogue. They were served on roasts, boiled with meat, chopped in sauces, pickled with cucumbers, preserved in salt, or served on fried fish, the hotter the better. Hot peppers were commonly called Guinea peppers to differentiate them from peppercorns and allspice (Jamaica pepper), both of which were ruthlessly inflicted on colonial stomachs.

121. Mangoes
(Mangoes)

Take very young, oval muskmelons, cut a round piece from the end or side of each, and remove the seeds. Then with thread tie the cut-out pieces to the melons and put them in strong salt water for 2 days. Dry the melons well, put them in a kettle covered above and below with grape or cabbage leaves, [add] a little alum, and let them turn green over a low fire. Cover the kettle carefully so that the steam does not escape, for steam hastens the greening of mangoes very much. After they have turned a nice green, stuff the melons with the following mixture, namely, grated horseradish, white mustard seed, mace, powdered nutmeg, finely chopped ginger root, pepper, turmeric, and olive oil. Into each mango stick a small clove of garlic. Tie up the mangoes well with thread and put them in stone crocks. Pour boiling vinegar over them, and cover the crocks carefully. In this same way, one may stuff [and pickle] green bell peppers.

The history of melon mango is one of those sidelights of early American cookery that has not been completely explored, yet insofar as the Pennsylvania Germans are concerned, it presents a fascinating story of assimilation and adaptation that ends in a most unusual way.

This recipe, of course, does not call for true tropical mangoes, but for the much less exotic muskmelons, which the Pennsylvania Dutch call *Muschmelune*. Old-fashioned muskmelons were actually a cousin of the true cantaloupe, and this distinction was once quite clear, although today cantaloupe and muskmelon often mean the same thing to many people. Muskmelons of a hundred years ago looked and tasted very different from melons grown in this country today; for those interested in making authentic melon mangoes, the Hoagen cantaloupe, with smooth skin and green flesh, and now sold commercially by several seed companies, approximates some of the features of the muskmelons raised by the Pennsylvania Dutch during the early nineteenth century.

Muskmelon

The Anglo-American character of this dish is evident from the fact that it was not well known in Germany and until the late nineteenth century did not appear in many German-American cookbooks. Melon mangoes were one feature of Pennsylvania-German cookery that differed considerably from later German-American cuisine, because, like the Pennsylvania Germans, melon mangoes arrived in Pennsylvania during the eighteenth century. The pickle appears to have reached America from India via England. In his illustrated German-American cookbook (1888), Charles Hellstern published a recipe that not only uses the basic mango stuffing but also directs our attention to this fact. It is called *Gurken wie ostindischen Mango einzumachen*— cucumbers pickled like East Indian mangoes.[149]

Pickles utilizing unripe mangoes have been made in India for many centuries. One traditional mango pickle, made by stuffing mangoes with mustard seed, horseradish, and other spices, is still made by the Parsees of western India and calls for more or less the same ingredients as those used in typical Pennsylvania-German melon mangoes. This same basic stuffing also appears in a recipe called "Mango or Pica-lilli" in William Kitchiner's *The Cook's Oracle* (1823).[150] Several versions of this "native" dish, called *bafena*, appeared in the *Indian Domestic Economy and Receipt Book*, published in Bombay in 1849. By that time, piccalilli, which developed out of the mango stuffing, had become a separate species of pickle.

True pickled mangoes may have been introduced to the English by the Portuguese of Goa. England and Portugal had a long history of close trading ties, and mango itself is a Portuguese loan word from the Tamil—*mangas*—one of thirty-two Tamil words for this fruit.

Although the word for mangoes could have reached England as early as 1563 via Garcia de Orta's classic work on Indian simples and drugs, the pickle itself seems to have reached England about a century later. It was probably something like *bafena*, made with unripe mangoes packed down in vinegar in crockery jars and sold among those expensive Eastern imports that became the rage among the English upper classes during the second half of the seventeenth century, when the East India Company flooded England with tea and other treasured exotica from the Orient.

Vegetable marrow

In 1690, the first hothouse mangoes were grown in England, but few people, aside from gentlemen gardeners, ever saw the fresh fruit. Counterfeiting mango pickle became a profitable enterprise, and fashion-conscious cooks came up with several passable substitutes, among them cucumbers and vegetable marrow. Mangoes were so widely copied that virtually any pickle using the basic mustard seed and horseradish stuffing was called a mango. For example, in the *Complete House-keeper and Professed Cook* (New Castle, 1786), Mary Smith included a recipe for "Onions in Mango."[151] Her recipe was nothing more than stuffed onions.

Upper-class colonists in North America were no less ardent for fashion and orientalia than their English cousins, and no doubt mango pickles found their way into the American diet through English cookbooks imported or reprinted in the colonies during the eighteenth century.

During this same period proper mangoes were introduced into several Caribbean and Latin American colonies: Brazil (by 1700); Barbados, West Indies (1742); Mexico (before 1779); and Jamaica (1782). In spite of this, fresh mangoes were not generally available even in port markets on the Atlantic coast until this century, so Americans were forced to find a number of substitutes of their own, including unripe peaches (a Creole favorite), muskmelons, baby watermelons—as Girardey suggests—and later green bell peppers. Again, as in England, the word mango was applied to any sort of pickle using the basic *bafena* stuffing.

American muskmelons were ideally suited for mango pickles,

both in flavor and texture, and they could be grown easily in many parts of the country, particularly in tidewater areas where summers are hot and the soil is sandy. For this reason melon mangoes were always much more popular in the South than in the North.

Thomas DeVoe noted in his *Market Assistant* (1867) that during the early 1800s, Philadelphia markets were considered the very best for muskmelons, but almost all of those melons were shipped in from South Jersey.[152] In Pennsylvania, muskmelons had to be started indoors in March and set out on hills in May. If May were warm, the plants would establish themselves quickly and begin producing melons by August. Cool September evenings, however, retard productivity, and many of the melons rot on the vine before they ripen. It was this problem with the weather more than anything else that caused the old-fashioned muskmelons to fall out of favor with the Pennsylvania Germans by the 1840s. By that time, many newer and less temperamental varieties of melon were available from nurserymen. Robert Buist of Philadelphia has described many of these new melons in his *Family Kitchen Gardener* of 1847.

Evidently there were a good many country cooks who avoided the trouble of growing muskmelons and simply substituted green bell peppers in the pickling recipe. A number of period cookbooks recommended this step, particularly for those regions where melons were difficult to grow.

The reference in *Die geschickte Hausfrau* to mangoes made with bell peppers is important, for pepper mangoes, as they were called, were so popular among the Pennsylvania Germans that the word *mango* became part of dialect speech, and even now appears as a general term for peppers in many modern Pennsylvania cookbooks. I need only mention Pat Parker's Radio WLTR cookbook (1949), with recipes drawn from Columbia and Northumberland counties. It boasts of a "Mango Relish" calling for red and green "mangoes."[153]

Today, mango can mean any kind of pepper, pickled or fresh, green or red. Long after pepper mangoes fell out of fashion, the word has continued in Pennsylvania dialect vocabularies. There are still some individuals in central Pennsylvania who use mango almost every day without realizing that there is a tropical fruit by the same name.

Mango

Pennsylvania-German pepper mangoes reached their ultimate conclusion in the sweet-and-sour "Hanover Mangoes" perfected at Hanover, Pennsylvania, in the 1880s. In addition to the basic mustard seed and horseradish stuffing, shredded cabbage, raisins, and dried currants were also included. Like other pepper mangoes, *Hanower-mangos* were at their best when served as a condiment with roast pork or veal.

122. Pepper Vinegar
(Pfeffer-Essig)

Take a dozen ripe peppers, cut off the stems, and cut them in pieces. Put them in a kettle with 3 pints of vinegar, boil until reduced to a quart, and press through a sieve. A little of this vinegar will give zest to any gravy or sauce.

The peppers required in this recipe are the cayenne or *hot* peppers. Like tarragon, garlic, shallot, and camp vinegar, pepper vinegar was among those articles recommended by Thomas Cooper as absolutely necessary for the well-furnished pantry, and for this reason, we may consider it more an item of upper-class Anglo-American cookery than a traditional Pennsylvania-German condiment. Its popularity in Philadelphia cookbooks may explain its presence in regional recipe anthologies like *Die geschickte Hausfrau*.

Among Philadelphians, pepper vinegar was used with the same frequency (and just as sparingly) as horseradish or its closest cousin tabasco. It was sometimes poured hot over salad greens, added to pickles and sauces, or even sprinkled over scrapple, sausage, and other pork products. It appears to have been one of those hot West Indian things that gained popularity in the United States during the late eighteenth and early nineteenth centuries but is now gratefully forgotten, retired by the much milder Creole chili sauces, which are now as popular among the Pennsylvania Germans as they are anywhere.

Chili pepper

123. To Put Up Red Cabbage
(Rothes Kraut einzumachen)

Shred the cabbage thin and make a layer of it in a stone crock. Sprinkle a little pepper and salt over this, then add another layer of shredded cabbage, sprinkling salt and pepper over it again, and continue in this manner until you have enough cabbage [to fill the crock]. Then pour cold vinegar over it, cover the cabbage with a pewter plate and tie the crock down carefully.

Red cabbage

George Girardey explained how red cabbage was served: "When one wishes to serve red cabbage, mix it with a little hot butter, pepper and vinegar, stir this all together well, and serve as a salad."[154]

124. Red Beets
(Rothe Rüben)

Take red beets of uniform size and wash them in cold water. Boil them from ¾ to 1½ hours according to their size, then put them into a bowl of cold water. Using your hands, rub the skins off, cut the beets in longish strips, and put them in cold vinegar with some peppercorns and salt. Beets should not be sliced up before they are cooked, but simply washed clean. Old beets that have been kept in the ground a long time must stand in water overnight before they can be cooked.

Pickled red beets—*gepickelte Rotriewe* in Pennsylvania Dutch—are still a Pennsylvania-German favorite, although today they are generally sliced into *Scheibche* (small round slices) rather than the *Schnittels*, thin strips so popular in the last century.

There was also another traditional way to preserve beets. It was a form of *Lattwaerrick*, much like apple butter, and was made in the following manner.[155]

George Girardey's Beet "Butter"

Cook red beets until they are completely soft, skin and wash them, and let them cook down in an equal quantity of sugar, the juice of one lemon, a little powdered cinnamon, nutmeg, and spices. Stir this constantly. This preserve is very light and looks attractive on the table.

125. Pickled Peaches
(Eingemachte Pfirsichen)

Take ripe peaches and rub the down off with a brush. Heat 1 gallon of good vinegar, add 4 pounds of brown sugar to it, boil, and skim it clear. Stick 5 or 6 cloves in each peach [and pour the vinegar over them]. Then pour off the vinegar, heat it, skim it well, and pour it again over the peaches. When cold, place the peaches in large canning jars and store in a cool place.

Pickled peaches were among the earliest fruit pickles made in Pennsylvania. Except for the glass canning jars, this recipe in particular is not very different from those used by the Pennsylvania Germans during the early 1700s—even to the typically tart flavor. But to make the recipe work according to the proportions given, one will need about thirty-two pounds (or ⅔ bushel) of small, ripe peaches, the sweeter the better. And instead of cloves, use cassia. That makes quite a difference and is much more authentic for nineteenth-century Pennsylvania.

126. Tomato Catsup
(Tomätoes Cätschup)

Pour boiling water over the tomatoes so that the skins come off easily. After this, cut them in pieces and put them in a stone crock, and add to each gallon 2 spoonfuls of salt. Set the crock in an iron pot full of boiling water, and let the tomatoes cook 3 hours. Then strain them through a strong, damp cloth. Mix 4 spoonfuls of peppercorns to each gallon of catsup, and let this cook 1 hour. After the catsup cools, put it in bottles and stop them up well. It will keep for years this way, the older the better. Should mold form on top of the catsup, cook it again and add some peppercorns.

Tomato catsup was originally used for improving sauces and soup broths, and before 1800, it was looked upon as something particularly French. In Philadelphia, it was often called "French sauce," for French and West Indian cooks were the first to introduce it on a large scale after 1793, when so many of them fled to this country. According to Philadelphia newspapers, tomato catsups were available in Pennsylvania as commercial imports from France, Italy, and the West Indies by the late 1790s. But tomato catsup remained more or less a curious luxury item until after the War of 1812 and the development of local commercial pickling houses. Catsup then became extremely cheap and widely imitated, at least as an urban food. In rural Pennsylvania, however, another twenty or thirty years passed before tomatoes in any form gained general acceptance.

One of the earliest recipes for tomato catsup to appear in a Pennsylvania-German periodical was published in the September 1839 issue of *Ceres*, a German-language agricultural monthly printed in Lebanon, Pennsylvania. That recipe was much more sophisticated than the one in *Die geschickte Hausfrau* in that it included cayenne pepper, black pepper, allspice, mustard, and two tablespoons of the juice pressed from garlic. For those who did not know, the recipe noted at the end that "Catsup schmeckt sehr gut zum Fleische"—catsup tastes very good on meat.[156]

Essig

127. To Make Vinegar
(Essig zu machen)

During warm weather, put an oak keg in the attic directly under the roof where it is hot. Add 1 or 2 gallons of clear, fermented cider, and leave the bung hole open. In 2 or 3 weeks, this will turn to sharp vinegar and develop enough mother so that more cider can be added. Continue from time to time to add a little cider until the keg is full.

———◆◆———

There are many Pennsylvania-German recipes for making vinegar, some more scientific than others. The first edition of *Die geschickte Hausfrau* ended with a long recipe for *Obstessig* (fruit vinegar) made from spoiled apples and pears. Even though that recipe was later dropped, it was a practical idea for fallen fruit or for fruit that was beginning to sour in storage. It was immeasurably more useful than the recipe given above, because the attic, after all, is not very convenient to the kitchen when pickling time comes around. And what Hausfrau was hardy enough to carry a keg of vinegar down winding stairs to the first floor? All objections are overruled by one plain fact: The recipe is a fail-safe method for making good vinegar.

128. To Make Sauerkraut
(Guter Kraut zu pöckeln)

Sauerkraut was something one learned to make as a child. For the Pennsylvania Germans, the art of sauerkraut making was practically second nature, which is why very few early recipes for sauerkraut have been preserved. This is also probably one good reason why there was no need to include a recipe for it in the original editions of *Die geschickte Hausfrau*. Yet sauerkraut was so basic to Pennsylvania-German cookery that it would be an inexcusable omission not to take notice of it in a culinary study such as this.

Philadelphia writer Eliza Leslie was one of the first to publicize Pennsylvania-German sauerkraut in her cookbooks, but the earliest recipes appeared in newspapers and agricultural journals. Farmers in other parts of the country heard that sauerkraut was a cheap and healthful dish, and so their letters to editors requesting recipes were answered, sometimes with amazing detail.

The recipe chosen here was one of these. It accomplished two things at once. It gave directions for making sauerkraut and suggested ways for cooking it. But best of all, it came directly from the country-side and was based on firsthand experience. The writer, whose identity was withheld in the original article, lived at Setzler's Store in Chester County, Pennsylvania. The recipe appeared under the heading of "Sour Krout" in the *Genesee Farmer* for September 1838.[157]

In the fall, after we have had two or three freezing nights, collect up as many solid heads of cabbage as you wish to preserve, salt up (say fifty for a family of 6 or 8 persons), take off all the green and imperfect leaves, cut each head lengthwise through the heart, and cut that clean out. A cabbage knife should now be procured on which the cabbage should be cut fine, and a strong cedar or other barrel, previously well soaked and cleaned at hand, the bottom of which to be laid over with cabbage leaves; fine salt now to be well mixed with portions of the cabbage in the proportion of a pint of the former to a heaped bushel of the latter, and these gradually packed in the barrel by gently stamping with a suitable wooden rammer. When the barrel is nearly full, it should be placed in a cool dry cellar, on boards, the bottom secured from pressing out; a barrel head or pieces of boards laid on the top of the cabbage, and a heavy weight laid on them. In a week or ten days the pickle should cover the cabbage, or a weak brine must be prepared and poured over, when fermentation will commence; and from this time to the end of the season, once a week, the froth should be

skimmed off, and the boards, weight, and sides of the barrel, cleanly washed. At the end of two weeks it will be fit to cook; and as much of its savoury and salutary quality depends on this, I will describe the manner I do it. I take up at a time as much as will make two messes (as warming up what is left the first day is no injury to it); put it in a tin boiler with a piece of fat pork; and, if I have it, a spoonful or two of goose or other dripping, and just sufficient water to boil nearly dry over a smart fire in 3 hours. Boiled potatoes should always be eaten along with sour krout, as alone it is too fat, cooked in this manner, to make a meal. The potatoes are better boiled in a separate vessel, but they can be boiled with the krout; though very apt to get heavy. Sour krout should be all used before the approach of warm weather, as the quantity of salt here recommended is too small to preserve it.

Those who wish to experiment with this recipe might be interested to know that the *Germantown Telegraph* for October 14, 1868, carried a similar article on making sauerkraut and noted the types of cabbage then generally in use. Savoy cabbage was considered the best by far in terms of the quality of sauerkraut it made. But as a plant, it was only half as productive as the "Drumhead" and "Flat Dutch" varieties. Thus, they were more popular with economy-minded cooks.

At one time, sauerkraut was viewed as one of the identifying foods that separated Pennsylvania Germans from their neighbors. Some writers have even gone so far as to suggest that one criterion for determining who is Pennsylvania Dutch and who is not is whether a person eats sauerkraut regularly. But this may be a piece of culinary chauvinism and little more. Nevertheless, sauerkraut is so intermeshed with Pennsylvania-German ethnic identity that it always makes its appearance anytime Pennsylvania-German foods are specifically called for. And, of course, during the Civil War, it gave birth to the name "Sauerkraut Yankees."

There is a twist of irony in this because history turned the joke around on the South. When Confederate troops captured Chambersburg in the summer of 1863, one of the first things the famished rebels demanded from the inhabitants were barrels of sauerkraut. The Dutch could only smile and shrug their shoulders. No one in his right mind made sauerkraut in the summer.

In the nineteenth century, sauerkraut was a cold-weather food. Sauerkraut with fresh pork was a fall dish. Sauerkraut with turkey was a Christmas dish. And sauerkraut with pork was eaten for good luck on New Year's Day, because, as the Dutch say, "the pig roots *forward*." Thus rooting forward into the new year, the Dutch ate sauerkraut with salt pork in the late winter, and finally, sauerkraut with fish in the early spring.

Generally, no matter what accompanied it, sauerkraut was thought best cooked plain. The method described in the recipe from Chester County was typical in this respect and not too different from the procedures found in eighteenth- and early nineteenth-century German cookbooks. For comparison, the following recipe is translated from Johann Fürst's *Simon Strüf*.[158] It appears to be based on a similar recipe in Friederike Löffler's *Handbuch für Frauenzimmer* of 1791.

To Cook Sauerkraut

Put good clean sauerkraut in water over the fire. Season it and let it simmer for two hours. In a sauce pan, heat some skimming grease, goose fat, drippings or pork lard. Sprinkle a little flour into it and let this turn straw color. (Onion lovers can also stir in a minced onion.) Add strong meat broth to this and then the sauerkraut, together with some of the liquid in which it cooked, so long as it is not too sour. If such is the case, ignore this step, pour off the liquid, and use more meat broth. Stir in more drippings or goose fat, if you have them, and let this cook together well.

9

Heady Punches and Small Beers

Fer was sollt mir schpaaren?
Kein Schetzel haben mir.
Das Geld, was mir versaufen,
Das haben mir nu nix!

Translation

If we don't have a honey,
why save our money?
The money we drink away
we never had anyway!

FROM AN OLD TAVERN SONG
"DRINKT, BUWE, DRINKT"

For Bacchus and common sense there are no substitutes. I need only quote the reliable, learned, and red-nosed Thomas Cooper for the Dutchy prognostication that a man "may eat or drink freely, without much precaution, and without more present inconvenience than what a good dose of magnesia may remove."[159] So in the face of a long and blessed history of stumbling feet and spinning heads, the hangover was one of the last of the grand maladies to exit from the Pennsylvania-German scene, or did it ever leave?

In his last will and testament, Johannes Weber, a well-to-do farmer who died near Lancaster in 1755, provided for his widow's thirst with an annual endowment of two bushels of malt for beer, two barrels of hard cider, two gallons of rum, and two gallons of peach brandy for the remainder of her life.

One may visualize the widow Weber with a rum sling in hand, giggling her way through quilting parties, spiking her son's pies with a smile, or dropping crockery all over the kitchen as that friendly cider warmed its way into her feet. But actually, with all due respect, this widow was no tippler. She was a quiet Mennonite, fond of riding, fond of her fine stone house, and fond of entertaining friends. It was simply that during the eighteenth century, most of the Pennsylvania Dutch were not abstainers, and a great many of them liked to imbibe more than once a day. This meant, of course, that sometimes some of them got out of hand.

Being the best distillers in the country, the Pennsylvania Dutch took part in the Whiskey Rebellion of 1794. It is said that federal intervention during that escapade turned many whiskey-loving Dutchmen into staunch Democrats. Like beer with pretzels, Berks County has mixed its whiskey with its Democrats ever since.

If Berks County could be called the heart of German Pennsylvania, then it follows that whiskey was its lifeblood. By whiskey, we mean *rye* whiskey, which was so common and so cheap in Pennsylvania that it was dispensed free to fieldhands, to customers in stores, to the crowds at "vendues," to the mourners at funerals, and to just about anyone who deserved special attention. Ministers inveighed against it, many a funeral was transformed into a drunken riot, and on some Sunday mornings, the aroma of rye was known to waft down from behind the pulpit.

Until the Civil War, the drinking habit was so much a part of Pennsylvania-German life that it was simply taken for granted. But to-

day, after a century or so of the Temperance Movement in our rural churches, it is difficult to imagine that this land of plenty was also a land of cordial shops and distilleries, of jolly country inns, of cake-and-mead shops, of beer gardens and vineyards. In a hundred years, all of this was swept away.

One of the earliest Pennsylvania-German works on the subject of alcoholic beverages was *Die wahre Brantwein-Brennerey; oder, Brantwein- Gin- und Cordialmacher-Kunst* (The True Brandy Distillery; or, the Art of Brandy, Gin, and Cordial Making) published in York in 1797. Although mostly a translation of English recipes, the German text is interesting for its use of the old Pennsylvania-German term for whiskey: *Dram.* Some of the other beverages would be considered odd today—lemon cordial, for example—but the recipe for cherry ratafia was none other than a model for Pennsylvania-style cherry bounce (recipe 134). Over the years, this book was followed by a long list of Pennsylvania-German works on brewing, distilling, and viticulture.

Christian Becker's *Unterricht für amerikanische Bauern, Weinberge anzulegen und zu unterhalten* (Instructions to American Farmers on Laying Out and Maintaining Vineyards), published in Easton in 1809, was the first Pennsylvania-German work devoted exclusively to viticulture and winemaking. But long before 1809 viticulture seems to have been well established among the Pennsylvania Dutch, so the book did not contain any great revelations in its day.

During the 1820s, a number of writers on temperance, particularly among the Quakers, advocated wine as a moderate and more healthful alternative to ardent spirits. This reasoning gave Pennsylvania-German viticulture such a boost in the 1830s and 1840s that by the time *Die geschickte Hausfrau* was published, many small private vineyards were producing Isabella and "Madeira" wines for local consumption. Except for the once-famous "Reading Red" (similar to Swabian Ramsthaler), most of these wines were approximations, from good to passable, of the white Rhine wines the Pennsylvania Germans loved so well.

Nearly all of these wines could be purchased at local *Weischtuppe* (wine parlors), cafés, and beer gardens throughout German Pennsylvania. One of the most famous was Lauer's in Reading, described by "Der Alte vom Berge" in his letter to the *Philadelphier Demokrat* of June 12, 1850: "In the arcaded beer garden of Herr Lauer, one can see thousands of delightful roses and other flowers in full bloom; one can see the friendly faces of our Reading folk and those of visitors, who mingle in this paradise, here and there, to sip on drinks of wine or beer."

By 1848, locally made wines, beers, whiskeys, and cordials are regularly mentioned in Pennsylvania-German newspapers. Awards for the best vintage or brew were handed out nearly every year at county and state agricultural fairs. The more discerning drinker could also choose from a vast array of imported beverages at the local *Weischtohr* (wine shop), and if it did not have in stock the precise item requested, then it was easy enough to send to Philadelphia for whatever one wanted.

Jacob Snider of Philadelphia, a Pennsylvania-German "cheap wine merchant" who catered to a large Pennsylvania-Dutch clientele (perhaps because he would pay freight for out-of-town deliveries), advertised in the *Germantown Telegraph* for New Year's Day of 1851 that he was selling Duff, Gordon & Co. sherries on draft; Manzanillas by the gallon; Amontillados by the sixteen-gallon cask; Extra-Amontillados by the bottle; various port wines; such Madeiras as "South Side," old "East India," "Sereial," all on draft or in bottles; clarets; burgundies; sparkling Moselles and Rhine wines from the firm of Deinhard & Jordan of Coblenz; still Hocks and "choice Steinbergs"; and a huge inventory of brandies, ranging from Otard, Dupuy & Co., vintage 1800; and Clavier, vintages 1821 and 1842; to Dubouche, vintage 1844—all by the hogshead no less!

Other wine merchants, such as Peter Wager of South Seventh Street, also operated wine shops in many large Pennsylvania-German towns. Wager, for example, owned a German wine shop on Center Square in Lancaster during the 1850s.

Aside from Pennsylvania-German brewery taverns, wine parlors, and country inns, which were patronized almost exclusively by men, homemade wines, beers, small beers, meads, and cordials were also served in cake-and-mead shops. The cake-and-mead shop was a species of café or teahouse, usually operated by single women or widows who converted part of their residences into places of business. Called *Kucheheiser* in Pennsylvania Dutch, these shops cultivated a pleasant, homey atmosphere, with menus offering an assortment of baked goods, candies, and cheeses. They were patterned after the old "cake houses" once fashionable in Philadelphia during the early part of the eighteenth century. Since it was illegal under most local ordinances for women to enter oyster houses and other drinking establishments patronized by men, it was here in the cake-and-mead shops that Pennsylvania-German women, their children, and even teenagers would gather to socialize, especially on fair days, such as Second Christmas (December 26) and Whitmonday (the day after Pentecost)—the unofficial beginning of summer in Pennsylvania-German folk culture.

On Whitmonday, girls put on new summer bonnets and went out with their beaux to a cake-and-mead shop for beer and a bite to eat.

But if a boy's father took him to the local tavern, then trysting at the cake-and-mead shop was over, for now he was accepted by the community as a man. If his girl friend valued her reputation, she would not follow him into the tavern unless escorted. Otherwise, she would become fair game for the amorous advances of any male present, and doubtless also subject to fine. This is probably why most Pennsylvania-German girls would not even consider going into a tavern, except perhaps to attend a chaperoned dance, a wedding, or some other community function. The Pennsylvania Germans were always rather strict about this division of drinking between the sexes, and these attitudes may be traced to Old World folk traditions.

Except for the *Glickdrinke*, or toasts—usually a table wine—weddings were generally low key, private, and more like suppers than lavish parties. Thus, drinking on fair days was exceeded only by the festivities of the militia muster and the funeral. At these events, beer and hard liquor were served in generous quantities, with rye whiskey and its more popular "improvement," cherry bounce, taking the lead over all other ardent spirits.

The great funeral banquet in particular was something Pennsylvania Germans looked forward to all their lives. In one grand debut, a simple farmer could make his mark in this world by leaving it. Tongues flapped, obituaries waxed poetic, and the Dutchman's soul, as one wag put it, was usually too soused to get into Heaven until after the vendue of his worldly goods.

In Christian Becker's *Sprachlehrer* of 1808 (the same Becker who wrote the first Pennsylvania-German book on viticulture), there is a conversation exercise between an innkeeper and a customer. The inn-

Battalion Day in Pennsylvania

keeper asks the customer if he would care to have his beer warmed, and in response, he is told: "Yes, warm it a little."[160]

Among the Pennsylvania Germans, it was customary to drink certain wines, most beers, and all liquors at room temperature or warmer. This included mixed drinks, such as punch and cider royal, as well as the numerous "slings," which were usually served piping hot. The *Schling*, from *schlingen*, "to swallow," was a German contribution as far as terminology was concerned and perhaps even in concept. In any case, the classic Pennsylvania-German slings were made by adding sugar and nutmeg to some sort of strong liquor and heating the mixture with a hot poker. It was necessary, then, to serve slings in heavy earthenware mugs. Only during the last half of the nineteenth century did the cold sling make its appearance in German Pennsylvania with other iced drinks. From the standpoint of health, cold drinks and crushed ice were considered unhealthy and therefore verboten.

As for the drinks in *Die geschickte Hausfrau*, the selection is modest in contrast to John Marquart's *600 Miscellaneous Valuable Receipts* (Lebanon, 1860), which included ninety-three recipes for alcoholic beverages, most of them ardent spirits or fruit brandies. Yet it is evident that, however modest, the recipes in *Die geschickte Hausfrau* were chosen to satisfy a wide variety of tastes. All of them were suitable for serving in cake-and-mead shops, and three of them could be classified as temperance drinks. Taken as a whole, the selection of beverages favored the Hausfrau over the tastes of her husband, which should be expected in a cookbook of this sort.

129. Spruce Beer
(Sprossen-Bier)

Mix 10 gallons of water, ¼ pound of hops, and 1 small teacup of ginger in a large kettle. Boil these ingredients until all the hops sink to the bottom. Then draw off a bucket of liquid and add 6 quarts of molasses and 3½ ounces of spruce essence. When the molasses and essence have completely dissolved, pour this back into the kettle, and then run it all through a hairsieve into a keg. Add ½ pint of good, strong yeast, and let this work 2 days. Then stop up the keg, and the next day, pour the beer into jugs or bottles. It should be ready to use in 1 week's time.

Instead of spruce essence, 2 pounds of small spruce twigs can be used if they are boiled 10 minutes in the liquid above.

To make spruce beer for immediate use, and not quite so much of it, boil 1 handful of hops in 2½ gallons of water until they sink to the bottom. Then strain the water, and when it is lukewarm, add 1 spoonful of powdered white ginger, 1 pint of molasses, 1 tablespoon of spruce essence, and ½ pint of yeast. Mix this thoroughly, and let it work in a stone crock 1½ to 2 days. Then pour it into bottles, each containing 3 or 4 raisins. This beer will be ready to drink in a very short time.

A cake-and-mead shop

During the eighteenth century, spruce beer was considered a diet drink by the English, and for this reason, it was never supposed to be intoxicating.

While the origin of spruce beer may be difficult to pinpoint, it is clear from historic evidence that it is extremely ancient in northern Europe, so there is no question that the very first European settlers in America knew about it. It was probably introduced in Pennsylvania by the Swedes and Finns, who settled along the Delaware many years before the English laid claim to the region.

According to John Marquart, two varieties of spruce beer were popular among the Pennsylvania Germans: one made with white spruce and the other with brown. By the 1850s, both were regular picnic standbys. Since fermentation was never allowed to go far enough to produce any great amount of alcohol, spruce beers were perfect refreshments for small children, who loved the bubbles, as well as for abstainers, who promoted them as temperance drinks.

130. Ginger Beer
(Imber-Bier)

Work 1½ pounds of loaf sugar to a fine powder, and mix it thoroughly with 3 ounces of white ginger and the grated rinds of 2 lemons. Place these ingredients in a stone crock and pour 2 gallons of boiling water over them. When this has become milk warm, strain it and add the juice of the lemons and 2 large tablespoons of strong yeast. Make the beer in the evening, let it stand overnight, then, the next morning, pour the beer into stone jugs and tie down the corks tightly with string.

Ginger was one of the earliest Eastern spices known to Europeans. It is even mentioned in the Anglo-Saxon Leech Books. Historically, ginger came in two basic forms: dry and "green." The green ginger was usually candied in sugar or honey, somewhat like modern crystalized ginger.

As a beverage, ginger beer was one of those late medieval drinks that survived the rising popularity of ardent spirits during the seventeenth and eighteenth centuries. Like spruce beer, it was made almost everywhere in northern Europe. Today in the United States, it is sold as ginger ale, an unfermented, artificially flavored drink that is quite inferior to old-fashioned ginger beer.

Among the Pennsylvania Germans, ginger beer was a popular refreshment in temperance families, who might often serve it to their fieldhands in lieu of whiskey. Beyond that, it was generally considered a drink for old people and children, hence its classification as a "small" beer. It was also listed among those drinks allowed the sick, who were thought to benefit from the medicinal virtues of the ginger.

131. Molasses Beer
(Syrup-Bier)

To 6 quarts of water, add 2 quarts of molasses, ½ pint of the best brewer's yeast, 2 tablespoons of powdered ginger, and 1 tablespoon of cream of tartar. Mix this thoroughly, let it stand 12 hours, then pour it into bottles into which 3 or 4 raisins have been placed. Instead of a spoonful of ginger, one may add the juice and finely grated rind of a large lemon, which much improves it. However, this beer keeps only 2 or 3 days.

According to George Girardey, spruce beer and molasses beer were the same thing, the latter merely lacking spruce essence for flavoring. Thus, being the simpler of the two, molasses beer was also the more popular. In fact, during the seventeenth and eighteenth centuries, homemade molasses beer was one of the most popular light beverages in rural Pennsylvania. West Indian molasses was cheap, and before the establishment of breweries outside of Philadelphia, molasses beer was sometimes the only form of beer country people could obtain; hence, the many complaints about its uneven quality.

In commenting on the small beers sold in Philadelphia, the author of *The Complete Family Brewer* (1805) has this to say about molasses beer:[161]

> As to treacle beer, I shall say very little; but let it speak for itself, only this, it is preferable to that sold at the Hucksters' shops in Philadelphia; I am persuaded they would have more custom if they were to sell it instead of the rot-gut stuff, imposed on them by their Brewers under the name of small beer; and with this advantage too, they may make it themselves for half the price.

Its cheapness undoubtedly made molasses beer attractive to the budget-minded Hausfrau, who realized its obvious advantages early in the eighteenth century.

In a German account of Pennsylvania published in Frankfurt in 1728, the author described molasses beer as "an exceedingly pleasant and thirst-quenching beverage, which tastes better to me than the pure water. This beer is composed of water, molasses, and hops, together with some wheat bran."[162] He took pains to mention it because molasses beer was not generally known in Germany. It was one of the very first beverages German settlers assimilated from the English when they came to Pennsylvania.

132. Currant Wine
(*Johannisbeer-Wein*)

White currants

Take 4 gallons of currants, stem them, and mash them with a long stick in a stone crock. Let this stand well covered for 24 hours. Then put the currants in a large linen bag and press the juice out. Next, boil 2½ gallons of water and 5½ pounds of the best loaf sugar, and skim it well. When no more scum forms, mix the currant juice with the syrup, and let it stand 2 or 3 weeks. Then pour it into another crock, but be careful not to stir up the sediment. Should the wine fail to become completely bright and clear, take 1 quart of it and dissolve the whites of 2 eggs and ½ ounce of cream of tartar in it, [first] beating the eggs to a stiff foam, then pouring it all into the keg gradually. After 10 days, pour this wine into bottles, which should be stored in sawdust. After a year the wine will be drinkable, but it will be very good after 3 or 4 years. One quart of brandy can also be added to [each] 6 gallons of wine.

The Pennsylvania Germans call currants *Kannsdrauwe*, which is dialect for *Johannestrauben*, or "St. John's grapes." Currants were given this folk name because they usually ripened by St. John's Day, or June 24th.

Currant wine was a traditional folk beverage in northern Europe, particularly in areas where viticulture did not thrive. The Pennsylvania Dutch brought this Old World love of currants with them to Pennsylvania, for nearly every Pennsylvania-German book on winemaking also mentions currant wine.

Currant wine was no less popular in rural England. Eighteenth-century cookbooks were full of instructions for making it, and the very best grade, made from white currants, was often called "English champagne." This is probably where Johann Georg Hohman got the idea for his Pennsylvania-Dutch recipe "equal to champagne," which he published in his *Land- und Haus-Apotheke* (House and Country Apothecary: Reading, 1818). I supply Hohman's recipe for comparative purposes, and also because it was extremely popular.[163]

To Make from Currants an Exceedingly Good Wine, Equal to Champagne

Take good, ripe currants, or half currants and half gooseberries, remove the stems, and press them in a fruit or wine press; lacking that, on a narrow board in a strong linen bag, using a rod as one would work out honey. When the berries are duly pressed, add the same quantity of pure spring or well water as juice, quart for quart, as required. For each quart of the water and juice mixture, add 1½ pounds of coarse loaf sugar, or some other ordinary sugar. If you intend to use this wine within the year, then you need use only a half pound of sugar to each quart instead. This must then be placed in a cask previously well scoured and fumigated with a nutmeg. But first cut the sugar into small pieces and then pour it, with the liquid, into the cask. When the cask is full, take it to a cellar and lay it on a sturdy rack where it must lie still without the slightest movement. After the course of some hours, or at most, the next day, this wine will begin to ferment. Once it has completely fermented, the cask should be filled again with additional pressing that has been reserved for this purpose in a jug. The bung is again closed, but not tightly, so that some air can be let into the cask until all sound of fermentation has ceased. Not until then is the bung driven in tight and the cask sufficiently secured. The wine should now remain in the cask without being touched or moved in the least until February of the following year, when it must be bottled off. At that time the following should be observed exactly: 1) That this wine must not be tapped with the usual bung, but with a quill; 2) That you guard against tapping the cask too low toward the bottom so that no lees get into the bottles; hence, the safest way to proceed is to tap the cask in the very beginning near the middle, and then tap progressively lower from time to time until the wine begins to show cloudiness.

The bottles must be well cleaned, and the day before using,

washed out with French brandy, then turned upside down so that nothing of the brandy remains in them. Once the wine is drawn off, the bottles should not be tightly stopped, although they must be watched closely because by very tight corking, they are certain to explode. After some days, when no more evidence of fermentation is detected in the wine, the bottles can be tightly corked and set very gently on dry shelves in the cellar. A wine prepared in this manner is often preferred by the greatest connoisseurs to the finest Madeira, to which it has a very great resemblance. Regarding the storage of currant wine, it should also be noted that when the currant bush is blooming [the following spring], this wine will begin to work again and then a little air must be let in by loosening the corks. Also, the bottles should never be filled above the neck.

This was the recipe of the same George Hohman, song peddler and occult healer, who compiled the famous Pennsylvania-German witchcraft book called *Der lange verborgene Freund* (The Long Lost Friend: Reading, 1820).

133. Mead
(Sommer-Bier)

To each gallon of hot water, add 5 pounds of honey, and let this boil ¾ hour, skimming it frequently. Then add hops tied up in a little bag (approximately 1 ounce or handful to each gallon) and boil ½ hour more. Run the beer through a strainer into a pot and let it stand 4 days. Then put it in a little keg or large stone jug, and to each gallon, add a gill of brandy and 1 chopped lemon. If the keg is large, do not bottle the beer until it has stood for 1 year.

This ancient and heady drink was originally made with the washings of honeycombs after the honey had been removed. In western England and Wales, mead was a winter drink, usually made in the early fall in order to have it ready by Christmas.[164] In Pennsylvania, however, it was a summer drink, hence the Pennsylvania-Dutch name: *Sommerbier*.

During the nineteenth century, mead was served at every Pennsylvania-German county fair and was always on tap in cake-and-mead shops, such as the widow Housum's in Chambersburg, famous during the 1840s for its good food and drink. Although the sign by her door proclaimed "Ale and Porter, Small Beer, Mead and Cakes," it was the widow's mead that drew them in like flies. We have been left with this pleasant description of it in John Cooper's *Recollections of Chambersburg* (1900):

> [Her] mead was a sparkling and very palatable beverage, when at the proper stage of ripeness, but when it got much beyond that stage, the drinker needed to keep his mouth open and his head thrown back if he did not wish to risk serious consequences, for if he kept his mouth closed, the rush of gas through his nose would produce a snort furious enough to scare a war horse.

134. Cherry Bounce
(Kirschen-Brandwein)

Put 6 pounds of ripe morello cherries and 6 pounds of large oxheart cherries in a wooden tub and mash them with a hammer until all the pits are broken. Add 3 pounds of white sugar to the cherries, and put them in a stone jug or large bottle. Add 2 gallons of the best double-distilled whiskey, and shake the bounce every day for the first month. At the end of 3 months, draw the bounce off into bottles. The longer it stands, the better it becomes.

There is probably no other Pennsylvania-German beverage that is now surrounded by so much lore as cherry bounce. *Baunz* or *Bauns*, as it is called in dialect, was almost as popular as the rye whiskey with which it was made, and in some places, it was drunk more freely and more openly than anything else. One needs no imagination to picture the results of John Badollet's visit with a Pennsylvania-German family in the wilds of central Pennsylvania in 1793. He wrote in his diary: "I spent the day as merry as I could, treated with wine by a rich Swizer, drinking cherry bounce & beer in the intervals."[165] Merry indeed! I cannot think of a deadlier combination than those three drinks.

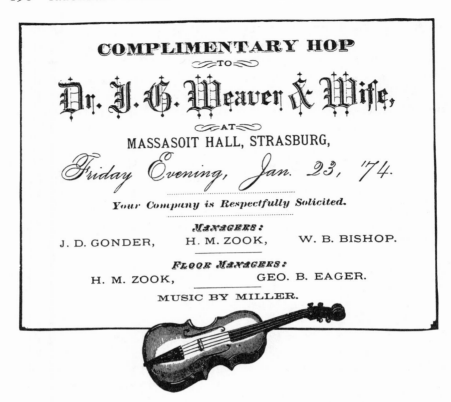

As a social drink, *Baunz* was served everywhere, much to the righteous discomfort of the temperance advocates. One nervous Victorian complained that "its use, as a drink, is attended with even more pernicious effects than plain brandy, rum or spirits. It is often made use of by females as a cordial, and besides destroying the health of their digestive organs, too often has led to habits of confirmed drunkenness."[166]

Bounce was originally an English approximation of Italian cherry ratafia. In England, it was generally a less elaborate affair made by infusing cherries in rectified spirits, often rum. Cordial waters, such as ratafia and sloe gin, became popular among the English upper classes in the seventeenth century. Judging from the method used to make *Baunz*, it is evident that the Pennsylvania-Dutch versions were based on older English models rather than on somewhat similar peasant drinks in Germany.

In Germany, it was common practice to infuse cherries or other fruit in brandy as a substitute for the more expensive fruit *Geist*, such as *Kirschwasser*, or cherry spirits. The similarity between the German fruit brandies and the English cordial waters may have been one important factor in the popularity of cherry bounce among the Pennsylvania Dutch. But perhaps more importantly, it was also the cheapness of the main ingredients. Rye whiskey was commonly distilled at home, and wild cherries were available everywhere. Because of their characteristic flavor, wild cherries were perfect in bounce, better even than the cherries called for in the recipe above. If allowed to infuse in the liquor for a year or more before straining off, they could produce a bounce tasting curiously like rich Madeira. Being heavy and sweet, bounce made with rye and wild cherries was a perfect accompaniment to those intensely chocolate cakes that some Pennsylvania-Dutch housewives called "Gugelhoops."

135. Punch
(Punsch)

Using your hand, roll 12 nice lemons on a table, then shave the rinds quite thin and boil them in 1 gallon of water until all the flavor is drawn out. Then place 2 pounds of fine white sugar in a large bowl and squeeze the juice of the lemons over it. After the water has boiled sufficiently, let it drain through a cloth. Add this to the lemon juice and sugar, and stir in 1 quart of rum or good whiskey.

Although we now use the word punch rather indiscriminately, at one time its meaning was more specific. Punch was a mixed drink made with lemons and spirits and was not generally served on ice until after the 1820s. In taste, it was something akin to a tepid whiskey or rum sour, or a bit like an old-fashioned English lemon shrub.

A shrub usually contained tea, and all of George Girardey's punches at least had this one ingredient in common. The ingredients in his "French Punch," however, are the most interesting, since they reproduce the recipe of the drink that originally gave punch its name.[167]

George Girardey's French Punch

Put 1 pound of white sugar and 2 sliced lemons in a bowl. Stir in 1 quart of hot tea and 1 pint of good arrack or rum, and mix this together well. Drink warm.

Punch came to colonial America not with the French, but with the English, who brought it in turn from India, where it was known as *panch*, meaning five, in reference to its five basic ingredients: arrack, tea, water, sugar, and lemons. In Pennsylvania, brandy or rum was almost universally substituted for the arrack, and, in conformity with local taste, a handful of juniper berries was added to the hot tea to give it an aromatic flavor.

Even in William Penn's time, punch was a beverage associated with taverns and hospitality among upper-class gentlemen. Among the well to do, it was common practice in the eighteenth century to have a tankard of punch made in the morning and placed in a cooler, if the weather were hot. Gentlemen visitors were invited to help themselves if they so desired. This custom never caught on among the Pennsylvania Germans. Even punch bowls were rare in Pennsylvania-Dutch inventories. But punch did become standard fare at many country taverns, where it remained strictly a man's drink, meant to be accompanied by a pipe of tobacco and talk of politics and the crops.

136. Mulled Cider
(Glüh-Wein)

Each quart of cider requires 6 eggs. [First,] add a handful of cloves to the cider and let it boil. While it is boiling, beat the eggs in a large jug and add enough sugar to make the cider very sweet. Then pour the boiling cider over the beaten eggs, and proceed to pour this mixture back and forth from one jug to the other until a fine foam forms. Then pour it warm into glasses and grate some nutmeg over it.

Contrary to the name given this recipe in the German, it is not *Glüh-Wein*, or mulled wine. Mulled cider, however, it is, and it was one of the most commonly requested drinks at Pennsylvania-Dutch social gatherings. Second Christmas (December 26) was one occasion in particular when mulled cider appeared in quantity, because that was the day the Belschnicklers went mumming from house to house.

These Belschnicklers were usually young men dressed in grotesque costumes who were an annual terror to small children and old maids. Yet it was all in fun, for the custom was to invite them in and serve mulled cider, perhaps even a cherry sling (made with hot cherry bounce), and, of course, always a few Christmas cakes. After several houses and many drinks later, the Belschnicklers would grow a bit rowdy, and some of them were known to shoot off guns and cause considerable mischief.

If mischief were not enough, some hosts with hybrid tastes would add a healthy slug of apple jack to the cider, thus converting it into lethal *Seitereil*, a fogger of many brains known in English as cider royal.

137. Egg Punch
(Eyer-Punsch)

Beat the whites and yolks of 6 eggs separately. Stir the yolks into 1 quart of rich milk and sweeten it with ½ pound of sugar. Then add ½ pint of rum or brandy. Season this with 1 grated nutmeg, then slowly fold in the beaten egg whites.

Like punch, egg punch (or eggnog) was yet another English social drink that was popular among the Pennsylvania Dutch. Although this recipe is based (almost verbatim) on George Girardey's *Familie Eier Warm*, an eggnog that was served *hot* from the punch bowl,[168] Johann Christian Eupel also published nearly the same thing in his *Vollkommene Conditor* (The Complete Confectioner: Ilmenau, 1823), a cookery book sold in Pennsylvania during the 1820s and 1830s. He called it *Eierpunsch*, which is how it usually appeared in German cookbooks. Mulled eggs, or eggnog, was extremely popular in Germany because it was basically a variation of *Glühwein*. The following recipe is provided for comparison.[169]

Eupel's Mulled Wine

Whisk 4 whole eggs and 4 egg yolks in a pan. Work this up into a foam and then add 2 measures of ordinary white wine. Next, add 6 ounces of sugar and a small stick of cinnamon, and beat this over a low fire until it foams up.

---

138. An Excellent Small Beer
(Vortreffliches Schmall-Bier)

Take 1 quart bottle of the best Porter, add 4 quarts of water, 1 pint of molasses, and a teaspoon of ginger. Pour this into bottles, which must be corked tightly, and in 3 or 4 days it will be ready to use.

As beverages, small beers were considered harmless, although sometimes Fish Berry (*Cocculus indicus*) was added to make them hallucinogenic, much to the scandal of abstainers. Since the author of *The Complete Family Brewer* made rather indiscriminate use of these berries in many of his recipes, we may conclude that this dangerous practice had its army of adherents as well as its critics. The harmless species, however, was served on occasions when we would normally

Der

vollkommene Conditor,

oder

gründliche Anweisung

zur Zubereitung aller Arten Bonbons, Stangenzucker,
Conserven, Zuckerkuchen, Essenzpasten, Gefrornen,
Cremes, Gelees, Marmeladen, Compotts u. s. w., so
wie auch zum Einmachen und Glasiren der Früchte,
nebst Abhandlungen vom Zucker, den Graden bei dem
Zuckerkochen und von den zur Conditorei nöthigen
Gefäßen und Geräthschaften,

imgleichen

erprobte Vorschriften und Rezepte

zu allen Gattungen der

Kunstbäckerei,

als zu Torten, Makronen, Marzipan, Biscuit, Auf=
läufen, Leb = oder Pfefferkuchen, Hohllippen, Hobel=
spähnen, Schmalz und anderm Backwerk, so wie auch den
schmackhaftesten Pasteten;

Ferner

zu den beliebtesten Arten

künstlicher Getränke und Chokoladen,

als zu den verschiedenen Obstweinen, Punschen, Eier=
punsch, Bischoff, Vin brulé, Nikus, Limonade, Mandel=
milch u. s. w. u. s. w.

von

Johann Christian Eupel,

Conditor in Gotha.

Dritte vermehrte und verbesserte Auflage.

Ilmenau, 1823.
Gedruckt und verlegt bei Bernhard Friedrich Voigt.

Copies of Eupel's popular confectionary cookbook were advertised for
sale in the Philadelphia *Amerikanischer Correspondent* for April 30,
1828.

serve carbonated soft drinks today—at outings, for example.

The *Sunbury American* of May 14, 1848, promised a long list of refreshments for a country militia muster on Battalion Day: "there will be plenty of extras on the grounds, in the shape of pretty girls, ginger cakes, small beer, peanuts and molasses candy." No doubt the small beer was sold to help settle those peanuts, ginger cakes, and molasses candies in the stomachs of the pretty but overindulgent maidens, for elsewhere, small beer was also known as *Krankbier*, or "sick" beer, a tonic for dyspeptics.

139. Lemonade
(*Lemonade*)

Squeeze the juice from 12 nice lemons over 1 pound of powdered sugar. Pour a little boiling water on the [lemon] rinds, and when this cools, stir it into the lemon juice and sugar, then store the lemonade in bottles. To each ½ pint of water, use 1 wineglass of lemon juice.

Lemon press

Lemons were extremely important to the Pennsylvania Germans, and lemonade in particular was of great use both as a summer drink and as a home remedy. Lemons were so precious that many Pennsylvania Germans resorted to growing lemon trees in pots, but there never seemed to be enough lemons to go around.

Those who did not have pots and sun porches (or patience and green thumbs!) had to buy "market" lemons imported from Spain or Portugal. But in order to preserve them in those days before refrigeration, it was necessary to store the lemons, stems down, in boxes of sand, which were then kept in a cool cellar.

Since the curative properties of lemonade were unquestioned in the nineteenth century, it is not surprising that lemons, lemon juice, and sugar, in various combinations, appeared prominently among the Pennsylvania-Dutch home remedies found in L. W. Weber's *Der kluge Land-Medicus* (The Shrewd Country Doctor), published in Chambersburg in 1846. It was in this vein, during hot summer weather when parents were drinking beer or a spot of something headier, that lemonade was served as a tonic to the children, the Pennsylvania-Dutch way: flavored with a sprig of tansy.

Of course, the story of Pennsylvania-German cookery does not end with a sprig of tansy—nor does the original *Geschickte Hausfrau*. The last few recipes, devoted to such household chores as making wallpaper paste and soap, ended with a recipe for fruit vinegar in the first edition of 1848. But this was replaced in 1851 with a wash formula that made fabulous promises about washday savings. By today's standards, it would terrorize even the bravest pair of dishpan hands. The formula came from Sheffield, England, but because New York hucksters were selling it for $1.00 (as though a great secret), Aunt Pall saw to it that it got into print, and there it remained in *Die geschickte Hausfrau* until the book went out of fashion. In her very last letter to *Der amerikanische Bauer*, Aunt Pall complained about this and other washday woes and noted that it was always *men* who invented the wash formulas but women who did the washing. She said she was fed up drudging all day long for the male half of humanity and declared that since it was a man's world after all, she would simply stop writing letters, "bei Tschimmini," because women would get nowhere until men started washing their own dirty linen. With that, Aunt Pall went back to her teapots and tubs.

Measurements

Doubtless there are a number of readers who would like to experiment with the recipes in this book. With so many recipes gathered from such a wide variety of sources, it is almost impossible to provide a standard system of measure that will apply to every situation. However, one of the most useful measurement charts I have seen for period German-American recipes was published in the 1904 edition of *German National Cookery for American Kitchens*, by Henrietta Davidis. For greater convenience, her table of measurements is reproduced here.

Table of Measures

2 saltspoonfuls	make	1 coffeespoonful.
2 coffeespoonfuls	"	1 teaspoonful.
4 teaspoonfuls (liquid)	"	1 tablespoonful.
3 teaspoonfuls (dry)	"	1 tablespoonful.
4 tablespoonfuls (liquid)	"	1 wineglassful.
2 tablespoonfuls (liquid)	"	1 ounce.
2 wineglassfuls	"	1 gill.
2 gills (or ½ pint)	"	1 cupful.
2 cupfuls	"	1 pint.
4 cupfuls	"	1 quart.
1 cupful butter (solid)	makes	½ pound.
1 cupful granulated sugar	"	½ pound.
1 round tablespoonful butter	"	1 ounce.
1 heaping teaspoonful sugar	"	1 ounce.
1 ounce salt	"	1 teaspoonful.
1 quart sifted flour	"	1 pound.

A dash of pepper is ¼ saltspoonful.

Notes

1. Fred Lewis Pattee, *The House of the Black Ring*, p. 1.
2. William Woys Weaver, *"Die geschickte Hausfrau,"* pp. 343–63.
3. William H. Egle, "Gustav Sigismund Peters," p. 311.
4. Alfred L. Shoemaker, "Biographical Sketches of the Dauphin County Publishers," p. 8.
5. Looft was sold both by the Sauers of Germantown and by Anton Armbruster. The first edition of Looft appeared in 1755.
6. A biographical sketch of Friederike Löffler by Hans-Christoph Bernhard appeared as a "Nachwort" to a 1977 facsimile edition of Löffler's cookbook. That edition was published by J. F. Steinkopf of Stuttgart.
7. Advertisements for most of the early editions of Löffler's cookbook can be found in Pennsylvania-German newspapers. The German Society of Pennsylvania possesses a copy of the 1824 edition. The 1826 edition was advertised in many issues of the Philadelphia *Amerikanischer Correspondent*.
8. J. C. Myers, *Sketches on a Tour Through the Northern and Eastern States*, pp. 436–37.
9. A biography of Beck appears in *Der deutsche Pionier* 13 (July 1881):166–67. This was later reprinted in Rattermann's *Deutsch-Amerikanisches Biographikon*.
10. "Brief von Aent Ball!", p. 211.
11. Ibid.
12. "Kumbish," George Girardey, *Höchst nützliches Handbuch über Kochkunst*, p. 4.
13. Albert Hauser, *Vom Essen und Trinken im alten Zürich*, p. 42.
14. Marianne Kaltenbach, *Ächti schwizer Chuchi*, p. 37.
15. Hugo Moser, *Schwäbischer Volkshumor*, pp. 236–39.
16. Gottlieb Mittelberger, *Gottlieb Mittelberger's Journey to Pennsylvania in the Year 1750*, p. 65.
17. Wilhelm Diehl, "Brief eines nach Amerika ausgewanderten Ehepaar aus Birkenau," pp. 83–86.
18. Hans-Jürgen Teuteberg, "Variations in Meat Consumption in Germany," pp. 131–40.
19. James T. Lemon, *The Best Poor Man's Country*, pp. 166–67.
20. Girardey, *Handbuch*, p. 73.
21. Hans Wiswe, *Kulturgeschichte der Kochkunst*, pp. 216–17.
22. Elizabeth Drinker, *Extracts from the Journal of Elizabeth Drinker*, p. 31.
23. Isaac Clarence Kulp, "A Dunker Weekend Love Feast of 100 Years Ago," p. 4.
24. Marcus Looft, *Nieder-Sächsisches Koch-Buch*, p. 151.
25. Girardey published a recipe in his *Handbuch* (see Girardey's p. 76); another recipe appeared in *Der amerikanische Bauer* 2(1851):298.
26. *The Kitchen Companion*; see the recipe for roast veal. (*The Kitchen Companion* is unpaginated.)
27. Girardey, *Handbuch*, p. 58.
28. Henrietta Davidis, *Praktisches Kochbuch für die Deutschen in Amerika*, p. 139.
29. Friederike Löffler, *Oekonomisches Handbuch für Frauenzimmer*, pp. 40–41.
30. H. L. Barnum, *Family Receipts*, p. 171.
31. Charles Elmé Francatelli, *The Modern Cook*, p. 193.
32. Girardey, *Handbuch*, p. 83.
33. Ibid., p. 30.
34. Edith M. Thomas, *Mary at the Farm and Cook Recipes Compiled During Her Visit Among the "Pennsylvania Germans,"* p. 251.

35. James Allport, "Diary," May 8, 1828.
36. Friederike Löffler, *Neues Kochbuch*, p. 277. This is the old cookbook under a new title.
37. Girardey, *Handbuch*, p. 26.
38. [Friederike Löffler,] *Vollständiges Kochbuch für die deutsch-amerikanische Küche*, p. 67.
39. Hannah Glasse, *The Art of Cookery Made Plain and Easy*, p. 281.
40. Anna Fürst, *Vollständiges Kochbuch für alle Stände*, p. 388.
41. *Lancaster Journal* (Lancaster, Pa.), Nov. 18, 1818.
42. Elizabeth Nicholson, *The Economical Cook and House-Book*, p. 18.
43. For a typical recipe in an easily accessible source, see Hans Karl Adam, *German Cookery*, p. 56.
44. Correspondence with Anke Wijnsma, Head Librarian, Rijksmuseum voor Volkskunde "Het Nederlands Openluchtmuseum"; specifically, letter to William Woys Weaver, dated Arnhem, June 9, 1982.
45. Marcus Lambert, *A Dictionary of the Non-English Words of the Pennsylvania-German Dialect*, pp. 117–18.
46. Henry Hexham, *A Copious English and Netherduytch Dictionarie*. See s.v. "scrape." (This work is unpaginated.)
47. John Marquart, *600 Miscellaneous Valuable Receipts*, p. 237.
48. *Pennsylvania State Grange Cook Book*, p. 155.
49. Richard Bradley, *General Treatise of Husbandry and Gardening*, vol. 1, pp. 115–16.
50. See, for example, H. Brockmann-Jerosch, *Schweizer Bauernhaus*, pp. 44–47; and Karl Baumgarten, *Das deutsche Bauernhaus*, p. 151.
51. William Woys Weaver, "A Blacksmith's 'Summerkich,'" pp. 22–26.
52. "Curing and Smoking Hams," *Germantown Telegraph*, Nov. 12, 1851.
53. Alfred L. Shoemaker, *Christmas in Pennsylvania*, pp. 31–34.
54. Jean Anthelme Brillat-Savarin, *The Physiology of Taste*, pp. 55–61.
55. Girardey, *Handbuch*, pp. 76–77.
56. "Days and Times," *Rules of Discipline of the Yearly Meeting of Friends* (Philadelphia, 1843), pp. 26–28.
57. Friedrich Schwarzentruber, *Eine ernste Betrachtung über die übertriebenen Mahlzeiten und Hochzeiten*, p. 4.
58. Phebe Earle Gibbons, *The "Pennsylvania Dutch" and Other Essays*, p. 47.
59. Henry D. Paxon, "The Last of the Wild Pigeons in Bucks County," pp. 367–82.
60. Girardey, *Handbuch*, p. 95.
61. Emma Seifert Weigley, *Sarah Tyson Rorer*, p. 73.
62. Wiswe, *Kulturgeschichte der Kochkunst*, p. 192.
63. This recipe was discovered in the back of an old German prayer book once belonging to the Zimmerman (Carpenter) family of Germantown.
64. Jacob Biernauer, *Das unentbehrliche Haus- und Kunst-Buch*, p. 29.
65. Alfred L. Shoemaker, "Semi-Annual Fairs," p. 2.
66. Girardey, *Handbuch*, p. 96.
67. William J. Buck, *History of Montgomery County*, p. 12.
68. William Woys Weaver, "La Chapelle's Fish with Sauerkraut," p. 63.
69. Löffler, *Oekonomisches Handbuch*, p. 76.
70. Schwarzentruber, *Betrachtung*, p. 4.
71. *Die cölner Köchinn*, pp. 29–30.
72. Girardey, *Handbuch*, pp. 108–9.
73. A. F. M. Willich, *The Domestic Encyclopedia*, vol. 3, ed. James Mease (Philadelphia, 1804), p. 504. He calls tomatoes "love apples."
74. Robert Buist, *The Family Kitchen Gardener*, pp. 125–26.
75. Thomas Bridgeman, *The Young Gardener's Assistant* (New York, 1835), p. 79.
76. Bridgeman, ibid. (New York, 1858), p. 100.
77. Günter Wiegelmann, *Alltags- und Festspeisen*, pp. 230–32.
78. Don Yoder, "Folk Cookery," p. 334.
79. Christian Becker, *Der Deutschen allgegenwärtiger Englischer Sprachlehrer des Wortes Gottes*, p. 139.

80. Thomas Hill, "Journey on Horseback from New Brunswick, N. J. to Lycoming County, Pennsylvania in 1799," pp. 176–79.
81. Solomon Gery, "Scrap Book," p. 169.
82. Looft, *Nieder-Sächsisches Koch-Buch*, p. 113–14.
83. Johann Evangelist Fürst, *Der verständige Bauer, Simon Strüf*, p. 176.
84. Kulp, "A Dunker Weekend Love Feast," pp. 2–9.
85. Thomas Cooper, "Domestic Cookery," in *The Domestic Encyclopedia*, vol. 3 (Appendix), p. 70.
86. Loofft, *Nieder-Sächsisches Koch-Buch*, pp. 109–10.
87. Johannes Reisner, "Scrap Book," p. 13.
88. Evelyn M. Acomb, ed., *The Revolutionary Journal of Baron Ludwig von Closen*, p. 119.
89. Richard Briggs, *The New Art of Cookery*, p. 54.
90. Anna Bergner, *Pfälzer Kochbuch*, pp. 51–52.
91. Girardey, *Handbuch*, pp. 17–18.
92. [Löffler,] *Vollständiges Kochbuch*, p. 48.
93. Hannah Bouvier Peterson, *The National Cook Book*, p. 145.
94. J. Thomas Huey, *The Household Treasure*, p. 120.
95. I. H. Mayer, *Domestic Economy*, p. 170.
96. Mary Smith, *The Complete House-keeper*, p. 241.
97. Briggs, *New Art of Cookery*, p. 427.
98. Maria Eliza Rundell, *A New System of Domestic Cookery*, p. 133.
99. Amelia Simmons, *American Cookery*, p. 32.
100. Master Sebastian, *Koch- und Kellermeisterey*, p. 41.
101. Wiegelmann, *Festspeisen*, pp. 131–34.
102. Anna Dorn, *Neuestes universal- oder grosses Wiener-Kochbuch*, p. 171.
103. Michel Morineau, "The Potato in the Eighteenth Century, pp. 17–36.
104. Wolfgang Kleinschmidt, "Die Einführung der Kartoffel in der Pfalz und in den angrenzenden Gebieten der ehemaligen Rheinprovinz," p. 210.
105. Hauser, *Essen und Trinken*, p. 50.
106. Thomas P. Cope, *Philadelphia Merchant*, p. 231.
107. Count Niemcewicz noted this in his journal for May 30, 1799. Several other visitors to Pennsylvania during this period also made similar observations. See Julian Ursyn Niemcewicz, *Under Their Vine and Fig Tree*, p. 215.
108. George A. Heffner, *The Youthful Wanderer*, pp. 120–21.
109. For the German origins of Pennsylvania-German baking habits, see Max Lohss, "Ofen und Herd in Württemberg," pp. 362–86.
110. John Umble, "The Amish Mennonites of Union County, Pennsylvania," p. 96.
111. Gibbons, *"Pennsylvania Dutch,"* p. 42.
112. Hannah Widdifield, *Widdifield's New Cook Book*, pp. 143–44.
113. Elizabeth Ellicott Lea, *Domestic Cookery*, p. 87.
114. Conrad Hagger, *Neues saltzburgisches Koch-Buch*, p. 278.
115. Ignatius Bratenwender, *Der kölnische Leckerfress*, pp. 103–4.
116. Simmons, *American Cookery*, p. 28.
117. Niemcewicz, *Under Their Vine and Fig Tree*, p. 118.
118. George Butz, *Peach Industry in Pennsylvania*, pp. 2–4.
119. Barbara Denlinger Leaman, *Cook Book and Diary*, p. 1.
120. Löffler, *Oekonomisches Handbuch*, pp. 447–48.
121. Josiah T. Marshall, *The Farmer's and Emigrant's Hand-Book*, p. 135.
122. Several informants born after 1900 have expressed these sentiments to me during the course of interviews, so this attitude evidently lingered into this century.
123. Peter Kalm, *Peter Kalm's Travels in North America*, vol. 2, pp. 516–17.
124. Alexander Graydon, *Memoirs of His Own Time*, p. 266.
125. Fred Kniffen, "The Outdoor Oven in Louisiana," pp. 25–35.
126. *Der neue amerikanische Landwirtschafts-Calender auf das Jahr 1854*, p. 11.
127. Wiswe, *Kulturgeschichte*, pp. 211–12.
128. Jakob F. Landis, *Lese und Prüfe*, p. 4.
129. *41 bewährte Recepte*, p. 30.
130. *The Family's Guide*, p. 5.

131. *Help for the Marthas*, p. 51.
132. Frances Harriet McDougall, *The Housekeeper's Book*, pp. 131–32.
133. Laura G. Abell, *The Skillful Housewife's Book*, p. 133.
134. Loofft, *Nieder-Sächsisches Koch-Buch*, pp. 424–25.
135. Jacob Graeff, "Reminiscences of Reading 70 Years Ago."
136. Johann Krauss, *Oeconomisches Haus- und Kunstbuch*, recipe 123. (This work is unpaginated.)
137. Wiswe, *Kulturgeschichte*, p. 146.
138. Karl Rhamm, *Ethnographische Beiträge zur germanisch-slawischen Alterthumskunde*, vol. 1, p. 139.
139. Herta Neunteufel, *Kochkunst im Barock*, p. 106.
140. *American Weekly Mercury* (Philadelphia), Dec. 29, 1719.
141. Alexander von Humboldt, *The Island of Cuba*, p. 258.
142. Girardey, *Handbuch*, p. 162.
143. Ibid., p. 159.
144. An excellent recipe for authentic Pennsylvania-German *Hutzelbrod* was published in *Der amerikanische Bauer* 3(1853):311.
145. "Byers Family Recipe Book," p. 82.
146. *Philadelphier Demokrat*, June 12, 1850.
147. *Der neue gemeinnützige Landwirthschafts Calender auf das Jahr 1798*, s.v. "Hausmittel." (This work is unpaginated.)
148. Marion Harland, *Common Sense in the Household*, p. 469.
149. Charles Hellstern, *Illustrirtes deutsch-amerikanisches Kochbuch*, no. 8, p. 361.
150. William Kitchiner, *The Cook's Oracle*, p. 43.
151. Smith, *Complete House-keeper*, p. 361.
152. Thomas F. DeVoe, *The Market Assistant*, p. 380.
153. Pat Parker, *WLTR Contributor's Cook Book*, p. 46.
154. Girardey, *Handbuch*, p. 4.
155. Ibid., pp. 164–65.
156. *Ceres* 1(September 1839):32.
157. "Sour Krout," p. 141.
158. Johann Fürst, *Simon Strüf*, p. 178.
159. Cooper, "Domestic Cookery," p. 73.
160. Becker, *Sprachlehrer*, p. 139.
161. *The Complete Family Brewer*, p. iv.
162. Julius Sachse, "A Missive from Pennsylvania in the Year of Grace 1728," p. 22.
163. Johann Georg Hohman, *Die Land- und Haus-Apotheke*, p. 57.
164. S. Minwel Tibbott, *Welsh Fare*, p. 81.
165. William A. Hunter, "John Badollet's 'Journal of the Time I Spent in Stoney Creek Glades, 1793–1794,'" p. 184.
166. E. G. Storke, *The Family, Farm and Gardens, and the Domestic Animals*, p. 169.
167. Girardey, *Handbuch*, p. 168.
168. Ibid., p. 167.
169. Johann Christian Eupel, *Der vollkommene Conditor*, p. 229.

Bibliography

Published Sources

Abell, Laura G. *The Skillful Housewife's Book*. New York: D. Newell, 1846.

Acomb, Evelyn M., ed. *The Revolutionary Journal of Baron Ludwig von Closen*. Chapel Hill: University of North Carolina Press, 1958.

Adam, Hans Karl. *German Cookery*. London/Cleveland: World Publishing Co., 1967.

Allentown Friedens-Bothe, December 12, 1850.

Allgemeines oeconomisches Lexicon. Leipzig: Johann Friedrich Gleditschens sel. Sohn, 1731.

Der amerikanische Bauer. Edited by Jacob M. Beck. 4 vols. Harrisburg, Pa.: Lutz and Scheffer, 1850–51; Scheffer and Beck, 1851–54.

Amerikanischer Correspondent für das In- und Ausland (Philadelphia), April 30, 1828.

The American Weekly Mercury (Philadelphia), December 29, 1719.

Appert, Nicolas. *L'art de conserver*. Paris: Patris et Cie., 1810.

Barnum, H. L. *Family Receipts*. Cincinnati: Lincoln & Co., 1831.

Baumgarten, Karl. *Das deutsche Bauernhaus*. Neumünster: Karl Wachholtz Verlag, 1980.

Beauvilliers, Antoine. *L'art du cuisinier*. 2 vols. Paris: Pillet, 1814.

Becker, Christian. *Der Deutschen allgegenwärtiger Englischer Sprachlehrer des Wortes Gottes*. Easton, Pa.: C. J. Hütter, 1808.

————. *Unterricht für amerikanische Bauern, Weinberge anzulegen und zu unterhalten*. Easton, Pa.: C. J. Hütter, 1809.

Bergner, Anna. *Pfälzer Kochbuch*. Mannheim: Tobias Löffler, 1858.

Biernauer, Jacob. *Das unentbehrliche Haus- und Kunst-Buch, für den Bauer und Stadtmann*. [Reading, Pa.]: for the common good, 1818.

Birlinger, Anton. "Küchen- und Kellerdeutsch." *Alemannia* 18(1890):244–66.

Bradley, Richard. *A General Treatise of Husbandry and Gardening*. London: T. Woodward and J. Peele, 1726.

Bratenwender, Ignatius. *Der kölnische Leckerfress, oder wohlgeordnetes Kochbuch*. Cologne: Imhof-Schwarz, 1819.

Bridgeman, Thomas. *The Young Gardener's Assistant*. New York: W. Mitchell, 1835. Also, the stereotype edition, New York: A. O. Moore, 1858.

Briggs, Richard. *The New Art of Cookery, According to the Present Practice*. Philadelphia: W. Spotswood, R. Campbell, and B. Johnson, 1792.

Brillat-Savarin, Jean Anthelme. *The Physiology of Taste*. London: Peter Davies Ltd., 1925.

Brockmann-Jerosch, H. *Schweizer Bauernhaus*. Bern: Verlag Hans Huber, 1933.

Buck, William J. *History of Montgomery County*. Norristown, Pa.: E. L. Acker, 1859.

Buist, Robert. *The Family Kitchen Gardener*. New York: J. C. Riker, 1847.

Daz buoch von guoter spize. Edited by Gerold Hayer. Göppingen: Alfred Kümmerle, 1976.

Burgstaller, Ernst. "Festtagsgebäcke." *Oesterreichisches Volkskundeatlas* 5(1959): 1–20.

Butz, George. *Peach Industry in Pennsylvania*. Harrisburg: Clarence M. Busch, 1897.

Ceres, eine Zeitschrift für den Landwirth. Edited by Dr. Adolf Bauer, 1(September 1839):32.

Child, Lydia Maria. *The Frugal Housewife*. Boston: March & Capen; Carter & Hendee, 1829.

The Complete Family Brewer. Philadelphia: B. Graves, 1805.

Cookery as It Should Be; A New Manual of Dining Room and Kitchen for Persons in

Moderate Circumstances. Philadelphia: Willis P. Hazard, 1853. Attributed to Mrs. Goodfellow, but written after her death.

Cooper, John M. *Recollections of Chambersburg, Pa., Chiefly Between the Years 1830–1850*. Chambersburg, Pa.: A. Nevin Pomeroy, 1900.

Cooper, Thomas. "Domestic Cookery." In *The Domestic Encyclopedia: Or A Dictionary of Facts and Useful Knowledge*, by A. F. M. Willich. 3d ed. Edited by Thomas Cooper. 3 vols. Philadelphia: Abraham Small, 1821.

———. *A Treatise of Domestic Medicine, Intended for Families*. Reading, Pa.: George Getz, 1824.

Cope, Thomas P. *Philadelphia Merchant: The Diary of Thomas P. Cope, 1800–1851*. Edited by E. Cope Harrison. South Bend, Ind.: Gateway Editions, 1978.

Davidis, Henrietta. *Praktisches Kochbuch für die Deutschen in Amerika*. Edited by Hedwig Voss. Milwaukee: George Brumder, 1897.

———. *German National Cookery for American Kitchens*. Milwaukee: C. N. Caspar Co. Book Emporium, 1904.

Dembińska, Maria. "Day ut ia pobrusa a ti poziwai." *Kwartalnik Historii Kultury Materialnej*, no. 4(1977), pp. 499–506.

DeVoe, Thomas F. *The Market Assistant*. [New York:] The Riverside Press, for the author, 1867. Only 100 copies printed.

Diehl, Wilhelm. "Brief eines nach Amerika ausgewanderten Ehepaar aus Birkenau." *Hessische Chronik* 17(1930):83–86.

Dorn, Anna. *Neuestes Universal- oder grosses Wiener-Kochbuch*. Vienna: Tendler und von Manstein, 1827.

Dorson, Richard M., ed. *Folklore and Folklife*. Chicago/London: University of Chicago Press, 1972.

Drechsler, Paul. *Sitte, Brauch und Volksglaube in Schlesien*. Leipzig: B. G. Teubner, 1903.

Drinker, Elizabeth. *Extracts from the Journal of Elizabeth Drinker*. Edited by Henry D. Biddle. Philadelphia: J. B. Lippincott, 1889.

Egle, William H. "Gustav Sigismund Peters." *Der deutsche Pionier* 15(November 1883):307–11.

Ein vortrefliches Kräuter-Buch für Haus-Väter und Mütter, nebst etlichen auserlesenen Recepten. Hanover, Pa.: Stark und Lange, 1809.

Eupel, Johann Christian. *Der vollkommene Conditor*. Ilmenau: Bernhardt Friedrich Voigt, 1823.

The Family's Guide; Comprising a Choice Variety of Very Useful Recipes, in Domestic Economy. Cortland, N.Y.: C. W. Mason, 1833. Reprinted Harrisburg, Pa.: G. S. Peters, 1848.

Forster, Robert, and Ranum, Orest, eds. *Food and Drink in History*. Baltimore/London: Johns Hopkins University Press, 1979.

Francatelli, Charles Elmé. *The Modern Cook*. London: Richard Bentley, 1846.

The Franklin Repository (Chambersburg, Pa.). June 15, 1824.

Funk, H. H. "Some Oldtime Breakfast-Cakes." *The Pennsylvania-German* 9(January 1908):37.

Fürst, Anna [Marianne Strüf]. *Vollständiges Kochbuch für alle Stände*. Stuttgart: Adolph Becher, 1846.

Fürst, Johann Evangelist. *Der verständige Bauer, Simon Strüf, eine Familien-Geschichte*. Brünn: J. G. Gastl [ca. 1820]. A popular book among the Pennsylvania-German Catholics.

Germantown Telegraph. January 1, 1851; January 8, 1851; February 19, 1851; June 25, 1851; September 24, 1851; November 5, 1851; November 12, 1851; October 14, 1868.

Gibbons, Phebe Earle. *The "Pennsylvania Dutch," and Other Essays*. Philadelphia: J. B. Lippincott & Co., 1882.

Girardey, George. *Höchst nützliches Handbuch über Kochkunst, Fabrication der Liqueren, Weine, Cider, Essig, &c*. Cincinnati: J. A. James, 1842. The first edition appeared in 1841, but thus far no copies have been located.

Glasse, Hannah. *The Art of Cookery Made Plain and Easy*. London: T. Longman, 1796.

Göbel, W. L. *Homöopathisches Kochbuch*. Edited by Arthur Lutze. Sonderhausen: Fr.

Aug. Eupel, 1861.

Graeff, Jacob. "Reminiscences of Reading 70 Years Ago." *The Reading Eagle*, November 8, 1896.

Graydon, Alexander. *Memoirs of His Own Time. With Reminiscences of the Men and Events of the Revolution.* Edited by John Stockton Littell. Philadelphia: Lindsay & Blakiston, 1846 (a reprint of the Harrisburg edition of 1811).

Hagger, Conrad. *Neues saltzburgisches Koch-Buch.* Augsburg: Johann Jacob Lotter, 1719.

Hark, Ann, and Barba, Preston A. *Pennsylvania German Cookery.* Allentown, Pa.: Schlechter's, 1950.

Harland, Marion. *Common Sense in the Household.* New York: Charles Scribner's Sons, 1884.

Hartley, Dorothy. *Food in England.* London: Macdonald and Jane's, 1975.

Hauser, Albert. *Vom Essen und Trinken im alten Zürich.* Zürich: Berichthaus, 1961.

Heffner, George A. *The Youthful Wanderer.* Orefield, Pa.: A. S. Heffner, 1876.

Hellstern, Charles. *Illustrirtes deutsch-amerikanisches Kochbuch.* New York: G. Heerbrandt, 1888. Issued in ten installments, each forming a chapter of the cookbook.

Hexham, Henry. *A Copious English and Netherduytch Dictionarie/Het Groot Woorden-Boeck.* Rotterdam: Aernout Leers, 1648.

Hill, Thomas. "A Journey on Horseback from New Brunswick, N.J. to Lycoming County, Pennsylvania, in 1799." *Now and Then: A Quarterly Magazine of History and Biography* 4(January–March 1931):176–79.

Hohman, Johann Georg. *Die Land- und Haus-Apotheke.* Reading, Pa.: Carl A. Bruckman, 1818.

———. *Der lange verborgene Freund.* Reading, Pa.: privately printed, 1820.

Hope's Philadelphia Price-Current, October 5, 1807.

Hörandner, Edith. "Küche und Kochen." *Wissenschaftliche Arbeiten BGLD* 56(1975): 159–90.

———. "The Recipe Book as a Cultural and Socio-Historical Document." In *Food in Perspective,* edited by Alexander Fenton and Trefor M. Owen. Edinburgh: John Donald Publishers, 1981.

———. *Model.* Munich: Callwey, 1982.

Howland, Esther Allen. *The New England Economical Housekeeper, and Family Receipt Book.* Worcester, Mass.: S. A. Howland, 1844.

Huey, J. Thomas. *The Household Treasure, or, The Young Housewife's Companion.* Philadelphia: J. Thomas Huey & Co., 1871.

Humboldt, Alexander von. *The Island of Cuba.* Translated by J. Thrasher. New York: Derby & Jackson, 1856.

Hunter, William A. "John Badollet's 'Journal of the Time I Spent in Stoney Creek Glades, 1793–1794.'" *Pennsylvania Magazine of History and Biography* 104(April 1980):162–99.

Indian Domestic Economy and Receipt Book. Bombay: Gentleman's Gazette Press, 1849.

Kalm, Peter. *Peter Kalm's Travels in North America.* Edited by A. Benson. New York: Dover Publications, Inc., 1966.

Kaltenbach, Marianne. *Ächti schwizer Chuchi.* Bern/Stuttgart: Hallwag Verlag, 1977.

Kemp, Ellwood L. *An Idyl of the War, The German Exiles, and Other Poems.* Philadelphia: John E. Potter, 1883.

The Keystone (Harrisburg, Pa.). August 1, 1848.

The Kitchen Companion, and House-Keeper's Own Book. Philadelphia: Turner & Fisher, 1844.

Kitchiner, William. *The Cook's Oracle.* Boston: Munroe and Francis, 1823. The first edition appeared in London in 1817.

Kleinschmidt, Wolfgang. "Die Einführung der Kartoffel in der Pfalz und in den angrenzenden Gebieten der ehemaligen Rheinprovinz." *Rheinisch-westfälische Zeitschrift für Volkskunde,* vol. 24, nos. 1–4(1978), pp. 208–30.

Knackwurst, Marcus. *Wurstologia et Durstologia.* Schweinfurt: Hanss Darm, 1662.

Kniffen, Fred. "The Outdoor Oven in Louisiana." *Louisiana History* 1(1960):25–35.

Kowalska-Lewicka, Anna. "Die Volksnahrung der Bauern in Polen." *Acta Ethnographica Academiae Scientiarum Hungaricae*, vol. 20, nos. 1–2(1971), pp. 45–84.

Krauss, Johann. *Oeconomisches Haus- und Kunstbuch.* Allentown, Pa.: Henrich Ebner, 1819.

Kulp, Isaac Clarence. "A Dunker Weekend Love Feast of 100 Years Ago." *Pennsylvania Folklife* 11(Spring 1960):2–9.

Kunst, P. J. *Ein amerikanisches Wörterbuch der englischen und deutschen Sprache.* Harrisburg, Pa.: Lutz & Scheffer, 1850.

Lambert, Marcus B. *A Dictionary of the Non-English Words of the Pennsylvania-German Dialect.* Lancaster, Pa.: Lancaster Press, Inc., 1924.

Landis, Jakob F. *Lese und Prüfe. Nahezu zweihundert werthvolle Rezepte.* Harrisburg, Pa.: Jakob F. Landis, 1882.

Lea, Elizabeth Ellicott. *Domestic Cookery, Useful Receipts, and Hints to Young Housekeepers.* Baltimore: Cushings and Bailey, 1853.

Lemon, James T. *The Best Poor Man's Country: A Geographical Study of Early Southeastern Pennsylvania.* Baltimore and London: The Johns Hopkins Press, 1972.

Leslie, Eliza. *Seventy-Five Receipts for Pastry, Cakes and Sweetmeats.* Boston: Munroe and Francis; New York: C. S. Francis, 1828.

———. *The Indian Meal Book.* Philadelphia: Carey and Hart, 1847.

———. *Miss Leslie's Lady's New Receipt-Book.* Philadelphia: A. Hart, late Carey & Hart, 1850.

Liechtenstein, Eleanora von. *Freywillig-auffgesprungener Granat-Apffel des Christlichen Samaritans.* Vienna: Leopold Voigt, 1696.

Löffler, Friederike. *Oekonomisches Handbuch für Frauenzimmer.* Stuttgart: Johann Friedrich Steinkopf, 1791 and 1795.

———. *Neues Kochbuch.* Stuttgart: Friederich Steinkopf, 1824. Copies of this edition sold widely in Pennsylvania.

[Löffler, Friederike.] *Vollständiges Kochbuch für die deutsch-amerikanische Küche.* Edited by Franz Loës. Philadelphia: Loës & Sebald, ca. 1856.

Lohss, Max. "Ofen und Herd in Württemberg." *Wörter und Sachen* (Heidelberg) 11(1929):362–86.

Loofft, Marcus. *Nieder-Sächsisches Koch-Buch.* Lübeck: Christian Iverson u. Co., 1778.

Lowenstein, Eleanor. *Bibliography of American Cookery Books, 1742–1860.* Worcester, Mass.: American Antiquarian Society, 1972.

McDougall, Frances Harriet. *The Housekeeper's Book.* Philadelphia: William Marshall & Co., 1837.

Marquart, John. *600 Miscellaneous Valuable Receipts, Worth Their Weight in Gold.* Lebanon, Pa.: Christian Henry, 1860.

Marshall, Josiah T. *The Farmer's and Emigrant's Hand-Book.* New York: D. Appleton & Co., 1845.

Mayer, I. H. *Domestic Cookery; Or How to Make Hard Times Good and Good Times Better.* Lancaster, Pa.: I. H. Mayer, 1893.

Menon. *La cuisinière bourgeoise.* Paris: P. M. Nyon, 1788.

Mittelberger, Gottlieb. *Gottlieb Mittelberger's Journey to Pennsylvania in the Year 1750.* Translated by Carl T. Eben. Philadelphia: John J. McVey, 1898.

Morineau, Michel. "The Potato in the Eighteenth Century." In *Food and Drink in History*, edited by Robert Forster and Orest Ranum. Baltimore/London: Johns Hopkins University Press, 1979.

Moser, Hugo. *Schwäbischer Volkshumor.* Stuttgart: W. Kohlhammer, 1950.

Myers, J. C. *Sketches on a Tour Through the Northern and Eastern States.* Harrisonburg, Va.: J. H. Wartmann and Brothers, 1849.

Der neue amerikanische Landwirtschafts-Calender auf das Jahr 1854. Edited by Carl Friederich Egelmann. Reading, Pa.: Ritter & Co., 1853.

Der neue gemeinnützige Landwirtschafts Calender auf das Jahr 1798. Lancaster, Pa.: Johann Albrecht und Comp., 1797.

Der neue Reading Calender auf das Jahr 1881. Reading, Pa.: Ritter & Co., 1880.

Neuer gemeinnütziger pennsylvanischer Calender auf das Jahr 1856. Lancaster, Pa.: Johann Bär, 1855.

Neunteufel, Herta. *Kochkunst im Barock*. Graz and Vienna: Leykam, 1976.

The New American Pocket Farrier and Farmer's Guide. Philadelphia: Leary & Getz, 1845.

The New Family Receipt Book. Philadelphia: Collins & Croft, 1818.

Nicholson, Elizabeth. *The Economical Cook and House-Book*. Philadelphia: Willis P. Hazard, 1855.

Niemcewicz, Julian Ursyn. *Under Their Vine and Fig Tree*. Translated by M. Budka. Elizabeth, N.J.: The Grassmann Publishing Co., 1965.

Parker, Pat. *WLTR Contributors' Cook Book*. [Bloomsburg, Pa.?]: WLTR Radio, 1949.

Pattee, Fred Lewis. *The House of the Black Ring*. Harrisburg, Pa.: Mt. Pleasant Press, 1916.

Paxon, Henry D. "The Last of the Wild Pigeons in Bucks County." *Papers Read Before the Bucks County Historical Society* 4(1917):367–82.

Pennsylvania Farm Journal 2(July 1852).

Pennsylvania State Grange Home Economics Committee. *Pennsylvania State Grange Cook Book*. Harrisburg, Pa.: The Evangelical Press, 1932.

Pennsylvanische Staats Zeitung, June 10, 1846; March 24, 1847.

Peterson, Hannah Bouvier. *The National Cook Book*. Philadelphia: Childs & Peterson, 1855.

Philadelphia Ledger, December 26, 1846.

Philadelphier Demokrat, January 11, 1850; June 12, 1850.

Randolph, Mary. *The Virginia House-Wife*. Washington, D.C.: Davis and Force, 1824. Also, Philadelphia: E. H. Butler & Co., 1851.

Rattermann, H. A. *Deutsch-Amerikanisches Biographikon und Dichter-Album der ersten Hälfte des 19. Jahrhunderts*. Cincinnati: privately printed, 1911.

Reading Adler, May 27, 1851.

Republikaner von Berks (Reading, Pa.), August 15, 1872.

Rhamm, Karl. *Ethnographische Beiträge zur germanisch-slawischen Altertumskunde*. Brunswick: Friederich Vieweg und Sohn, 1905.

Rhiner, Oskar. "Dünne, Wähe, Kuchen, Fladen, Zelten. Die Wortgeographie des Flachkuchens mit Belag und ihre volkskundliche Hintergründe in der deutschen Schweiz." *Beiträge zur schweizerdeutschen Mundartforschung* 9(1958).

Rumohr, Karl Friedrich von. *Geist der Kochkunst*. Stuttgart and Tübingen: Cotta'schen Buchhandlung, 1822.

Rumpolt, Marx. *Ein new Kochbuch*. Frankfurt: Johann Feyerabend, 1587.

Rundell, Maria Eliza. *A New System of Domestic Cookery*. Philadelphia: Benjamin C. Busby, 1807.

Rutledge, Sarah. *The Carolina Housewife, or House and Home*. Charleston: W. R. Babcock & Co., 1847.

Sachse, Julius. "A Missive from Pennsylvania in the Year of Grace 1728." *Proceedings of the Pennsylvania German Society* 8(1909):1–25.

Sauer, Christopher. *Kurtzgefasstes Kräuterbuch*. Germantown: Christopher Sauer, 1762–78. Issued in installments.

Schepers, Josef. *Haus und Hof westfälischer Bauern*. Münster: Aschendorff, 1973.

Schoepf, Johann David. *Travels in the Confederation (1783–1784)*. Translated by Alfred J. Morrison. New York: Burt Franklin, Pub., 1968 (reprint of Philadelphia edition of 1911).

Schumacher-Voelker, Uta. "German Cookery Books, 1485–1800." *Petits Propos Culinaires* 6(1980):34–46.

Schwarzentruber, Friedrich. *Eine ernste Betrachtung über die übertriebenen Mahlzeiten und Hochzeiten*. Arthur, Ill.: A. M. Publishing Association, 1937.

Sebastian, Master. *Koch- und Kellermeisterey*. Frankfurt: Sigmund Feyerabend, 1581.

Shoemaker, Alfred L. "Biographical Sketches of the Dauphin County Publishers." *The Pennsylvania Dutchman* 3(April 1952):8.

———. "Semi-Annual Fairs." *The Pennsylvania Dutchman* 4(October 1953):2.

———. *Christmas in Pennsylvania. A Folk-Cultural Study*. Kutztown, Pa.: Pennsylvania Folklife Society, 1959.

Siegfried, Samuel and Solomon. *41 bewährte Recepte: für Handwerker und Hausväter*. Millgrove, Pa.: Samuel und Solomon Siegfried, 1834.

Simmons, Amelia. *American Cookery, or the Art of Dressing Viands, Fish, Poultry and Vegetables*. Hartford: Hudson & Goodwin, 1796.

Smith, Mary. *The Complete House-keeper, and Professed Cook*. New Castle, England: S. Hodgson, and G. G. J. and J. Robinson, 1786.

"Sour Krout." *Genesee Farmer* 3(September 1838):141.

The State Capital Gazette (Harrisburg, Pa.), March 9, 1842.

Storke, E. G. *The Family, Farm and Gardens, and the Domestic Animals*. Auburn, N.Y.: The Auburn Publishing Company, 1860. Three works published as one.

Strüf, Marianne. *See* Anna Fürst.

"Sugar Consumption in the United States." *The Inglenook*, January 31, 1911.

The Sunbury American, May 15, 1848.

Teuteberg, Hans-Jürgen. "Variations in Meat Consumption in Germany." *Ethnologia Scandinavica* 1(1971):131–40.

Thiele, Ernst. *Waffeleisen und Waffelgebäcke*. Cologne: Oda-Verlag, 1959.

Thomas, Edith M. *Mary at the Farm and Cook Recipes Compiled During Her Visit Among the "Pennsylvania Germans."* Norristown, Pa.: H. Hartenstein, 1915.

Tibbot, S. Minwel. *Welsh Fare*. Cowbridge and Bridgend: Welsh Folk Museum, 1976.

Ude, Louis Eustache. *The French Cook*. Philadelphia: Carey, Lea and Carey, 1828.

Umble, John. "The Amish Mennonites of Union County, Pennsylvania." *The Diary* 7(March 1975):60.

Van Winter, Johanna Maria. *Van Soeter Cokene. Recepten uit de Oudheid en Middeleeuwen*. Haarlem: Fibula-Van Dishoeck, 1976.

Der Volksfreund (Lancaster, Pa.), July 30, 1850.

Vollmer, Wilhelm. *Vollständiges deutsches Vereinigten Staaten Kochbuch*. Philadelphia: John Weik, 1856.

von Sazenhofen, Carl J., and Wigand, Horst D. *Gerätefibel: Bauernküche*. Munich: L. Staackmann, 1979.

Die wahre Brantwein-Brennerey; oder Brantwein- Gin- und Cordialmacher-Kunst. York, Pa.: Solomon Meyer, 1797.

Weaver, William Woys. "A Blacksmith's 'Summerkich.'" *Pennsylvania Folklife* 22(Summer 1973):22–26.

————. "Swiss Foods and Foodways in Early Pennsylvania." *Newsletter: Swiss American Historical Society* 16(June 1980):4–17.

————. "*Die geschickte Hausfrau*: The First Ethnic Cookbook in the United States." In *Food in Perspective: Proceedings of the Third International Conference on Ethnological Food Research*, edited by Alexander Fenton and Trefor M. Owen, pp. 343–63. Edinburgh: John Donald Publishers, 1981.

————. "La Chapelle's Fish with Sauerkraut." *Petits Propos Culinaires* 9(1981):63.

————. "Early Printed Cookbooks of the Pennsylvania Germans: Their Sources and Their Legacy." In *Pfälzer/Palatines: Festschrift für Fritz Braun*, edited by Karl Scherer, pp. 361–74. Kaiserslautern: Heimatstelle Pfalz, 1981.

————. "Schinckel's Spice Powder." *Petits Propos Culinaires* 10(1982):39–40.

————. "When Shad Came In: Shad Cookery in Old Philadelphia." *Petits Propos Culinaires* 11(1982):7–19.

Weaver, William Woys, ed. *A Quaker Woman's Cookbook: The Domestic Cookery of Elizabeth Ellicott Lea*. Philadelphia: University of Pennsylvania Press, 1982.

Weber, L. W. *Der kluge Land-Medicus und Haus-Apotheke*. Chambersburg, Pa.: privately printed, 1846.

Weigley, Emma Seifert. *Sarah Tyson Rorer*. Philadelphia: American Philosophical Society, 1977.

White, Joseph J. *Cranberry Culture*. New York: Orange Judd Company, 1870.

Widdifield, Hannah. *Widdifield's New Cook Book*. Philadelphia: T. B. Peterson & Bros., 1856.

Wiegelmann, Günter. *Alltags- und Festspeisen, Wandel und gegenwärtige Stellung*. Marburg: N. G. Elwert, 1967.

Willich, A. F. M. *The Domestic Encyclopaedia*. Edited by James Mease. Philadelphia: William Young Birch and Abraham Small, 1803–1804.

Wilson, C. Anne. "Burnt Wine and Cordial Waters: The Early Days of Distilling." *Folk Life* 18(1975):54–65.

Wiswe, Hans. *Kulturgeschichte der Kochkunst*. Munich: Heinz Moos, 1970.

Wollenweber, Ludwig. *Gemälde aus dem pennsylvanischen Volksleben*. Philadelphia and Leipzig: Schäfer und Koradi, 1869.

Wurmbach, Annemarie. "Kuchen-Fladen-Torte. Eine wort- und sach-kundliche Untersuchung." *Zeitschrift für Volkskunde* 56(1960):20–40.

Yearly Meeting of Friends. *Rules of Discipline of the Yearly Meeting of Friends*. Philadelphia: John Richards, 1843.

Yoder, Don. "Sauerkraut in the Pennsylvania Folk-Culture." *Pennsylvania Folklife* 12(Summer 1961):56–69.

———. "Historical Sources for American Traditional Cookery: Examples from the Pennsylvania German Culture." *Pennsylvania Folklife* 20(Spring 1971):16–29.

———. "Folk Cookery." In *Folklore and Folklife*, edited by Richard M. Dorson, pp. 325–50. Chicago/London: University of Chicago Press, 1972.

Young Ladies of Class No. 9, St. Paul's Reformed Sunday School. *Help for the Marthas*. Reading, Pa.: Daniel Miller, 1892.

Manuscript and Unpublished Sources

Allport, James. "Diary of James Allport: April-May, 1828." Five-page typescript. Genealogical Department, Pennsylvania State Library, Harrisburg.

"Byers Family Recipe Book." Upper Strasburg Township, Franklin County, Pennsylvania (ca. 1870–1915), 114pp. Recipes collected by "R" and "S" Byers, probably mother and daughter. Some of the recipes trace to sources printed in the 1840s and 1850s. Private collection.

Gery, Solomon. "Scrap Book." Harlem, Berks County, Pennsylvania (ca. 1868–72), 324pp. Clippings and ephemera in English and German mounted into a mill account book from the 1820s. Most of the culinary material dates from the period 1868–72, but several of the recipes can be traced to Friederike Löffler and *Der amerikanische Bauer* (Harrisburg, 1850–54). Gery was evidently a farmer. Private collection.

Leaman, Barbara Denlinger. "Cook Book and Diary." East Lampeter Township, Lancaster County, Pennsylvania (mostly 1867–69, with a few entries dated 1877), 120pp. Born in 1851, Barbara Leaman married John L. Groff of Lancaster County in 1870. The cookbook originally belonged to her mother, Elizabeth Denlinger Leaman (1824–1902), who wrote a few recipes in German. The rest of the recipes are in English. Private collection.

Leber, Mrs. George. "Receipt Book." 2 vols. unpaginated. York County, Pennsylvania (ca. 1875–80). Culinary recipes in English but with many dialect spellings. Private collection.

Pastorius, Franz Daniel. "Medicus dilectus oder Artzney-Büchlein." Germantown, Pa.: ca. 1695. Collection of the Historical Society of Pennsylvania, Philadelphia.

Peters, Gustav Sigismund. "Will." Dated November 17, 1845. Probated March 25, 1847. *Will Book F*, vol. 1, 50. Dauphin County Court House, Harrisburg, Pennsylvania.

———. "Inventory." Dated March 30 and 31, 1847; and April 1, 2, and 3, 1847. Filed April 3, 1847. Office of the Probate of Wills, Dauphin County Court House, Harrisburg, Pennsylvania.

Reisner, Johannes. "Scrap Book." Tulpehocken Township, Berks County, Pennsylvania. Begun 1832, continued by a descendant until 1908. German and English ephemera and recipes, some of which trace to Wilhelm Vollmer's *Vollständiges deutsches Vereinigten Staaten Kochbuch*. Private collection.

ter Braeck, Anna. "Receipt Book." East Friesland, ca. seventeenth-eighteenth centuries. Manuscript 347, East Friesland State Museum. Emden, Federal Republic of Germany.

Weber, Hans (John Weaver). "Will." Dated January 8, 1755. Probated April 29, 1755. *Will Book B*, vol. 1, 102. Archive, Lancaster County Court House, Lancaster, Pennsylvania.

Wijnsma, Anke. Correspondence with William Woys Weaver concerning Holland Dutch foods and foodways in America. Letter dated Arnhem, Holland, June 9, 1982. Anke Wijnsma is librarian of the "Nederlands Openluchtmuseum" at Arnhem.

Index